Praise for

A Practical Guide to
Mental Health
& Learning Disorders
for Every Educator

"*A Practical Guide to Mental Health & Learning Disorders for Every Educator* by Dr. Myles L. Cooley is just that: a comprehensive resource that is invaluable for all educators. New teachers will benefit from the range of topics such as setting up an effective classroom using PBIS strategies, to learning how to incorporate social-emotional learning approaches within the classroom structure, to unpacking popular education buzzwords such as *grit* and *growth mindset*. Veteran teachers and administrators will learn new tangible interventions rooted in best practices that can be immediately implemented to help address the ever-changing social-emotional needs of students with mental health challenges. As a school psychologist and former school counselor, I am most excited about the well-thought-out interventions and reproducible forms that I plan on using in both individual and group counseling settings. If you are looking for help in navigating the growing social, emotional, behavioral, and mental health demands that are being placed on educators, then this is the book for you."

—*Jennifer D. Beardslee, M.Ed., Ed.S., NCSP, elementary school psychologist in Wakefield, Massachusetts*

· ·

"Dr. Cooley provides educational professionals with a down-to-earth guide to understanding mental health disorders in adolescents. *A Practical Guide to Mental Health & Learning Disorders for Every Educator* is a comprehensive collection of forms, statistics, and anecdotes. Beyond that, Cooley offers what other publications on this topic have failed to provide: He dispenses valuable information on culturally responsive pedagogy and disproportionality in disciplinary practices for minority students. I highly recommend this guide to every educator and teacher-preparation program."

—*Ruba Monem, Ed.D., K–12 educator in Miami, Florida*

"When it comes to finding effective strategies to help with behavior and academic difficulties in the classroom, every teacher longs for a 'go-to' reference. That is what you get with *A Practical Guide to Mental Health & Learning Disorders for Every Educator*. Part one provides interventions that are proactive, preventative, and beneficial to all students. Dr. Cooley guides readers in effectively creating classroom policies and procedures as well as fostering cultural awareness. He stresses that early intervention is equally important for children with mental health disorders as it is for children with learning disorders, and he shares sensible approaches to help teachers communicate with parents as well as collaborate with school personnel. Part two of the book contains descriptions of mental health and learning disorders. Dr. Cooley starts by defining each disorder and then presents behaviors and symptoms that school staff may observe. Next, he provides strategies and interventions to try in the classroom, followed by appropriate professional treatments. Teaching is one of the most challenging professions, but with a book like this at their disposal, teachers can be confident that they have a tool to help them be successful."

—Amy Peters, M.A.Ed., *elementary special education teacher in Sioux City, Iowa*

. . . .

"This book is a must-have resource for any educator! Not only does it discuss many learning differences faced by today's educators, it also lists behaviors and symptoms to look for as well as provides practical strategies and interventions for educators to use in the classroom. This book speaks the educator's language and provides us with a tool that can be used in any grade."

—Dana Smith, *504 coordinator and high school English teacher in Hot Springs, Arkansas*

A Practical Guide to
Mental Health
& Learning Disorders
for Every Educator

How to Recognize, Understand, and Help
Challenged (and Challenging) Students Succeed

Revised & Updated Edition

MYLES L. COOLEY, PH.D.

free spirit
PUBLISHING®

Text copyright © 2018, 2007 by Myles L. Cooley, Ph.D.

The first edition of *A Practical Guide to Mental Health & Learning Disorders for Every Educator* was published in 2007 under the title *Teaching Kids with Mental Health & Learning Disorders in the Regular Classroom.*

Library of Congress Cataloging-in-Publication Data
Names: Cooley, Myles L., author.
Title: A Practical Guide to Mental Health & Learning Disorders for Every Educator : How to Recognize, Understand, and Help Challenged (and Challenging) Students Succeed / Myles L. Cooley, Ph.D.
Other titles: Teaching kids with mental health & learning disorders in the regular classroom
Description: Revised and updated edition. | Minneapolis, MN : Free Spirit Publishing, [2018] | Revised and updated edition of : Teaching kids with mental health and learning disorders in the regular classroom : how to recognize, understand, and help challenged (and challenging) students succeed / Myles L. Cooley. c2007. | Includes bibliographical references and index.
Identifiers: LCCN 2018021377 (print) | LCCN 2018002530 (ebook) | ISBN 9781631981760 (paperback) | ISBN 1631981765 (paperback) | ISBN 9781631983412 (Web PDF) | ISBN 9781631983429 (ePub)
Subjects: LCSH: Children with mental disabilities—Education—United States. | Learning disabled children—Education—United States. | Inclusive education—United States. | BISAC: EDUCATION / Special Education / Learning Disabilities. | EDUCATION / Special Education / Social Disabilities. | EDUCATION / Special Education / Mental Disabilities.
Classification: LCC LC4031 .C663 2018 (ebook) | LCC LC4031 (print) | DDC 371.92—dc23
LC record available at https://lccn.loc.gov/2018021377

Edited by Douglas J. Fehlen and Christine Zuchora-Walske
Cover and interior design by Emily Dyer

10 9 8 7 6 5 4 3 2 1
Printed in the United States of America

Free Spirit Publishing Inc.
6325 Sandburg Road, Suite 100
Minneapolis, MN 55427-3674
(612) 338-2068
help4kids@freespirit.com
www.freespirit.com

SUSTAINABLE FORESTRY INITIATIVE
Certified Chain of Custody
Promoting Sustainable Forestry
www.sfiprogram.org
SFI-01268
SFI label applies to the text stock

Free Spirit offers competitive pricing.
Contact edsales@freespirit.com for pricing information on multiple quantity purchases.

Dedication

To the thousands of kids I've tried to help, who have taught me much of what I know today.

Acknowledgments

I would like to thank Free Spirit Publishing for the opportunity to write a revised and updated edition of this book. Christine Zuchora-Walske edited this edition and was invaluable in the writing process. She is responsible for much of the accuracy and readability of this book. Thanks also to the thousands of children and adolescents I've seen over the years, who have taught me more than all the books on my bookshelf have.

CONTENTS

Part 1: The Role of Schools in Addressing Mental Health and Learning Disorders

List of Reproducible Forms

FOREWORD

by Sharon A. Hoover, Ph.D.

Two decades ago, as a frontline psychologist in schools, I often felt that my impact on student mental health was minimal compared to the influence of teachers. Now, as codirector of the Center for School Mental Health at the University of Maryland School of Medicine, I am convinced that this is true. Schools are among the most important venues in which to support students' well-being and mental health, and educators are key to the success of this work. Those with specialty mental health training—such as school social workers, counselors, psychologists, and school-based community mental health clinicians—are integral to student mental health, but student mental health is a shared responsibility. Teachers have enormous opportunity to promote the social and emotional health of students and to tailor their instruction to those with special mental health and learning needs. However, the tools for carrying out this endeavor are not always easy to find.

That's one reason why, when asked to write this foreword, I first needed to see for myself that this practical guide was indeed practical. Far too often I have seen efforts to "train" educators in the area of mental health that are well-intentioned yet miss the mark, either by relying only on classroom management strategies to elicit positive behaviors or by focusing too much on diagnostic criteria and pathology beyond the scope of educators' training and responsibilities. I was glad to see that here, by contrast, Dr. Cooley has thoughtfully laid out some fundamental frameworks and concepts in the school mental health field, including social-emotional learning (SEL) and Multi-Tiered Systems of Support (MTSS), and that he has supplemented basic mental health information with practical strategies to promote social and emotional health, identify students' mental health challenges, and individualize teaching for students with diverse needs.

This type of accessible, ready-to-use information is of the utmost importance as schools have become de facto settings for mental health care, with educators playing an ever-increasing role in the identification and treatment of students with mental health needs. The situation is growing, but not new. In fact, almost two decades ago, the US surgeon general identified teachers as "frontline" mental health workers who should be trained to recognize and manage child and adolescent mental health difficulties, in addition to supporting positive social-emotional development for all students. With current estimates of up to one in five young people meeting criteria for a diagnosable mental health condition, approximately four to six students in each classroom will present with serious challenges. Even more students will engage in risk behaviors such as physical fighting, bullying, substance use, and unprotected sex. Teachers have the immense task of providing effective academic instruction for the whole classroom while meeting each student's social, emotional, and behavioral needs, yet are often provided with little training to help them address some of the mental health difficulties they may face. Nevertheless, most of the educators I speak with are looking for opportunities to meaningfully improve their students' lives beyond the classroom and could benefit greatly from tools to do so in the realm of mental health. While teaching the academic fundamentals of education is foundational to the work of schools, it's also imperative to recognize that true success—academic and otherwise—will not be achieved without attention to students' mental health. The mission of schools must be not only to instill critical thinking and academic skills, but also to foster healthy, connected human beings with the capacity to live meaningful and productive lives. And to succeed in promoting this mission, educators must be attuned to the unique mental health and learning needs of each student and provided with tools to translate their understanding into useful supports in the classroom. This book gives teachers those tools.

Additionally, while most teachers embrace their role in addressing students' mental health needs, all too often this aspect of their job—particularly managing challenging behavior—contributes to stress and burnout. I encourage educators not only to put into practice the information and strategies Dr. Cooley presents for supporting students, but also to attend to their own social and emotional health and development. Our Center for School Mental Health is increasingly responding to assistance requests from schools and districts seeking to enhance wellness among their staff, recognizing that educator well-being is directly related to student well-being and performance. Dr. Cooley mentions these efforts in his book, including mindfulness techniques that educators are adopting to deal with the stressors of teaching. It is well worth exploring the specific strategies that districts, schools, teachers, counselors, and others can use to promote their own health and satisfaction—which will, in turn, promote students' mental health. Just as we need to put the oxygen mask on ourselves before we put it on our children, the same goes for the mental health supports we provide to our students. So, educators, I urge you to embrace the mission you committed to at the start of your teaching careers: to teach and support the whole child and to make a meaningful difference in each student's life. The strategies outlined in this book, paired with techniques to foster your own wellness, will improve your students' school experiences and their lives beyond school walls, and will also bolster your own teaching practice and professional quality of life.

Sharon A. Hoover, Ph.D.

Codirector, Center for School Mental Health, University of Maryland School of Medicine

Associate Professor, University of Maryland School of Medicine, Division of Child and Adolescent Psychiatry

"Good teaching means being responsive to the hand you've been dealt."
—*Ross W. Greene, Ph.D., psychologist and author*

As the ancient Greek philosopher Heraclitus of Ephesus said, change is the only constant in life.[1] So, in addition to teaching your students academic skills using effective, tried-and-true methods, you must also keep up with the changes occurring in education. Since the original publication of this book in 2007, new and modified educational philosophies and best practices have developed. These changes may require you to learn new skills. This process can be time consuming, and—like all change—will likely involve some initial discomfort.

Changes have occurred in multiple areas of education. First, an increase in the diversity of students in the United States means that teachers and students need to be more sensitive to one another. Educators must modify teaching practices for students of different ethnicities, cultures, sexual identities, and abilities (see chapter 4). Second, the numbers of English language learners in classrooms are increasing. Improving these students' academic skills, test scores, and high school graduation rates and reducing the numbers of dropouts is a growing challenge.[2] Third, increased standardized testing has teachers more concerned about their salaries and job security.[3]

Some changes have resulted in problems for students, particularly teens. Teens spend more time with smartphones than ever before. Attachment to their phones causes teens to experience increased loneliness, depression, and sleep deprivation, as well as cyberbullying, which has almost doubled since 2007.[4] More and more educators are recognizing the importance of teaching social-emotional skills as an effective intervention to counter students' current stress and improve their chances of success in their adult lives.[5]

Another development since 2007 that's relevant to schools was the publication of the *Diagnostic and Statistical Manual of Mental Disorders: Fifth Edition (DSM-5)* in 2013. The *DSM-5* updated the definitions of and criteria for certain diagnoses and added new diagnoses. These revisions have improved our understanding of many mental health and learning disorders. The *DSM-5* has resulted in changes in the ways schools qualify students for accommodations or for special education services.

In addition to responding to these changes in education, another challenge you face as an educator is the expectation that you teach many students who have difficulties with learning or with mood or anxiety. These challenges may interfere not only with students' learning, but also with your ability to teach. The extra attention you must devote to these students makes your job considerably more difficult.

In other words, you've got a tough job—one of the toughest there is. The fact that you're reading this book shows your deep concern for students' learning and mental health. In my work with children and families, I've come to know and admire many dedicated teachers. Like you, they are hungry for information they can use to help students who struggle with various difficulties. That's why I wrote this book. I want to help educators identify students with possible mental health and learning disorders and provide them with practical classroom strategies to teach and support those students.

Mainstreaming and Inclusion in Classrooms

What is it that makes your job so demanding? Without a doubt, you are expected to teach students with a wide spectrum of abilities and needs. Some of your students come to you with academic and behavioral difficulties. This results partly from the practices of mainstreaming and inclusion of children with special needs. Mainstreaming involves placing students from self-contained special education classrooms or pull-out instruction in general education classes for part of their school day. Inclusion allows special education students to be taught in regular classrooms, with a special education teacher providing occasional support in the classroom. Research shows that these practices have many advantages for students with certain disabilities, including higher academic performance, more positive self-esteem, and better social skills.[6]

While good intentions underlie mainstreaming and inclusion, you can imagine—or may have experienced—some major challenges in these classrooms. Educator and education journalist Jackie Mader points out that "a national push to take students with disabilities out of isolation means most now spend the majority of their days in general education classrooms. That means general education teachers are teaching students with disabilities. But training programs are doing little to prepare teachers."[7] So how can you help all kids succeed academically, especially in the current environment of high-stakes testing? How do you deal with children's social and emotional development? What about training for you? How can you respond to children with mental health challenges? This book will help you answer these questions.

HOW COMMON ARE MENTAL HEALTH AND LEARNING DISORDERS?

- One in five students in the United States has a mental health disorder.[8] Some of these students have two or more diagnosable disorders.

- One in two students in the child welfare system has a mental health disorder.[9]

- In the United States, 5 percent of students are identified as having a learning disability, and an additional 15 percent have unidentified learning and attention challenges.[10]

- Students with mental health issues may be absent up to twenty-two days a year.[11]

- Rates of expulsion and suspension are three times higher among students with mental health disorders.[12]

- Numbers of school psychologists, school counselors, and school social workers fall well below levels recommended by national associations.[13]

The Challenge for Teachers

Helping students with mental health, behavioral, and learning challenges may seem daunting. Educators are often the first people students come to when they're facing difficulties of many kinds, but teachers may be ill prepared to identify and refer students suspected of having mental health disorders. Teachers are trained in cardiopulmonary resuscitation (CPR), epinephrine autoinjectors (such as the EpiPen), bodily fluid cleanup, and a variety of other safety measures, but many receive little to no training around mental health disorders.[14] Fifty percent of teachers leave the profession within their first four years, primarily because of students with behavior problems.[15]

CAN YOU RELATE TO THIS?

Forty-six percent of teachers report high daily stress, which affects their health, quality of life, and teaching ability.[16] Patricia A. Jennings, an authority on how teacher stress affects the social-emotional classroom environment and well-being of students, summarizes the multiple factors causing this stress:

"We ask an awful lot of teachers these days. . . . Beyond just conveying the course material, teachers are supposed to provide a nurturing learning environment; be responsive to students, parents, and colleagues; juggle the demands of standardized testing; coach students through conflicts with peers; be exemplars of emotion regulation; handle disruptive behavior and generally be great role models. . . . The problem is we rarely give teachers training or resources for any of them."[17]

The good news is that there are many strategies you can use to support students. *A Practical Guide to Mental Health & Learning Disorders for Every Educator* provides interventions for regular classroom teachers as well as advice for determining when students may need help from other school staff or outside professionals. You'll learn the signs and symptoms of many mental health disorders to help you recognize whether a child might need additional assistance or evaluation. In addition to helping you with your students, if you are a parent, I hope the information in this book is useful in relation to your own child.

More and more educators and researchers understand that academic difficulties often spring from significant differences in *how* students learn, as well as from social and emotional difficulties students may be facing. Teachers are using innovative instructional techniques to engage learners. Rather than simply penalizing students for misbehavior or low achievement, educators are looking more deeply into what might be causing these issues. To prevent these issues, schools increasingly are implementing Positive Behavioral Interventions and Supports, or PBIS. (For more information on PBIS, see chapter 2.) Research has shown that when students' psychological or learning challenges are identified and addressed, students not only feel and behave better, but also achieve at higher academic levels.[18]

Addressing certain students' differences can seem to be a great challenge when, at the same time, you're accountable for the performance of all your students. You might fear that giving too much attention to these students will keep you from helping the majority of your class achieve state standards and reach grade-level proficiency. The information and strategies presented in this book will allow you to give individual attention to those students who need it with minimal negative impact on the rest of the class. Many of the strategies will benefit all students.

How to Use This Book

You can use the information and strategies in this book regardless of whether you know a student has a disorder. If you already know what disorder a student has, you can find relevant information by searching for that disorder in the contents. When you're not sure whether a child has a disorder, you can identify potentially helpful strategies by searching the index for behaviors you have observed. A student who is always disorganized, for example, may benefit from some of the strategies you'll find for helping students with executive function difficulties. A very shy student who is reluctant to participate in class or socialize with others may struggle with anxiety, and you might find the information in chapter 8 useful.

I have written this book with regular classroom teachers in mind, but the information can be helpful to all school personnel. School counselors and psychologists will learn techniques they can use with students in guidance settings. Classroom aides and special educators who work in pull-out settings will find strategies to help students improve academic performance and to promote appropriate classroom behaviors. Administrators can benefit from the information on a school's legal responsibilities in educating and caring for students with certain disorders. Parents and others involved in children's care and education can gain insight into the difficulties that may underlie a child's behavior. Here's what you'll find in this book:

PART 1: THE ROLE OF SCHOOLS IN ADDRESSING MENTAL HEALTH AND LEARNING DISORDERS

The first part of the book contains information about schoolwide and classroom practices and procedures that benefit all students. Many of these interventions are proactive and preventive: They minimize the likelihood of behavior and academic problems.

Chapter 1 addresses classroom rules and student compliance. Identifying students' academic or behavior difficulties and communicating them to parents is covered in chapter 3, while chapter 2 discusses addressing these issues with a Multi-Tiered System of Supports (MTSS). In chapter 4, readers can learn how to respond to increasingly diverse student populations with culturally sensitive classrooms and curricula. Chapter 5 includes multiple ways to enhance social-emotional learning, which is considered by many to be essential for lifelong success. Finally, many students have executive function difficulties. Chapter 6 discusses identifying and accommodating students with these challenges. Chapter 7 discusses how to describe students with disabilities, the different terminology used by different professionals, and the use of gender pronouns and other terms in the book.

PART 2: MENTAL HEALTH AND LEARNING DISORDERS

In the second part of the book, you'll find detailed information on specific mental health and learning disorders. All the chapters are laid out in a uniform way, so you can easily find the information you need. Each chapter defines the disorder (or disorders) with its symptoms and gives helpful strategies for working with students who have (or may have) the disorder. Also included are statistics on how common disorders are among children, in-the-trenches stories, treatments professionals may use, and other information that can be helpful in your work with children. You'll also see anecdotes about individual students or parents. All these examples come from my experiences with kids, but I have changed the names to protect students' privacy.

The book concludes with sections you can use to find out more about conditions. The glossary offers a handy guide to key terms used in this book. The source notes provide the sources for factual statements that appear throughout the book. The resources—organized by disorder—include information on related books, organizations, and websites for adults and children.

Digital Content

At the end of some chapters, you will find reproducible handouts that you can use in the classroom. Please feel free to use these forms as you see fit. You can photocopy them from the book or download and print them out. See page 243 for downloading instructions

What's New in This Edition

New or updated content makes up more than half of this edition. You'll find new chapters, new disorders, and the latest information, research, and interventions for existing disorders. Here's a look at what's new:

Part 1: The Role of Schools in Addressing Mental Health and Learning Disorders

- Chapter 2: Schoolwide Behavior and Academic Supports discusses Positive Behavioral Interventions and Supports (PBIS), Response to Intervention (RTI), and 504 education plan accommodations for students requiring additional academic or behavioral support.

- Chapter 4: Culturally Responsive Education addresses the increasing cultural diversity of today's students. It discusses ways to modify your classroom environment and curriculum to include references to multiple cultures. Culturally responsive teaching uses the cultural knowledge, prior experiences, and frames of reference of diverse students to make learning encounters more relevant and effective for them.[19]

- Chapter 5: Social-Emotional Learning describes the increased recognition of noncognitive skills that contribute to students' development. These include self-control, mindfulness, a growth mindset, grit, and social skills.

- Chapter 6: Identifying and Supporting Students with Executive Function Difficulties describes helpful accommodations for students with ADHD, learning disabilities, and autism, as well as other students who exhibit executive function difficulties.

Part 2: Mental Health and Learning Disorders

- Part 2 lists and defines disorders according to the latest (fifth) edition of the American Psychiatric Association's *Diagnostic and Statistical Manual of Mental Disorders*, the *DSM-5*.[20] In some cases, the ways disorders are categorized have changed. The *DSM-5* has revised the symptoms for other diagnoses and has also added new diagnoses.

- Chapter 10: Depressive Disorders describes a new diagnosis, disruptive mood dysregulation disorder. This diagnosis arose as a result of the increasing numbers of children diagnosed with bipolar disorder. Because these students were not necessarily exhibiting manic episodes, researchers questioned whether these students met the criteria for bipolar disorder. This new diagnosis allows students with intense mood and behavior issues *without* manic episodes to be diagnosed and treated. The new diagnosis is expected to reduce the numbers of children diagnosed with bipolar disorder, which is often treated with powerful medications.

- A new *DSM-5* category, neurodevelopmental disorders (chapter 12), includes many disorders exhibited in the early developmental period. They are characterized by developmental deficits that impair a child's functioning. These disorders are ADHD, tic disorders, autism spectrum disorder, specific learning disorder, and communication disorders. One major change in the *DSM-5* is that autism is now considered a spectrum disorder. Students can have low- or high-functioning autism, in which the types and degrees of symptoms may vary. The *DSM-5* has eliminated Asperger's syndrome as a diagnosis. Students formerly diagnosed with Asperger's syndrome are now considered to have a high-functioning autism spectrum disorder.

- Students who injure or harm themselves have never had a separate diagnosis. Chapter 14: Self-Injury and Suicide describes a proposed diagnosis in the *DSM-5* of nonsuicidal self-injury. This proposed diagnosis enables more research and study on self-injury to be conducted prior to the next edition of the *Diagnostic and Statistical Manual of Mental Disorders*, when a more refined diagnosis may become permanent.

- Chapter 16: Trauma and Stressor-Related Disorders describes a range of traumatic events some children experience that may or may not result in classic post-traumatic stress disorder (PTSD). These events include adverse childhood experiences (ACEs), bullying, and violence. The chapter describes the effects of these events on students' behavior and learning and offers strategies to respond to these students.

Your Power to Make a Difference

Our youngest daughter, Lisa, was about seven years old when a teacher told me and my wife that she was concerned because she thought Lisa looked sad. The teacher suggested that maybe Lisa was depressed. Another teacher asked us if Lisa was afraid of teachers. When we asked why, the teacher said that Lisa didn't talk to her as much as other students did.

These comments came as quite a surprise to us. We were used to a bubbling chatterbox at home. We found out that Lisa had considerable anxiety in the classroom, which was showing up as shyness. This story demonstrates both the importance of avoiding diagnosing students (Lisa was not depressed) and the benefit families receive from knowing that something is "not right" at school. A school counselor helped Lisa with her shyness and anxiety, and Lisa was able to be more comfortable and successful in school.

This story also highlights the important role teachers play in the lives of students. As an educator, you may spend as much waking time with children as their parents do. As a result, you'll often be among the first to observe potential problems. While it's important to avoid rushing to judgment, your ability and willingness to share your concerns with families is crucial. Early intervention in mental health and learning disorders can mean fewer and less severe academic, emotional, and behavioral difficulties.

Like most teachers, you probably came to this job knowing that it wouldn't always be easy. You probably knew about teaching's challenges but chose to teach anyway because you recognized the importance of this profession and couldn't pass up the opportunity to enrich children's lives. Along the way, you've probably realized another truth of the trade: teaching is one of the most rewarding professions there is. Your work with children makes you a very influential person in their futures. Lisa can attest to this; she is currently an elementary school counselor.

I hope this book helps make your work even more rewarding. I'd enjoy hearing about how you're using the strategies in your classroom. I'd also like to learn about any other methods you have found effective. You may share your thoughts with me in care of my publisher:

Free Spirit Publishing Inc.
6325 Sandburg Road, Suite 100
Minneapolis, MN 55427-3674
help4kids@freespirit.com

Keep up your important work.

Myles L. Cooley, Ph.D.

PART 1

· · ·

The Role of Schools in Addressing Mental Health and Learning Disorders

CHAPTER 1

Effective Classroom Policies and Procedures

"The least intrusive prevention strategy is to teach students rules and routines that will facilitate their success."

—*Mary Margaret Kerr and C. Michael Nelson, educators and authors*

Students with mental health and learning disorders often have challenges at school that extend beyond academics. Much of the time, they need accommodations and additional supports to help them function in the classroom. Depending on a student's disorder and its severity, you may even need to teach basic classroom expectations and consistently reinforce them. Otherwise, a student's behavioral or learning difficulties can interfere with your teaching—and test your patience.

It's important to remember that inappropriate behaviors are not often the result of students consciously disregarding rules. Instead, these students may be experiencing effects of disorders that make it difficult for them to comply with classroom expectations. For example, a child with ADHD may understand rules and try to obey them but find it very hard to control impulsive urges. A student with language deficits might have difficulty understanding or remembering rules. There are many possible ways in which students' disorders can affect their abilities to show appropriate behavior and academic skills.

It's important to acknowledge students' difficulties, and also to proactively help students develop strategies to comply with expectations. This chapter offers some basic classroom management information to keep in mind when working with children who have mental health and learning disorders. You will also find specific supports, accommodations, and interventions within the respective disorder chapters.

School Rules

Educators should develop school rules in conjunction with a mission statement that clarifies their school's purpose and goals. It's important that teachers, counselors, administrators, and other school staff participate in developing rules and disciplinary policies. In a school with a Multi-Tiered System of Supports, or MTSS (see chapter 2), teaching rules is an essential first step.

Many schools and districts involve children and families in creating student codes of conduct. Initiatives to address bullying, in particular, bring school staff, students, and parents together in efforts to build respectful school communities. This collaborative approach can increase staff and student buy-in and ensure that expectations for appropriate behavior are clear to the entire school community.

While conduct guidelines will vary between schools, there are some important principles to remember when establishing school rules.

Rules should be realistic. It's important that behavior expectations are appropriate for children's age and development.

Rules should be consistent. Rules are most effective when school staff apply them consistently in multiple settings. When teachers have very different standards, children receive mixed messages about expected behavior. Behavior expectations in some settings, such as in the lunchroom or on the playground, need to be more flexible to accommodate nonclassroom activities. However, even these rules should be consistent with the school's general behavior code.

Rules should be concise. Some students with mental health and learning disorders have difficulty understanding and remembering rules. The more straightforward and concise rules are, the better all students will be able to remember and follow them.

Rules should be explicit. Rules should refer to concrete behaviors, not abstract ideas. For example, "Speak in a respectful way" is a directive that students must interpret. Instead, a clearer rule might be, "Raise your hand if you would like to speak during class. If you are called on, speak in a calm voice." Different settings, such as small-group work, may require similarly specific rules.

Rules should be stated in the positive. Telling students what they *shouldn't* do doesn't indicate how they *should* act. For example, instead of "No hitting," a rule might read, "Always keep your hands and feet to yourself."

Rules should be discussed and agreed upon. Rules should be posted in all areas of the school. Teachers and other staff should go over rules with students to ensure that students understand the rules. Consider distributing handouts with classroom rules (or a school code of conduct) when discussing them. Ask students to take this handout home, discuss the rules with a parent, and return the sheet to you with a parent's signature. Also provide space for students to sign to indicate that they understand the rules.

Encouraging Rule Following

Even when schools clearly communicate and enforce positive, concise, and explicit rules, some students may still have difficulty behaving appropriately at school. Children with mental health and learning disorders face a variety of challenges that can make it hard for them to remember, understand, and comply with rules. Many will need ongoing supportive strategies.

If your school has implemented a Positive Behavioral Intervention and Supports (PBIS) system (see chapter 2), your strategies should align with that system. If your school has not begun a PBIS system, you will want to consult with a counselor or school psychologist to develop strategies. Following are some supportive strategies that will help students display positive behavior.

Teach students social skills. In the book *Lost at School*, Ross W. Greene maintains that "kids do well if they can," but frequently they can't because they don't have the necessary skills.[1] For instance, students with autism spectrum disorder may not have the skills to socialize appropriately, so these students may hit other kids to get their attention. Other students may blurt out answers without raising their hands because they have difficulty controlling their impulses. Children with anxiety may never raise their hands, so their grades for class participation might be low. (For guidance on teaching students these skills, see "Social Skills" on page 45.)

Provide positive reinforcement. One of the most powerful ways to encourage desired behavior is to regularly praise students when they behave appropriately. In other words, catch them being good. This is a simple yet effective way teachers can help students follow rules. Be specific in your praise so students know exactly what they did to earn it. You might also reward them for positive behaviors by granting a privilege or through some other tangible form of acknowledgment. You'll find a reproducible "Certificate of Respectful Behavior" on page 16.

Practice rule compliance. Students learn behaviors when they practice them. Verbal reinforcement for rule compliance motivates students to continue following rules. For rules that students have difficulty following, repeated practice is effective. For example, if the rule is to raise your hand to answer questions and some students blurt out answers, you could announce a practice session on hand raising. Tell the class that you're going to ask them three questions in a row and you want to see hands go up to answer. Doing this a few times a day can encourage that behavior.

Sample Certificate of Respectful Behavior

Certificate of Respectful Behavior

On this _____8th_____ day of _____May_____ ,
     (date)   (month)

_____Jonas_____ has earned this Certificate of Respectful Behavior.
     (student's name)

_____Jonas_____ has earned this certificate for

terrific behavior on the playground during lunch recess. When a

disagreement came up in the baseball game, Jonas talked it out

with the other player without raising his voice or getting physical.

Keep up the respectful behavior, _____Jonas_____!

_____Mr. Alvarez_____
     (Teacher signature)

Keep parents informed. Parents should know about their children's behavior—the good as well as the bad. Sharing positive comments with parents about their children is a pleasant way to let parents know that your approach to behavior is balanced. You'll give credit where credit is due, and you'll also hold students accountable when their behavior is unacceptable. One of the simplest ways to achieve this balance is to call or send positive notes or emails to the families of at least four students each week, rotating through your roster. Not only do parents appreciate hearing positive information from you about their children, but it also increases your credibility when you have to send home negative information. Even when you're reporting a student's difficulties, include some positive information. For example: "Xiang has always been an excellent all-around student—and he continues to read and write at a very high level. I'm concerned, however, about his recent poor performance in math. I'd like us to work together to help him do as well in math as he does in reading and writing." Here's an example regarding behavior: "Jalisa is much more cooperative when I ask her to do something in class. She still wants to play only what *she* wants to play on the playground, though. I can see that other kids are less eager to play with her. Let's see if we can come up with some ideas to encourage her to be a little more flexible."

COMMUNICATE WITH PARENTS EARLY

The most frequent complaint I hear from parents is that teachers wait too long to inform parents of concerns about a child's academic skills or behavior. Many parents report hearing from teachers at the end of the school year that their children's academic skills are weak. At that point, children may be at risk of retention. At the very least, valuable time has been lost in getting children additional help.

Include students in designing strategies. A behavior contract can be an effective approach to helping students focus on improving one or more inappropriate behaviors they are exhibiting at school. When children feel they play a role in how they are treated (as opposed to simply being disciplined by authority figures), they are more likely to take personal responsibility for their behavior. Reinforce appropriate behaviors with rewards. Parents and other school staff should be aware of and involved in designing behavior contracts. You can find a reproducible "Behavior Contract" on page 17.

Teach children to monitor their own behavior. Having students monitor their own actions is another way to give them responsibility and teach them self-control. Ask a student to focus on decreasing one negative behavior. When students are on the lookout for specific behaviors, they are more likely to notice when they engage in these behaviors. Being aware of a behavior is an essential first step

Sample Behavior Contract

Behavior Contract

This behavior contract between ___Cheryl___
(student's name)
and ___Mrs. Jacobson___
(teacher's name)
is for the period of ___March 1___ through ___March 5___.
(start date)   (end date)

The behavior(s) ___Cheryl___ agrees to show:
1. Standing in line quietly before lunch.
2. Keeping her hands to herself in the lunch line.
_____
_____
_____

If ___Cheryl___ is able to show these behavior(s), ___she___ will earn:
1. The chance to decide what game the class plays on
Friday, March 5.
_____
_____
_____

Date: ___March 1___
Student signature: ___Cheryl Hawkins___
Guardian signature: ___LaDonna Hawkins___
Teacher signature: ___Mrs. Jacobson___

in modifying it. Discuss a silent signal you can use during class to let students know when they have engaged in negative behavior, and have them mark it down on a self-monitoring checklist. You'll find a reproducible "Self-Monitoring Checklist" on page 18. Help students set daily or weekly goals in conjunction with a behavior contract.

Help students consider a different strategy if they repeatedly fail to comply with a rule. Students will not always initially succeed when they attempt to change their behavior. Help them understand what they did incorrectly and how they can respond differently next time. You'll find a reproducible "Behavior Improvement Plan" on page 19.

Establish provisions for times when students feel overwhelmed. Set up a quiet place in or near your classroom where students can go to calm down when they are upset or explosive. Allow students to visit a counselor if one is available. Consider developing a coping plan for students who feel overwhelmed. You'll find a reproducible "Student Coping Plan" on page 20.

Downplay minor misbehavior. Keep comments to a minimum and try to give feedback in nonverbal ways (such as a look or a hand gesture). This can help you minimize the behavior's impact on other students and avoid putting a spotlight on a child who's behaving inappropriately to get attention.

Stay calm. It's important not to take negative behavior personally. Some children have problems that greatly influence their behavior. It's your responsibility to stay calm, positive, and proactive in addressing student behavior.

Sample Self-Monitoring Checklist

Self-Monitoring Checklist

Self-monitoring checklist for: _____Ron_____
(student's name)

The behavior I am trying to stop is _speaking without being called on in class._

_____

_____

_____

I will make a checkmark each time I make a mistake.

Monday: __9/17__ ✓✓✓✓

Tuesday: __9/18__ ✓✓✓✓✓✓

Wednesday: __9/19__ ✓✓✓

Thursday: __9/20__ ✓✓✓

Friday: __9/21__ ✓

Notes: __If I make a mistake and speak without raising my__
__hand, Mr. Mouhasha will touch his earlobe to remind me__
__to make a checkmark.__

_____

_____

_____

_____

WHAT WORKS FOR ONE STUDENT MAY NOT WORK FOR ANOTHER

Differentiated academic instruction recognizes that students need different approaches to learning. In *Lost at School*, Ross W. Greene proposes that educators consider "differentiated discipline" when considering approaches to students' behavior.[2] This means using different strategies to modify different students' behavior.

Sample Behavior Improvement Plan

Behavior Improvement Plan

Behavior improvement plan for: __melinda__
(student's name)

What did I do that is against the rules? __I hit Tom in the arm.__

What rule did I break? __Keep your hands and feet to yourself.__

Why did I break this rule? __Tom would not let me have a turn on the computer.__

How did my behavior affect others? __I hurt Tom.__

What will I do next time I face a similar situation? __If I want to play on the computer, I will wait for my turn.__

How can my teacher help me do this? __Mr. Lofflin can listen to me when I have a problem and try to help me.__

Date: __January 11__

Student signature: __melinda martinez__

Guardian signature: __Elias Fernandez__

Teacher signature: __mr. Lofflin__

Sample Student Coping Plan

Student Coping Plan

Coping plan for: __Elijah__

When I am feeling upset or overwhelmed, I will:

1. Ask my teacher if I can sit in the back of the room away from others. I will do breathing exercises until I feel I can rejoin the class.

2. If I am still feeling frustrated, I can ask my teacher if I may see the school counselor. If he is available, I will go to his office to talk right away.

3. If, after all these steps, I don't think I can return to class and be calm, I can call Grandma to pick me up. I understand I will have to make up the work I miss.

Date: __February 20__

Student signature: __Elijah Bachman__

Guardian signature: __Glenda Bachman__

Teacher signature: __Mr. Roberts__

Rewards and Consequences

After behavioral plans are implemented, children need to be held accountable for their behavior. Usually, consequences for misbehavior should be combined with rewards for positive behavior. A good rule of thumb is that students should receive more praise and rewards than reprimands and penalties. Reward the slightest improvement in frequent misbehavior. Teacher educator Laura A. Riffel has compiled a list of hundreds of rewards appropriate for students in elementary through high school at www.wisconsinpbisnetwork.org. Just click on "Educators," then "PBIS in Action," then "Reinforcers." Finally, click on "Free or Inexpensive Rewards for Students and Staff."

Following is an example of a discipline plan for mild misbehavior in elementary school. This discipline plan is most effective if used in a self-contained class. It follows a hierarchy of increasing penalties for additional violations of a rule. However, it's important to be sure that students know and understand rules before administering negative consequences for infractions.

First violation: Write the student's name on the board. Make no verbal comment while writing the name. This helps you avoid disrupting your teaching or reinforcing a negative behavior by giving it attention.

Second violation: Put a checkmark beside the student's name on the board.

Third violation: Put a second checkmark by the student's name on the board. The student loses a privilege, such as free time after lunch.

Fourth violation: Put a third checkmark next to the student's name and send a note home to the student's family. A parent must sign the note and send it back to school.

Fifth violation: Put a fourth checkmark by the student's name. Call a parent the same day to discuss the student's difficulty following rules.

A modified version of this plan is necessary for students in upper grades who have multiple classes and teachers or for students who might be out of the general classroom for some portion of the day. Teachers could record infractions on an in-school online system. With this method, one teacher or counselor needs to be responsible for reviewing the student's daily performance and dispensing any needed consequences.

Behavior plans are effective for most students if implemented consistently. It's best if all staff members who are involved with a student use the same rewards and penalties. Severe violations of rules often require more severe consequences. Work with school counselors, administrators, and other staff to determine appropriate disciplinary actions for students with severe violations. You'll find strategies for addressing severe behaviors in chapters 2 and 13.

Certificate of Respectful Behavior

On this _____ , _____ day of _____
(date)   (month)

_____ has earned this Certificate of Respectful Behavior.
(student's name)

_____ has earned this certificate for

_____

_____

Keep up the respectful behavior, _____ !

_____
(Teacher signature)

Behavior Contract

....

This behavior contract between _____
(student's name)

and _____
(teacher's name)

is for the period of _____ through _____.
(start date)   (end date)

The behavior(s) _____ agrees to show:
(student's name)

_____

_____

_____

_____

_____

If _____ is able to show these behavior(s), _____ will earn:

_____

_____

_____

_____

_____

_____

Date: _____

Student signature: _____

Guardian signature: _____

Teacher signature: _____

Self-Monitoring Checklist

Self-monitoring checklist for _____
(student's name)

The behavior I am trying to stop is _____

_____

_____

_____

I will make a checkmark each time I make a mistake.

Monday: _____

Tuesday: _____

Wednesday: _____

Thursday: _____

Friday: _____

Notes: _____

_____

_____

_____

_____

Behavior Improvement Plan

Behavior improvement plan for _____
(student's name)

What did I do that is against the rules? _____

_____

What rule did I break? _____

_____

Why did I break this rule? _____

_____

How did my behavior affect others? _____

_____

What will I do next time I face a similar situation? _____

_____

How can my teacher help me do this? _____

_____

Date: _____

Student signature: _____

Guardian signature: _____

Teacher signature: _____

Student Coping Plan

Coping plan for _____
(student's name)

When I am feeling upset or overwhelmed, I will:

1. _____

_____

_____

_____

2. _____

_____

_____

_____

3. _____

_____

_____

_____

Date: _____

Student signature: _____

Guardian signature: _____

Teacher signature: _____

CHAPTER 2

Schoolwide Behavior and Academic Supports

....

"Students don't care how much you know until they know how much you care."
—*John C. Maxwell, author and leadership expert*

....

Historically, students with mental health and learning disorders have been at higher risk for special education referrals. The Individuals with Disabilities Education Act (IDEA) of 1997 and the reauthorized Act of 2004 recommended proactive and preventive behavioral and academic interventions to decrease these referrals. Referrals had been steadily increasing over the years, and there were good reasons for educators to reduce them. First, special education is expensive and is frequently ineffective in improving academic performance. Second, students from racial and ethnic minority groups are disproportionately represented in special education.[1]

Multi-Tiered System of Supports (MTSS)

In 1997, IDEA encouraged educators to use "positive behavioral interventions, strategies, and supports" and "positive academic and social learning opportunities" when students' behaviors interfered with their or others' learning.[2] In 2004, Congress formalized the language in IDEA to consistently use the phrase *Positive Behavioral Interventions and Supports*. This terminology became commonly known as PBIS.

The 2004 IDEA reauthorization introduced another approach for identifying students with learning disabilities. It stated that for students with possible learning difficulties, school districts would benefit from first determining whether the students would respond to scientific, research-based interventions. If students did not reach academic goals with increasingly intensive interventions, then they might have learning disabilities and be eligible for special education. This model, called *Response to Intervention (RTI)*, was very different from earlier methods of determining the need for support, in which students often had to "wait to fail" before being evaluated for learning disabilities. If that evaluation satisfied a district's criteria for a learning disability, only then might the student qualify for special education and receive some additional academic assistance.

The RTI approach has succeeded in decreasing the numbers of students qualifying for special education. From 2004 to 2013, the numbers of students identified as having learning disabilities decreased from 13.8 percent to 12.9 percent.[3] Advocates of reducing the special education population argue that many students who would once have been removed from the general classroom can, in fact, be adequately taught in inclusion classes with a general education teacher and a special education teacher. Many students in these inclusion classes show increased academic performance, positive self-esteem, and social skills.[4] Inclusion also reduces the stigma of segregating special education students for all or part of the day.

PBIS and RTI share many common features:

- Both processes provide training and support for all teachers.
- Both are considered preventive. If educators explicitly teach all students academic and social skills, many problems in these areas never develop.
- Students learn behavioral and academic curricula, which are equally important.
- Both establish a continuum of increasingly intensive, evidence-based interventions for students who need them.
- Teachers gather data to monitor and evaluate students' performance during each level of intervention, and team decisions determine students' needs for more intensive intervention.
- Both approaches emphasize the fidelity or integrity of interventions. This means that interventions must be implemented the same way they were "planned, intended, or originally designed."[5]

Because PBIS and RTI are similar, the current preferred term incorporating both approaches is Multi-Tiered System of Supports (MTSS). MTSS is the "integration of a number of multiple-tiered systems into one coherent, strategically combined system meant to address multiple domains or content areas in education (e.g., literacy and social-emotional competence)."[6]

Before the term *MTSS* came along, PBIS was the framework for responding to behavior and RTI was the approach for responding to academic difficulties. The following discussion separates the terms *PBIS* and *RTI* in this way for the purpose of describing MTSS in schools.

Positive Behavioral Interventions and Supports (PBIS)

PBIS is a prevention-oriented way for school personnel to:

- organize evidence-based practices for behavior and academic support
- improve their implementation of those practices
- enhance academic and social behavior outcomes for all students

PBIS emphasizes the establishment of organizational supports or systems that enable educators to use effective interventions accurately and successfully at the school, district, and state levels. These supports include:[7]

- team-based leadership
- data-based problem-solving
- continuous monitoring of student behavior
- regular screening of all students
- effective ongoing professional development

What PBIS Tiers Look Like

Tier 1: Universal PBIS

Tier 1 processes and procedures reflect schoolwide expectations for all students' behavior. Teachers implement a variety of strategies to teach and encourage these behaviors, such as:

- All classrooms are physically arranged to facilitate learning.
- Staff teach classroom expectations, rules, and routines. (See chapter 13.)
- Teachers define, post, and teach three to five positive classroom expectations.
- Teachers circulate in the classroom, interacting with students and monitoring behavior.
- Teachers provide opportunities for students to ask questions or make statements.
- Teachers provide frequent praise to reinforce positive behavior.
- Teachers remind students of appropriate behavior when transitioning from one environment to another.
- Teachers use brief, specific requests or statements to correct behaviors.
- Teachers respond to minor misbehavior by ignoring it or removing privileges.
- Teachers offer redirection and alternative behaviors to help students comply with expectations.

In schools that implement PBIS consistently, Tier 1 interventions ideally could resolve 80 percent of behavior problems and office discipline referrals. In schools where many students are struggling, 50 to 70 percent of problems may be resolved.[8]

Tier 2: Supplemental PBIS

Tier 2 interventions address about 10 to 15 percent of students—those who don't respond favorably to Tier 1 interventions. To identify students in need of Tier 2 support, teachers can gather data via classroom tracking forms listing minor classroom misbehavior, classroom interventions, and office discipline referrals. Screening instruments also help teachers identify these students.

Teachers then use strategies that address the behavioral issues of groups of students with similar behavior problems or behaviors that occur for the same reasons. For example, a teacher might create two separate Tier 2 intervention groups: one for students who seek excessive attention and one for students who try to avoid academic work.

Tier 2 interventions usually involve additional instruction and practice.[9] Common interventions at this level are the behavior education program (BEP) or check-in/check-out (CICO), social skills groups, mentoring, and contracts.[10] (See chapter 1 for more information on best practices for classroom behavior management.)

Tier 3: Intensive PBIS

A remaining 1 to 5 percent of students may require interventions that address individuals' problematic behaviors.[11] School teams meet to develop an individual behavior plan for each student using a four-step problem-solving process:[12]

1. Identify the problem. What is the problem? What do we want the student to do instead of the problem behavior?

2. Analyze the problem. Why is the problem occurring?

3. Design an intervention. What are we going to do to solve the problem?

4. Evaluate the student's response to the intervention. Did the intervention work?

Student interventions are based on what each student requires to be successful at school. Students receiving Tier 3 supports can continue to receive Tier 1 and 2 supports as needed.

FUNCTIONAL BEHAVIOR ASSESSMENT (FBA)

To more precisely determine the purpose of a student's behavior, educators may decide to conduct a functional behavior assessment (FBA) at any tier of intervention to collect additional information. An FBA is based on several assumptions:[13]

- Behavior is a response to an event (antecedent).

- Behavior is a form of communication.

- Behavior is strengthened or weakened by the consequences that follow it.

- Behavior is, most often, designed to obtain something desirable or avoid something unpleasant or punishing.

The procedure for conducting an FBA usually includes the following steps:[14]

1. Identify and define the problem behavior.

2. Collect information about when the behavior occurs through observation, data collection, and interviews with the student, parents, and staff.

3. Identify what happens before the student's problem behavior and what happens after the behavior.

4. Come to an agreement about the purpose of the behavior.

5. Develop a statement that explains why and when the team thinks the student uses the problem behavior.

Response to Intervention (RTI)

As in the PBIS framework, in which social and behavioral rules are taught to all students, in the RTI framework, all academic subjects are taught using a core curriculum that is research-based as much as possible. In Tier 1 of the RTI framework, teachers gather data from curriculum-based assessments administered to all students a few times a year to identify those at risk of academic failure. Teachers then provide at-risk students more instruction with Tier 2 interventions. Evidence-based instruction at this level is usually given in small groups that meet three or four times a week for twenty to forty minutes each time.[15] A small number of students will require Tier 3 intervention. This involves longer and more frequent sessions in smaller groups targeting individual needs. The data teachers record at each level drives their decisions to provide different levels of intervention. Students whose initial screenings show them to be severely lacking in skills compared to their classmates can be moved immediately into a higher tier of interventions.[16]

MTSS Is Helpful But Does Not Identify or Solve All Problems

In the mental health world, professionals sometimes label disorders as *externalizing* or *internalizing*. Externalizing disorders usually cause disruptive behaviors that directly affect others. Internalizing disorders usually cause behaviors that individuals experience inside and are not frequently observed by others. For example, anxiety or depressive disorders are internalizing disorders. An MTSS approach can help identify externalizing disorders but cannot identify invisible internalizing disorders. Later chapters in this book offer ways educators can identify and respond to students with internalizing disorders.

Despite the introduction and progress of MTSS, "it is untrue and misleading to claim that we currently have a necessary and sufficient knowledge base to guide the implementation of RTI as a process of early intervention and disability identification across all grades, for all academic skills, in all content areas, and for all children and youth."[17] Educators should rely on those practices that have been identified as evidence-based and effective to address specific challenges.[18]

In addition, educators must, of course, comply with existing requirements regarding the accommodations provided to students with special needs, including those with 504 plans or individualized education programs (IEPs). MTSS is a *recommended* process that addresses all students' behavioral and academic difficulties. The Rehabilitation Act of 1973 *requires* that schools provide accommodations for students with disabilities. This civil rights law prevents discrimination against students with disabilities by requiring schools to meet the needs of these students as adequately as they meet the needs of nondisabled students. This requirement affords students with disabilities an equal opportunity for an education. The law provides classroom services or accommodations for students with physical or mental disabilities if their disability "substantially limits" a major life activity (learning).[19] In 2008, the Americans with Disabilities Act was amended to make it easier for students to declare a disability. The amendment said that the term *substantially limits* should be interpreted broadly and not require an extensive analysis.[20] Later chapters in this book will provide teaching strategies and classroom accommodations for many mental health and learning disorders.

CHAPTER 3

Identifying and Communicating Students' Needs

"There is no health without mental health; mental health is too important to be left to the professionals alone, and mental health is everyone's business."

—*Vikram Patel, psychiatrist and Harvard professor*

You may learn in any number of ways that students have mental health or learning disorders. With some children, you may spot signs of possible disorders on your own. With other children, someone will inform you of their difficulties. For example, an administrator might ask you to pick up where another teacher has left off in providing accommodations or special services for a student who has a learning disability or depression. Or perhaps parents report a disorder when their child joins your class.

When someone informs you of a student's problem, it can help a great deal to get familiar with any data on the student that school staff have already collected. This might include the student's academic history, information on behavior and social skills, and past 504 plans or individualized education programs (IEPs). (All students receiving special education services have IEPs.) You can also gather anecdotal data by talking to other staff members who have taught or counseled the student in the past.

Regardless of whether you have prior information about a student's disability or disorder, early intervention can make a significant difference in the progress the child makes during the school year. For example, a prompt change in instructional approach might help you engage a student in a new way and prevent the need for special services. In another scenario, a referral for special education assessment might be necessary. The more quickly educators provide students with instructional strategies or accommodations that best respond to students' needs, the more likely all students are to be successful.

SCHOOL REGISTRATION FORMS

Your school's registration form is a great first opportunity to gather important information about students. Registration forms are usually standard throughout school districts. These forms request general information about students, including any mental health, behavioral, speech, or learning problems that may affect students' education. (The forms should always include a confidentiality statement.)

To minimize the possibility of families forgetting to note children's conditions, it's best if registration forms list common problems, such as learning disabilities, ADHD, mood and anxiety disorders, tics, seizures, and speech or language difficulties. Ideally, forms should provide an additional "other" space for writing in unlisted conditions. Forms should also offer space for families to list physical illnesses, such as allergies and diabetes. Allow plenty of space for parents to write relevant comments about students' problems.

If students are not required to register yearly, distribute a form annually that asks parents to inform the school of any changes in medical history or other special circumstances affecting a child. Also be sure an emergency contact form is on file for every student.

Early intervention is just as important for children with mental health disorders as it is for children with learning disorders. Emotional distress due to a mood disorder or another condition affects students in multiple ways. Academic performance can suffer, as can self-concept and relationships with others. Some educators may be reluctant to intervene in issues related to a child's emotional well-being. Indeed, making the decision to intervene requires good judgment. Remember, however, that students' difficulties are seldom resolved without intervention from caring adults. Your role is important.

What should you do if you observe a child having difficulties? You might be able to resolve a minor problem alone. For more serious problems, it's important to consult with colleagues. Counselors, school psychologists, other specialists, and administrators can all provide significant insight. Often they will have background information on a student that you might not be privy to. These people are also responsible for knowing the ins and outs of school procedures and important legal considerations that determine the next steps for helping a child.

 IMPORTANT! When you are speaking with students or their parents about behaviors, avoid diagnosing disorders. Diagnosing goes beyond your qualifications as a teacher. Your responsibility is to report behavior you observe—not to diagnose a condition that may be causing the behavior. Involve counselors, school psychologists, and other specialists in your conversations with parents as needed.

It's best if the policies and forms for reporting behavior problems are uniform within your school or district. If your school does not have guidelines for responding to these issues, collaborating with other school staff in a team approach is especially crucial.

Working with Counselors and School Psychologists

If your school uses a Multi-Tiered System of Supports (MTSS), you'll be implementing interventions from that system. (See chapter 2 for more on MTSS.) If you have not been trained in MTSS, check with counselors, school psychologists, and other specialists before deciding on interventions for students. There are many ways in which you can reach out for this help:

- If you don't completely understand a student's behavior, consider asking a counselor, school psychologist, or special educator to observe your class. This person may be able to offer insight into why a student is acting a certain way or could conduct additional assessments to help determine what's happening.

- Sometimes a student's difficulties won't present you with an obvious intervention strategy. Rely on counselors, school psychologists, and other specialists to suggest interventions.

- For students facing certain sensitive problems, such as social problems or difficulties dealing with divorce, the loss of a loved one, or other major life changes, request that a specialist intervene. Particularly in elementary schools, counselors often conduct groups for students who may be experiencing such problems.

- Call on school psychologists, counselors, and other specially trained staff to manage crises with students. Consider including in any student coping plan (see page 20) a provision allowing students to visit a specialist to talk and calm down during emotional times.

- A counselor, school psychologist, or other specialist can be a great resource during parent meetings in which you are discussing a student's problem.

Also remember to make full use of any other specialists in your school—the school nurse, the speech-language pathologist, the occupational therapist, and any others who may be able to help with a student's behavior. Consult these staff members when their areas of specialty correspond with needs you observe in students.

 IMPORTANT! Although it's essential to communicate about students with other staff, be cautious about revealing information students have told you in confidence. A high school girl may tell you a certain boy has been calling her a lot. A fifth grader might confide to you that he dislikes another teacher at school. By sharing too much, you could damage a student's trust in you and jeopardize the relationship. However, in some situations—such as in the case of abuse or talk of suicide—you are legally obligated to report information.

Communicating with Parents

Sharing sensitive information with parents may be one of the most challenging parts of your job. When you're speaking with parents, you may find it helpful to limit your reporting to the ways in which problems are negatively affecting the child emotionally, socially, or academically. Using this approach, you'll be more likely to avoid saying anything that may sound like a value judgment of the student's abilities or of the parents' child-rearing. If you're lucky, a parent will respond to your comments with something like, "Thank you for sharing this information. I've noticed this behavior, too, and I'm concerned about it. I appreciate how much you care about my child."

Even when you've made your best effort to show sensitivity, parents may not react favorably. A parent may disagree with what you have to say ("Are you saying that my child has a problem?"). Or a parent may blame you for the student's difficulty ("If school were more interesting and you were a better teacher, my child wouldn't behave this way!"). If you hear such remarks, remember that you're not alone. During difficult times like this, another member of the school staff can be especially helpful. A colleague can verify what you are saying about a student and serve as a witness to the conversation you—and, by extension, your school—are having with a parent.

What can you do if a parent becomes defensive or even confrontational? First, stop and take a deep breath. It's your responsibility to stay calm and listen to what the parent has to say. It's possible that a parent's claims are true—that a child doesn't show a behavior at home. Acknowledge this and say you're glad to hear that the parent hasn't observed this behavior outside of school. You may want to add, however, that for whatever reason, the student is showing certain behaviors in your classroom that are affecting learning—not only of the child in question, but also of other students.

YOUR COMMENTS ARE NEVER IN VAIN

If you're a teacher of a young child and the first to express concerns about a behavior, the child's parents may minimize or deny your concern. Parents sometimes feel their child will "grow out of it." If the child continues to exhibit the concerning behavior, parents will likely hear about it from subsequent teachers. When this happens several times, parents are more likely to acknowledge the concern and take some action. So even if you feel at times that your efforts do not yield the outcomes you hope for, take heart knowing that speaking up is still the right course of action.

In some situations, you may know that a student also behaves in a certain way outside of school. Don't debate a parent who tells you otherwise, since this may cause greater tension. Remember that a child's behavior is a sensitive topic for parents. They may struggle to come to terms with their child behaving in an inappropriate way or having an emotional problem. It may take more than you (or other school staff) sharing information about the student for parents to acknowledge certain realities. In some cases, parents simply do not want to face the idea that a problem exists.

In difficult times, remember why you have brought up concerns with parents. You're looking out for the welfare and successful education of your student. Also remember that in your interactions with parents, you need to work with them to address a child's problem. The best way to help students is to use a team approach—with you, other school staff, parents, and outside professionals working together to address a student's difficulties.

Following are some examples of inappropriate suggestions and appropriate alternatives for speaking to parents.

Instead of . . .	Try . . .
"I think your child is depressed."	"I'm a little concerned about Sayén. She doesn't laugh or get excited anymore when all the other students are having a good time in class. Have you noticed anything different about her behavior lately?"
"Jamie's awfully shy."	"I've noticed that Jamie sometimes has trouble joining others at playtime, and looks down at the floor much of the time. Have you noticed any of these behaviors when Jamie is with others outside school?"
"Eric never stops running around. I think he might have ADHD."	"Sometimes Eric seems to have a hard time paying attention and staying still. I notice that he also forgets instructions much of the time and often seems distracted. Have you ever noticed behavior like this at home?"

CHILD ABUSE AND NEGLECT

There may be times when you suspect parental mistreatment as a cause of a student's difficulties. Teachers are legally obligated to report suspicions of child abuse or neglect. You can find statutes and reporting information for all US states and territories at www.childwelfare.gov.

You don't have to be certain that abuse is occurring. The law requires reporting only a reasonable suspicion. Your state agency will conduct an inquiry to determine the validity of a suspicion. Informants are kept anonymous. Make sure you or your school administrator has checked the applicable laws in your state. If you do not report suspected child abuse or neglect, you and your school could be held liable.

Medication

School officials should be aware of any medications students are taking. Side effects of medications (such as stomachaches, appetite changes, mood changes, headaches, and agitation) can affect children at school. When you are reporting potential medication side effects to parents, follow guidelines similar to those for discussing behavior. At first it's best to make behavioral observations ("Sam was very sleepy today." "Luis keeps complaining of headaches."). Let the parent respond with an explanation. If the parent does not mention a connection with medication, you might ask whether a medication the student is taking may be causing the problem. You might find it helpful to involve a school specialist in these conversations.

Even when you are very tactful, some parents may misinterpret your comments about medication. They might think you either favor or oppose its use. Remember that your job is to manage students in the classroom as effectively as you can, regardless of other treatments or interventions parents pursue. Medical treatment is the parents' responsibility and choice.

NEVER SUGGEST THAT A STUDENT TAKE MEDICATION

You probably know that medication can be helpful for students who have ADHD, as well as for students who have some other disorders. But just as you should never mention a diagnosis to parents, you should also refrain from suggesting medication treatment.

CHAPTER 4

Culturally Responsive Education

....

"[Educators] must accept the existence of cultural pluralism
in this country and respect differences without equating them with
inferiorities or tolerating them with an air of condescension."

—Geneva Gay, education professor and author

....

Today's students are more diverse than ever, and that diversity is increasing. In 2015, for the first time in US history, the majority of babies younger than one year old were children of color.[1] By the year 2023, 55 percent of US students are projected to be children of color.[2] While the population of students of color continues to grow in the United States, 90 percent of teachers in twenty-four states are white.[3] Most of these teachers have not been trained in culturally and linguistically responsive teaching techniques.

A culture is a group of people with shared experiences, interests, and beliefs. Cultures can be based on racial, ethnic, and language differences, but there are also other cultures in schools that contribute to diversity. For example, students who identify as LGBTQ share a culture.[4] Similarly, students who come from economically diverse backgrounds and different types of families may also share other things in common. Students may identify with different religious groups that represent different cultures. Some students may pray quietly during the school day, refuse to eat certain foods, or wear clothing that is traditional in their families. All of these things represent different aspects of culture.

Culturally responsive teaching is "using cultural knowledge, prior experiences, frames of reference, and performance styles of . . . diverse students to make learning encounters more relevant to and effective for them."[5] The need for culturally responsive teaching is not simply a politically correct theory. Without a culturally responsive school environment, some students can experience the following negative consequences:

- They may encounter unintentional slights against their backgrounds.[6]
- Teachers may have lower tolerance for and expectations of these students.[7]
- Teachers may resort to disciplinary actions more frequently with these students.[8]

Fostering Cultural Awareness

To foster cultural and linguistic responsiveness in your classroom, you can use the following strategies:[9]

Inquire about your students' backgrounds. Encourage them to share information about their family histories, customs, and beliefs.

Ask students about what interests them. Encourage students to select reading materials, projects, and experiences to share with the class. Some of these selections may be culturally relevant and interesting for all students.

Be sensitive to language differences. Respect English language learners and be patient with any difficulty you have understanding these students' spoken or written English.

Maintain high expectations for all students. Teachers sometimes assume that students from different cultures or backgrounds will perform worse than students from teachers' own cultures. But these students are equally capable if teachers give them comparable instruction. If English knowledge is an impediment, provide instructional materials at the students' level of English mastery.

Develop a curriculum that recognizes many cultures. Help students develop pride in their cultures and in their individual identities within those cultures, as well as respect for people from other cultures and backgrounds.

The reproducible "Classroom Checklist" on page 37 can help you evaluate the cultural sensitivity of your classroom, and the reproducible "Curriculum Checklist" on page 38 offers suggestions for incorporating information from various cultures into your curriculum.

CULTURALLY RESPONSIVE EDUCATION STARTS WITH TEACHERS AND STAFF

Teachers and staff learn and practice cultural sensitivity by:[10]

- understanding their own cultural identities and how these identities influence their teaching

- inviting community members from all cultures and backgrounds to participate in school activities and leadership roles

- learning about students' backgrounds, families, cultures, values, and customs

- encouraging students to learn about one another's cultures

- affirming that culturally specific behaviors in students' homes and communities are legitimate and valuable

Embedding Culturally Responsive Practices Within a Multi-Tiered System of Supports (MTSS)

One important reason for implementing MTSS in schools is to decrease disproportionality in disciplinary practices. Disciplinary disproportionality is "an over-representation of minorities, often African Americans, in the use of disciplinary, exclusionary, and punitive consequences."[11] Numerous studies have shown no evidence that black students' behavior is worse than white students' behavior, so disciplinary statistics should be the same for both groups.

DISPROPORTIONATE DISCIPLINE

- Black students are more frequently disciplined than white students are.[12]

- Black students are 30 percent more likely to receive office referrals.[12]

- Black students are suspended and expelled more often and are suspended for longer durations.[13]

- Black girls are twice as likely to receive office referrals and five times more likely to be suspended compared to white girls.[12]

- In elementary schools, suspension rates of black students are six times higher than the suspension rates of white students.[12]

Researchers have suggested that some of these excessive disciplinary practices are a result of teachers lacking cultural awareness. The following suggestions can help you craft a culturally responsive disciplinary approach. A school's MTSS can include these criteria, or a school without MTSS can implement these criteria independently.[14]

- The severity of discipline procedures matches the severity of the infraction.
- Disciplinary actions are based on the infraction, not the student.
- The same rules are applied to all students.
- Students receive the same discipline for breaking the same rules.

Members of minority cultures are vulnerable to ostracism, harassment, and bullying. Bullying and cyberbullying continue to be problems in schools, and traditional rules and punishments have not reduced the problem. Zero-tolerance policies have backfired, worsening bullying.[15]

A broader approach to bullying that appears to be effective is creating a whole-school climate that encourages empathy and positive interactions among students and between students and teachers.[16]

Other strategies for implementing a whole-school anti-bullying climate are as follows:

Encourage influential students to take the lead in changing the school culture.
One study showed that middle school students with lots of social connections created anti-bullying messages that reduced bullying.[17]

Implement social-emotional learning experiences. Teach students how to self-regulate, handle conflict, and empathize. For example, a student could ask a peer who has been bullied how he or she felt about the situation.

Encourage bystanders to speak up. Students who don't bully are more likely to stand up for peers in schools that emphasize a caring environment.

Ensure that teachers, coaches, and administrators don't bully students. Teachers and coaches humiliate students when they scream or yell at them. Adults model a positive school climate through caring and empathetic responses to students. Positive teacher-student relationships are associated with reduced bullying and increased feelings of safety among students.

Incorporate positive, empathetic, caring attitudes into the curriculum. For example, when you are discussing a current tragic or historical event, ask students how it might affect them and their families if it happened locally.

AN ALTERNATIVE TO PUNISHMENT FOR BULLYING

Restorative justice principles provide an alternative to punishment. These principles are as follows:[18]

- recognizing that misbehavior is an opportunity for social-emotional learning

- bringing together everyone who is immediately affected by the incident

- creating dialogues that lead to understanding and actions that restore relationships

These principles are put into action through restorative discussion circles facilitated by a teacher or counselor. In these discussions, students take responsibility for their actions, resolve the harm, repair the relationship, and internalize a moral message. Agreements are typically signed at the conclusion of a session. Participation is voluntary, but punishment is the alternative for students who refuse to participate. This intervention has shown preliminary results in improving many aspects of students' and teachers' lives in school. Educators should receive training and practice in this intervention prior to implementing it. For a good primer, see the guide *Teaching Restorative Practices with Classroom Circles* at studentsatthecenterhub.org /resource/teaching-restorative-practices-with-classroom-circles.

An MTSS is not complete until it is responsive to all cultures. Your challenge is to contribute to your classroom's and school's implementation of culturally sensitive practices. The checklists on pages 37–38 will enable you to make your classroom and teaching more responsive to students from diverse cultures.

Classroom Checklist

Does my classroom ...

- ☐ Value and respect differences in gender, religion, ethnicity, sexual identity, family composition, socioeconomic status, and student ability?

- ☐ Teach and model empathy, acceptance, kindness, generosity, respect, and responsibility?

- ☐ Display writings, artwork, projects, maps, and flags from many cultures?

- ☐ Have a large calendar with multicultural holidays and local events?

- ☐ Have seating and responsibility assignments that are not based on factors such as race, ethnicity, gender, and sexual identity?

- ☐ Have pictures of different people from many cultures?

- ☐ Offer books reflecting cultural diversity?

- ☐ Welcome parental and community involvement that bring diverse points of view?

- ☐ Ensure that participation in class field trips and other school sponsored activities does not depend on financial ability?

Curriculum Checklist

Does my academic curriculum ...

- ☐ Include literature, art, music, and well-known athletes or artists from many cultures?

- ☐ Discuss customs, traditions, holidays, clothing, and sports from around the world?

- ☐ Present male and female role models?

- ☐ Provide reading opportunities presenting material about different cultures, including religions, races, sexual identities, and blended and single-parent families?

- ☐ Encourage classroom discussions in which students can relate what they've read to their own experiences?

- ☐ Allow students to choose writing topics based on their own cultural experiences?

- ☐ Present and discuss examples in the media of stereotypes and bias to increase students' appreciation of diversity?

- ☐ Show sensitivity to students with a background of trauma, refugee experience, and family crisis and adjust assignments and evaluation methods accordingly?

CHAPTER 5

Social-Emotional Learning

"A growing body of research suggests that noncognitive factors can have just as strong an influence on academic performance and professional attainment as intellectual factors."

—US Department of Education

The Collaborative for Academic, Social, and Emotional Learning (CASEL) defines social-emotional learning (SEL) as "the process through which children and adults acquire the knowledge, attitudes, and skills to recognize and manage their emotions, set and achieve positive goals, demonstrate caring and concern for others, establish and maintain positive relationships, make responsible decisions, and handle interpersonal situations effectively."[1] You can incorporate social-emotional skills training into your school's Multi-Tiered System of Supports or MTSS (see chapter 2) or teach these skills independently.

THE PREDICTIVE POWER OF KINDERGARTEN BEHAVIOR

SEL begins early and has long-term effects. Studies show that kindergartners who were "socially and behaviorally 'not ready' for school" were much more likely to be retained, referred for special education, and suspended or expelled by the time they reached fourth grade.[2] Research also indicates that kindergarten students with higher social competence earn more high school and college degrees.[3]

Can social-emotional skills be taught? CASEL contends that "SEL programs are among the most successful interventions ever offered to school-aged youth."[4] Researchers have conducted hundreds of studies on SEL among students in grades K through 8. Programs following the recommended evidence-based practices improved these students' social-emotional skills, attitudes, social behavior, conduct, emotional well-being, and academic performance.[5] Teens who participated in SEL programs had lower rates of delinquency, substance abuse, and dropping out.[6] You can find detailed information on twenty-five leading SEL programs for elementary schools in the resources section (page 211).

This chapter discusses the following social-emotional skills and activities:

- self-control and self-regulation
- mindfulness
- mindset
- grit
- social skills
- yoga
- physical exercise

The social-emotional skills covered in this chapter, along with yoga and other physical exercise, complement academic learning so students can maximize their success in life.

Self-Control and Self-Regulation

You may remember the famous longitudinal study of preschoolers trying to resist eating marshmallows. In this study, researchers placed a marshmallow in front of each four-year-old participant. The children were told that if they didn't eat the marshmallow, they'd receive a second marshmallow in a few minutes. Kids who couldn't delay their gratification and ate the marshmallow went on to have lower reading and math levels in elementary school. They were at greater risk for oppositional behavior, aggression, and temper tantrums. As adults, they had poorer academic, health, and vocational outcomes.[7]

In addition to the terms *self-control* and *self-regulation*, you will see other terms used to describe these skills, including *self-discipline* and *willpower*. All these terms describe the ability to control one's impulses, attention, and emotions in order to sustain effort toward a goal. Poor self-control can lead to a variety of problems. For example, when students can't control their anger, they may lash out at teachers or other students. When students are distracted by classroom noise, it's hard for them to complete work in class. Students who don't have skills to deal with frustration may give up on many academic tasks.

In 2016, the Administration for Children and Families at the US Department of Health and Human Services published a report recommending that schools teach students self-regulation skills. These skills were defined as helping children "manage their thoughts and feelings, control impulses, and problem-solve."[8] Research has shown that these skills are better predictors of academic success than intelligence is.[9]

TEACHING SELF-CONTROL

The following strategies and accommodations may be useful for students with impulsive or hyperactive behaviors:

Emphasize the benefits of self-control. After a student exhibits self-control, point out the benefit of achieving the goal with self-discipline.

Play games that emphasize self-control with young students. Some examples are red light green light, Simon says, and freeze tag.[10]

Provide breaks between tasks that require self-control. Research has shown that willpower decreases the more it is used. Providing breaks allows the brain to recharge.[11]

Minimize distractions in your classroom. That pet guinea pig in a cage is cute, but it can be a major distraction.

Find ways to help students *want* to do work, rather than feel like they *have* to do it. The more you involve students in decisions about topics they work on, the more likely they will be to enjoy their work, and the less likely they'll be to grow distracted and frustrated.[12]

Empathize when you see frustration. Telling students who are frustrated with a task that "it's not that hard" or to "just keep trying" doesn't acknowledge their strong emotions. Such comments might increase students' frustration by implying that you are intolerant of their feelings. Instead, you could say, "That's really got you stumped, huh?" or, "Looks like you're frustrated." These statements validate students' feelings and encourage them to tell you why they're frustrated. They are then more likely to come up with a solution.

Let students move in ways that do not distract others. Let students stretch quietly or play with an object (such as a stress ball) when they feel the urge to move. You might also suggest students twirl their thumbs, tap a leg, or otherwise expend energy quietly.

Provide opportunities for physical activity. It can be difficult for children to stay still for an entire class period. When possible, incorporate physical activity into your lessons. This may be as simple as asking students to walk to the front of the class to respond to questions or write answers on the board.

Prevent students from turning in work or tests too quickly. Some children may rush through assignments and tests and make careless mistakes. Other students are competitive and may try to be the first to turn in their work. The quality of their work may suffer because they don't pay enough attention to detail. Tell these students you will not accept work if you think they have rushed to get it done.

Ask students to run errands for you. Let children who struggle with staying seated run errands periodically (like bringing something to the school office). If you notice that a student needs to move, invent an errand. Arrange for a student to occasionally drop off or pick up mail at the office and then return to class.

Let students move at their desks or tables. Allow students to sit on exercise balls, kneel on their chairs, or stand while they work.

Closely monitor behavior during transitions and unstructured activities. Some students may struggle to behave appropriately during lunch, recess, and other unstructured times. Reiterate rules for these periods and closely supervise these students when activities are under way.

Address misbehavior with minimal attention. Some children enjoy negative attention. If you become upset by their misbehavior, the behavior may increase. As much as possible, address inappropriate behavior without drawing a lot of attention to it. Keep verbal comments to a minimum, and try to give feedback through eye contact, a light touch on the shoulder, walking by a student's desk, or pointing at the student's work as a reminder to stay on task.

Set up behavior contracts. Focusing on one or two behaviors at a time, work with students to diminish inappropriate classroom actions. Create a behavior contract (see page 17) that specifically spells out what a student agrees to do, as well as the reward for meeting this goal. For an example of a filled-out behavior contract, see page 12.

Provide positive reinforcement for appropriate behavior. Even when students are not behaving perfectly, encourage and reinforce progress they make. Be specific in your praise. For example: "It's great the way you lined up this morning without touching anyone else."

Mindfulness

The practice of mindfulness originated in Buddhism more than two thousand years ago. Professor of medicine Jon Kabat-Zinn introduced it to the United States as a nonreligious practice in 1979. He defined mindfulness as "paying attention on purpose, in the present moment, and nonjudgmentally to the unfolding of experience moment by moment."[13]

Meditation is one process for achieving mindfulness. You begin by sitting quietly, paying attention to your breathing. Your mind will start to drift off to various thoughts about the past and the future. You accept these thoughts without any emotional reaction or judgment, let them pass, and return attention to your breathing. Does that sound simple? It's not. After just a few minutes, it becomes obvious how your thoughts constantly intrude to prevent you from being in the present moment. It takes lots of practice—weeks or months—to learn how to stay in the moment. It becomes easier over time, though, and the cognitive, emotional, and physical benefits appear to be numerous.[14]

Since 2000, the practice of mindfulness meditation has increased in schools.[15] Evidence is accumulating that K through 12 students who learn and practice mindfulness meditation experience some improvement in attention, social skills, and academic performance and that they have lower rates of anxiety, depression, anger, and possibly even ADHD.[16] Several mindfulness training programs now exist for teachers and students.[17] The potential benefits of mindfulness meditation for students convinced the United Kingdom in 2015 to launch a five-year, $8 million study of more than six thousand students between ages eleven and fourteen.[18]

MEDITATION FOR YOUNGER STUDENTS

Dr. Amy Saltzman, a holistic physician, wrote the meditation practice on page 43. It is not meant to be read as a script. Rather, it offers an example of language for young children that promotes tranquility. It will give you a sense of the words a teacher might use with students in grades K through 2. Teachers practice this exercise with students for five to ten minutes per day, and students are advised to practice at home as well. Teachers should not teach any meditative practice unless they have had training. Some adults mistakenly consider meditation to be only a religious practice. For this reason, it is important to get consent from your school and from families before introducing this practice.

"Today I would like to share one of my favorite places with you. It is called Still Quiet Place. It's not a place you travel to in a car, or a train, or a plane. It is a place inside you that you can find just by breathing.

Let's find it now. If you feel safe, close your eyes. Whether your eyes are open or closed, take some slow, deep breaths. See if you can feel a kind of warm smile in your body. Do you feel it? This is your Still Quiet Place. Take some more deep breaths, and really snuggle in.

The best thing about your Still Quiet Place is that it's always inside you. And you can visit it whenever you like. It is nice to visit your Still Quiet Place and feel the love that is there. It is especially helpful to visit your Still Quiet Place if you are feeling angry, or sad, or afraid. The Still Quiet Place is a good place to talk with these feelings and to make friends with them. When you rest in your Still Quiet Place and talk to your feelings, you may find that the feelings are not as big or as powerful as they seem. Remember, you can come here whenever you want, and stay as long as you like."*

*Amy Saltzman, *Mindfulness: A Guide for Teachers*, www.contemplativemind.org/Mindfulness-A_Teachers_Guide.pdf. Used with permission.

MEDITATION FOR OLDER STUDENTS

Students in fifth grade and older can learn Dr. Saltzman's PEACE process. After being trained and practicing breathing, students learn and practice the following steps to use in response to minor daily irritations. When students become more proficient at this process, they can use it to deal with more complex or challenging situations. PEACE* is an acronym for:[19]

P—Pause when you become aware that something is difficult.

E—Exhale and let out a sigh if you feel like it, then inhale.

A—Accept the situation as it is. As you continue to breathe, accept the situation and your reaction to it. It doesn't mean you're happy about it; just that you acknowledge it.

C—Choose how you'll respond.

E—Engage. After you've done the previous steps, you're now ready to interact with people and deal with the situation.

You can listen to Dr. Saltzman describe the theory and practice of meditation for teens at www.stillquietplace.com/still-quiet-place.

MEDITATION FOR TEACHERS

More than half of teachers feel their jobs negatively affect their mental and physical health.[20] To ease such stress, mindfulness meditation may be helpful for teachers, just as it is for students. A study of hundreds of urban elementary school teachers trained in mindfulness meditation by the Cultivating Awareness and Resilience in Education (CARE) program found that the program improved their sense of well-being, mindfulness, and sensitivity to students' needs.[21] Whether a teacher is

*Amy Saltzman, *Mindfulness: A Guide for Teachers*, www.contemplativemind.org/Mindfulness-A_Teachers_Guide.pdf. Used with permission.

trained in a school program or outside school, it appears that teachers may benefit personally and professionally from mindfulness meditation. This practice may be part of the solution to teacher burnout.

Mindset

Mindset refers to the perspective a person takes when approaching a task. In her 2016 book *Mindset: The New Psychology of Success*, psychologist Carol S. Dweck describes the difference between a fixed mindset and a growth mindset.[22] A fixed mindset is a belief that intelligence or natural ability is inborn and that this innate ability limits what you can accomplish. A growth mindset is a belief that effort and additional strategies can increase your abilities and accomplishments over time.

What are the consequences of a fixed mindset versus a growth mindset? Students with a fixed mindset tend to become discouraged when they encounter difficulty, because they believe that they have maximized their abilities. They may avoid difficult subjects or challenging tasks. If they are often told they are really smart, they may avoid tasks they fear might show that they are not so smart.[23]

Students with a growth mindset believe they are always capable of doing better. They respond to difficulty by figuring out how or why they weren't successful and then increasing their efforts. They see setbacks as opportunities to learn. A growth mindset may be particularly important for girls, who as early as age six tend to think boys are smarter than girls are. Girls with a fixed mindset may avoid some tasks because they don't believe they have the ability to be successful.[24]

It probably won't surprise you to learn that students with a growth mindset accomplish more than students with a fixed mindset do. So how do you teach and encourage students to have a growth mindset? You do this with the language you use and the way you talk to students. When you are commenting on students' work, instead of praising ability or intelligence, praise the processes and strategies students use. Here are some examples of teacher statements and responses to students that emphasize either a fixed or growth mindset:[25]

Praise
Fixed mindset response: "You wrote a great paper!"
Growth mindset response: "I can tell you put a lot of time and effort into that paper. It really shows."

Reminder to get back on task
Fixed mindset response: "Let's get back to work."
Growth mindset response: "If you're having difficulty, you can ask me for some help. Try to remember the techniques we talked about in class. I saw you do a similar problem yesterday, and I'm pretty sure you can solve this one."

Motivation
Fixed mindset response: "That was a pretty low test score. Maybe those problems were too difficult for you."
Growth mindset response: "You might be disappointed with your grade on that test. Let's figure out a strategy to help you get ready for the next test. I know that with a little bit more time and effort, you can do better."

Assigning work

Fixed mindset statement: "Class, this assignment is a tough one and may be difficult for some of you."

Growth mindset statement: "Class, when you first look at this assignment, it's going to seem very challenging. But if you spend a bit more time than usual on this work and use some of the ideas we've talked about in class, you'll be able to do this."

Grit

Psychologist Angela Duckworth popularized the term *grit* in her 2016 book *Grit: The Power of Passion and Perseverance*. People with grit have the self-discipline, determination, and resilience to keep pursuing goals despite frustration and failure, and they usually have a passion for their tasks and goals. These traits may be as important to success as intelligence is.[26] Individuals with grit usually have a growth mindset. They believe that if they persist with more effort and additional strategies, they can reach their goals despite setbacks.

How can you foster grit in your students? First, teach and reinforce a growth mindset. Second, let students pursue topics they're interested in. Interest is the first step in developing a passion. Third, encourage students to take on challenging tasks. Fourth, teach and model the idea that setbacks and failures are normal and should be expected and that students can overcome these obstacles with hard work and self-discipline. Setbacks and failures are learning experiences that reinforce resilience. Last, provide support for students when they encounter difficulties.[27] A teacher, website, or reference book could serve as a resource that reinforces the importance of finding alternative strategies when students' initial attempts fail.

Social Skills

Social skills can either facilitate or hinder students' relationships. These skills are sometimes included in Tier 2 of an MTSS (see chapter 2), but they can also be taught independently. The National Association of School Psychologists has organized these skills into the following categories:[28]

basic, essential skills: listening, following directions, talking nicely

interpersonal skills: asking for permission, sharing, inviting, waiting, being empathetic, working with others

problem-solving skills: asking for help, taking responsibility for actions, apologizing, evaluating alternative solutions, making decisions

conflict resolution skills: identifying emotions and dealing with bullying, peer pressure, and losing

Assessing Young Children's Social Competence

The pace of social development varies among students, so it's important to evaluate children's progress on key social abilities. The following lists of qualities and skills come from the ERIC Clearinghouse on Elementary and Early Childhood Education.[29] A particular student will not necessarily exhibit all these qualities and skills. But the more skills a student exhibits by age six, the more likely the student will be to have positive academic and social relationships as a child and as an adult. Students who do not possess many of these skills will benefit the most from social-emotional programs.

Individual Qualities

- is usually in a positive mood
- is not excessively dependent on adults
- usually comes to the program willingly
- usually copes with rebuffs adequately
- shows the capacity to empathize
- has positive relationships with one or two peers; shows the capacity to really care about these peers and misses them if they are absent
- displays the capacity for humor
- does not seem to be acutely lonely

Social Skills

- approaches others positively
- expresses wishes and preferences clearly; gives reasons for actions and positions
- asserts own rights and needs appropriately
- is not easily intimidated by bullying
- expresses frustrations and anger effectively and without escalating disagreements or harming others
- gains access to ongoing groups at play and in schoolwork
- enters ongoing discussion on a subject; makes relevant contributions to ongoing activities
- takes turns fairly easily
- shows interest in others; exchanges information with and requests information from others appropriately
- negotiates and compromises with others appropriately
- does not draw inappropriate attention to self
- accepts and enjoys peers and adults of other ethnic groups
- interacts nonverbally with other children using smiles, waves, nods, and so on

Peer Relationship Qualities

- is usually accepted, not neglected or rejected, by other children
- is sometimes invited by other children to join them in play, friendship, and schoolwork
- is named by other children as someone they are friends with or like to play and work with

TEACHING SOCIAL SKILLS

Teaching a social skill in the classroom involves a set of sequential steps:

1. Name the skill.
2. Create a rule about the skill. For example, "You use this skill when you want to . . ."
3. Break down the skill into small steps.
4. Demonstrate and model the skill.
5. Rehearse or role-play the skill in action.
6. Practice, practice, practice.

STEP-BY-STEP BREAKDOWN OF HOW TO JOIN A GROUP

Following are rules or steps teachers can teach children for joining a group:

1. Look at the person you want to speak to.
2. If necessary, wait until that person is finished talking.
3. Tap the person on the shoulder or arm.
4. When the person turns to you, say, "Can I play?" or, "Do you have room for one more?" or, "I heard you guys talking, and I think I might know the answer to that question."
5. Wait until the person responds.
6. If the person says "Okay" or something else that tells you that you can join or speak, say, "Thanks."
7. If the person ignores you or doesn't invite you to join or want you to speak, say, "Okay," and walk away. Try not to take this rejection personally. There might be lots of reasons, not having to do with you, for why this person didn't want to include you.

Yoga

Teaching and practicing yoga in schools is on the rise. Preliminary research is quite promising regarding yoga's benefits for students' academic and social-emotional behavior.[30] Both mindfulness meditation and yoga produce physical and cognitive benefits. Yoga teaches physical postures, breathing exercises, and relaxation techniques.[31] Its physical benefits include increased flexibility, strength, balance, and coordination.[32] The cognitive benefits are seen in improved concentration and executive functioning (see chapter 6). Other benefits include improved mood and self-control, decreased anxiety and emotional arousal, and improved self-esteem. An added benefit is that practicing yoga in schools can help reduce stress among teachers and other staff.[33]

Physical Exercise

It is well known that exercise leads to improved cognitive and emotional functioning in adults.[34] Evidence is accumulating that shows similar effects in children.[35] But the majority of children are not exercising enough. In 2012, one out of every three children age two to nineteen was overweight. One in six children was obese. And studies in 2006 and 2009 found that only about one in four children got the sixty minutes of daily physical exercise recommended by the *2008 Physical Activity Guidelines for Americans*.[36] Schools can help by increasing the amount of physical activity students receive at recess and after school. In 2013, the American Academy of Pediatrics issued a statement that "recess is a crucial and necessary component of a child's development and, as such, it should not be withheld for punitive or academic reasons."[37]

A report by the Institute of Medicine titled *Educating the Student Body: Taking Physical Activity and Physical Education to School* recommends a whole-school approach to increasing opportunities for physical exercise. The report includes the following recommendations:[38]

- The US Department of Education should designate physical education as a core subject.

- Teacher training and continuing education programs should provide multiple opportunities for K to 12 classroom and physical education teachers to promote physical activities in their curricula.

- High-quality physical education classes devote at least 50 percent of class time to providing high-intensity physical activity. Elementary students should participate in 150 minutes of physical education per week, and middle schoolers and high schoolers 225 minutes per week.

- Additional opportunities for physical activity should be accessible to all students before and after school hours.

A guide from the Centers for Disease Control and Prevention, *Strategies for Recess in Schools*, notes that only eight states require recess in school. This report provides specific guidelines for implementing recess in schools.[39]

Recess alone does not provide sufficient physical activity for students to meet the recommended guidelines. Activity after school and on weekends is also necessary to counter students' sedentary lifestyles. But taking away electronics and getting children moving is a major challenge for today's parents. Suggestions that educators can give parents include:[40]

Consider activities other than organized sports. Dancing, martial arts, swimming, ice skating, skateboarding, jumping rope, yoga, or climbing at a playground are possibilities for children who are better at non-ball activities.

Join children in play. Children love having adults play with them. Shoot hoops, kick a ball, bike, or walk with kids.

Limit screen time. The American Academy of Pediatrics recommends that children get no more than one to two hours of screen time a day.

Lead by example. If you spend a lot of time in front of the TV, you may not be practicing what you preach. You've got to model physical activity. Walk instead of driving somewhere and climb stairs instead of taking an elevator. When you go to the gym or for a run, explain to children why this activity is important.

Praise children for the smallest effort. Anything is better than nothing. Some children who aren't naturally athletic may be self-conscious about attempting physical activities. Movement, not proficiency, is the goal.

Bring a friend. Most kids enjoy activities they can play with other children.

Establish a routine. If children know that every Saturday morning means a bike ride and two evenings a week involve a brisk walk, they'll be more accepting of these activities.

Make exercise nonnegotiable. Exercise should be required, just like brushing teeth and wearing seatbelts are. All these activities promote children's health and well-being.

Allow children to have input. Children won't necessarily prefer an idea adults came up with. Let children suggest activities.

Make it fun. Children will resist exercising if it's not enjoyable. Find ways to make activities fun. Turn activities into some kind of game.

Evidence continues to accumulate showing that the skills and activities covered in this chapter complement academic learning so students can maximize their success in life. Principals and administrators remain highly interested in SEL programs and are eager to learn implementation strategies.[41] But our current educational system places enormous emphasis on teaching academic skills so students pass achievement and competency tests. Due to these priorities, only 25 percent of principals said their schools were "high implementers" of SEL programs.[42] How much more progress SEL programs can make in schools remains to be seen.

The most comprehensive health and wellness curriculum, the Compassionate Schools Project, is incorporating many of these social-emotional skills as well as yoga and other exercise. In Louisville, Kentucky, SEL skills are being taught to more than twenty thousand K to 5 students in fifty schools. Results of this instruction will be analyzed between 2019 and 2021, and student outcomes will be compared with those of students who did not participate in the program during the same period of time. This comparison will hopefully yield valuable information about the benefits of this type of social-emotional instruction for elementary students.[43]

CHAPTER 6

Identifying and Supporting Students with Executive Function Difficulties

"You can be truly smart and still struggle in life if you lack the ability to plan, organize time and space, initiate projects and see them through to completion, and you cannot resist temptations in favor of later better rewards."

—*Richard C. Saltus, science writer*

Executive function (EF) skills are cognitive skills governed by the prefrontal area of the brain and are necessary to managing behaviors leading to a goal. This is a very broad definition. EF skills include many cognitive, behavioral, and emotional regulation skills that are difficult to capture under a single definition. The EF skills covered in this chapter are cognitive skills. Emotional and behavioral regulation skills are discussed in Chapter 5: Social-Emotional Learning. Any student can have problems with EF, but those with ADHD, learning disabilities, and autism spectrum disorder (ASD) are at higher risk for challenges in this area.

Executive Function and Related Academic Problems

Weaknesses in different executive function skills cause different academic problems. Following is a list of some EF skills students may lack and common related academic problems.

Executive Function Skill	Common Related Academic Problems
sustaining attention: paying attention and resisting distractions for long enough to accomplish a goal related to tasks requiring effort	difficulty following directions
initiating: starting tasks in a timely manner	not completing classwork and homework
planning: planning and prioritizing what needs to be done and when (time management)	difficulty finishing homework, long-term assignments, and projects
organizing: keeping track of materials	not having appropriate materials available at the right time in school and at home not completing assignments

Executive Function Skill	Common Related Academic Problems
working memory: holding onto information while manipulating that information or performing another task	difficulty recalling sequential directions or multistep tasks
	forgetting what you're doing while doing it
	forgetting what you were going to say or write
shifting: changing activities or seeing something from another point of view	difficulty changing from one subject or activity to another
	thinking rigidly
self-monitoring: evaluating how you're doing as you proceed through a task	making careless errors
	using incorrect strategies
	not keeping track of time

EF weaknesses can cause problems in all academic subjects. Following are some examples.

Academic Task	Common EF-Related Problems
reading comprehension	difficulty sustaining attention to uninteresting material
	comprehension difficulty from lack of focus; taking longer to read due to necessity to reread
	forgetting what was read
writing a paper	difficulty organizing, holding ideas in memory, and arranging ideas in a logical sequence
	difficulty planning steps in the writing process
	difficulty starting a paper and managing time
	producing insufficient content
	making language mechanics errors due to focus on content and lack of self-monitoring
solving math problems	difficulty recalling procedural steps
	comprehension difficulties with word problems
	careless errors

It doesn't take students very long to recognize that their executive function difficulties make certain academic tasks difficult and frustrating. This leads to task procrastination and avoidance problems with initiating work. Addressing these difficulties can improve students' confidence and abilities to produce higher quality academic work.

How Can You Help Students with EF Difficulties?

First, try to distinguish between students who just don't want to perform certain tasks and students who seem to care but are unable to perform these tasks. (Some students may present a combination of these characteristics.) It is important not to penalize students who are less able to perform certain tasks. If you suspect students have brain-based EF difficulties, you can teach some EF skills or accommodate these students regardless of whether they have 504 plans (see chapter 2).

Following are some ways to help students strengthen their EF skills, depending on their specific areas of challenge.

SUSTAINING ATTENTION

Be thoughtful about where you seat students. As much as possible, seat inattentive students away from distractions such as doors and windows, and near attentive students who can serve as role models. It can also be helpful to seat an inattentive student near you at the front of the room.

Develop a system of signals with students. In private, tell inattentive students that you will signal when you'd like them to do something. A signal might be an index finger to the mouth or a tug on your left ear as a reminder to remain quiet or stay on task.

Make direct eye contact with students. Frequent eye contact can help keep students engaged in classroom discussion. If students are distracted, say their names and ask them to look at you as you teach.

Write instructions on the board. If students miss verbal instructions because they weren't paying attention, instructions written on the board can direct them. You might also give students a printed handout with detailed instructions.

Give students copies of class notes. Despite your best efforts to engage distractible students, they may miss important information they're supposed to be recording. As necessary, provide children with class notes so that they have the information they need to take tests or do course work.

Minimize text on tests and assignments; be concise. Make sure there's more white than black on any handout. The fewer words are on a page, the easier it will be for visually overwhelmed students to maintain focus.

Use technology in instruction. Most students enjoy working with computers. Learning software may be more engaging for children who are motivated to learn using technology. Use these programs to promote interest in content and reinforce your lessons.

Teach to multiple learning modalities. It is best to teach in all sensory modalities, including visual, auditory, and kinesthetic. Much attention was paid in the past to teaching students according to their individual learning styles or strongest modality. Research has not shown that this differentiation affects how students learn, and this theory is now considered a "neuromyth."[1] However, varying your instructional styles and methods can still help all learners do their best.

Be patient with students who ask for repetition or clarification. These students may not have been paying attention through no fault of their own.

INITIATING

Monitor all students. Go to a student's desk, inquire about difficulty starting or finishing work, and assist as needed.

Use a timer. A timer reinforces to students that they have a limited amount of time to complete classwork. Remind the class of time left at regular intervals.

Consider offering extended time. Some students will be slower to complete work due to difficulties with starting, sustaining attention, memory, and processing speed. Consider giving these students extended time on tests. These students may take more time doing homework, too. Consider reducing the amount of homework for them.

PLANNING

Teach students how to plan. Use examples of various assignments to illustrate how to create a plan. Provide questions students can ask themselves when they're planning: "What do I need to do?" "What materials or information do I need to accomplish this task?" "When do I need to have certain parts completed so I meet the deadline?" "How will I fit this work in with my other work?"

Break down assignments into shorter chunks with clear time frames and deadlines. For example, give several sequential deadlines for parts of an assignment due in three weeks. Check work at each deadline and troubleshoot with students who did not meet the deadline.

ORGANIZING

Have students organize their assignments. All students can benefit from using an assignment notebook, planner, or an organizing app on a smartphone, tablet, or computer. You can ask parents to check daily assignments online, students' completion of homework, and that students placed homework in binders or backpacks.

Encourage students to use three-ring binders. Binders should be separated by subject with dividers and include loose-leaf paper and a small pouch containing pens, pencils, erasers, highlighters, and other common supplies students need. Binders should have separate folders or compartments for items students need to take home, items that return to school, and completed work.

Make it clear where students can find items in the classroom. Share with students where supplies are stored and set up specific places where students can turn in work. Keep these locations consistent.

Help students organize their desks or lockers. Give extra assistance to students who struggle with organization. Encourage them to clean out their desks or lockers regularly. Help students decide what they can recycle, bring home, or leave at school.

Provide checklists for students and encourage their use. Checklists can help guide children through routines. For example, if first thing each morning you want students to turn in homework and take out their math books, math notebooks, rulers, and pencils, you might write down each of these steps under a heading "First Things." Your first instruction of the day could be to say, "First things!" and have students look at the "First Things" list on a poster.

Have students color-code and coordinate objects to aid memory and organization. Using a different color folder and notebook for each subject makes it easy for students to group and organize class information.

Working Memory

Approximately 10 percent of students have working memory problems.[2] This weakness may be one of the biggest impediments to academic functioning. Research suggests that working memory may be a better predictor of academic success than IQ is.[3]

Establish routines and clarify expectations. When events happen consistently or tasks are required at a certain time and place every day, students remember them more easily. However, some students will still forget to turn in their homework at the beginning of the school day despite being reminded frequently of this responsibility. These students may have working memory problems. They have forgotten what to do while doing something else. (Or they haven't done their homework.) Consider posting a daily schedule and pointing to items on the schedule at various times during the day.

Encourage parents to check homework assignments online and to provide an extra set of books at home. Many students with memory difficulties often forget to write down their homework assignments. Tell parents that there are no excuses for students not knowing their homework. They can look it up online if this technology is available, or they can call or text a classmate. At the beginning of the year, have students exchange phone numbers with at least one other student in class for this purpose. Students with memory problems may also forget to bring the right books home. If parents can afford it, an extra set of used books at home can address this problem.

Teach mnemonic techniques. Mnemonic strategies help students associate the information to be remembered with an image, tune, or word.[4]

Recognize how working memory deficits can affect academic performance in various subjects. (See the table on pages 51–52.) Teach memory skills to students, and make appropriate accommodations in the classroom.

Shifting

Prepare the class in advance for transitions. Some students get so interested in or hyperfocused on activities that they have difficulty stopping. Prepare students with at least one announcement of a transition several minutes before the change of activity.

Teach your class that sometimes the schedule or plan changes. Some students thrive in classrooms with structure and predictability. They may have trouble with changes in the schedule or with a substitute teacher. Students with autism spectrum disorder frequently have trouble with changes. Have a general policy that you announce and post at the beginning of the year: "Sometimes the schedule changes." Before a change occurs, repeat this policy to prepare students and reduce their anxiety.

Self-Monitoring

Encourage students to check their work. Ask them to look over assignments or tests before handing them in. Some students rush through work and are often the first to turn it in. Their work is frequently inaccurate and careless. Require these students to wait to turn in work or a test until at least half the class has finished. Encourage them to use this time to check their work.

Provide self-monitoring forms. Work with the student to agree on a target behavior. If the behavior pertains to classwork, the title of target behavior on a form might be "Am I doing my work right now?" (See page 57 for a reproducible form you can use.) Divide the form into sections reflecting the moment a timer or bell will randomly sound. Each time the student hears the cue, he or she writes a Y for yes or N for no in the appropriate section. Knowing they will be monitoring their own behavior helps keep students on task, increasing their academic production and quality.[5] If the behavior to be self-monitored occurs only at certain times during the day, the student could check off items or tasks on a checklist after completing them. Rewards for students are optional. Use them only if student self-satisfaction with success is insufficient to increase the target behavior.

Self-Monitoring Form

Name: _____

Subject: _____

Date: _____

Target behavior: _____

Am I doing my target behavior right now?	Yes	No
Cue 1		
Cue 2		
Cue 3		
Cue 4		
Cue 5		
Cue 6		

CHAPTER 7

Language Used in This Book

. . . .

"I'm a normal person whose mind may be a little abnormal,
but my mental health problems aren't me. They don't define me.
They are a part of me but they aren't part of my identity."

—Sophie Dishman, twenty-two-year-old with obsessive-compulsive disorder and anxiety

. . . .

This book refers to mental health and learning disorders by the formal terms under which they are classified in the *Diagnostic and Statistical Manual of Mental Disorders: Fifth Edition* (*DSM-5*). Published in 2013 by the American Psychiatric Association (APA), this classification system is the most universally used system for categorizing mental disorders. While the APA's classifications are not perfect due to the complexity of human behavior and the overlap among disorders, the *DSM-5* is the best tool currently available to diagnose disorders.

WHAT CAUSES DISORDERS?

Mental health and learning disorders can be the result of nature (biology), nurture (environment), or both. Evidence for a biological basis comes from research on structural, chemical, and electrical differences in the brains of people with certain disorders. Other research suggests genetic links, since many disorders occur more often in families and twins.

Environmental influences can affect mental and cognitive health as powerfully as biology does. Negative environmental factors—such as physical, sexual or emotional abuse; household violence; substance abuse; mental illness; divorce; or parental incarceration—can lead to the onset of disorders.[1] (For more information on the impact of adverse childhood experiences, see chapter 16.) On the flip side, some people who are biologically predisposed to certain disorders may not develop them because of positive environmental factors—such as parental or peer influence— that create resilience. This is one of the reasons why a teacher can be so critical in students' lives.

Different Professionals, Different Terms

Mental health professionals diagnose and treat disorders, while educators seek to identify and qualify students for special services or accommodations. Consequently, these different professionals may use different terms. For example, think of a student who has severe difficulties in reading. A psychologist working outside the school district might diagnose this student as having dyslexia, while the school district might use the term *specific learning disability (SLD)*. Another student might be diagnosed with multiple psychological disorders by an outside mental health professional but be termed *emotionally disturbed (ED)* by a school district.

Because of differing terminology, sometimes students don't get the help they need. An outside psychologist may diagnose a child with dyslexia, which is a relatively severe reading disability. Meanwhile, a school district may not provide services to the student, because his or her reading levels or responses to intervention do not meet the district's definition of or criteria for SLD. In this situation, parents may not believe there is reason to pursue outside interventions (such as tutoring), and the student may not receive adequate support.

THE CONFUSING WORLD OF A LEARNING DISABILITY

School psychologist: "Mrs. Gomez, Juan has a processing problem that causes some of his reading difficulties."

Mrs. Gomez: "But a psychologist who evaluated him told me he had a learning disability called *dyslexia*."

School psychologist: "Well, people inside and outside school districts don't necessarily use the same language to describe similar problems."

Mrs. Gomez: "I'm confused. What is Juan's problem, then?"

School psychologist: "I can understand your confusion. When a school psychologist says a student may have a learning disability, this means the student has not succeeded in an academic area after receiving the most intensive interventions. A comprehensive evaluation is then required, using a variety of assessments to determine that the student's underperformance is not due to lack of adequate instruction or any other disability.[2] At that point, a student may be categorized as *learning disabled* for the purpose of providing special education. But this categorization or label is not a diagnosis. School psychologists are not allowed to diagnose learning disabilities or mental health disorders. A child can be diagnosed with a learning disability only by a psychologist not employed by a school district. That diagnosis is determined by a specific pattern of reading deficits on tests."

Other Notes on Language

THE POWER OF LABELS

Throughout this book, I use labels in a way that recognizes that children are more than the mental health or learning disorders they may have. This means I do not call children "ADHD," "autistic," or "obsessive-compulsive." Instead, I refer to children affected by those disorders as "children with ADHD," "students with autism," or "young people with obsessive-compulsive disorder." This is consistent with the practice of "person-first language," which is the current standard used by government agencies as well as academic journals and other publications.[3] Labeling children ("He's learning disabled," for example) may seem more convenient, but it does a disservice to human beings, who are complex individuals with specific strengths and weaknesses. Calling people by labels implies that a condition characterizes their entire being and doesn't allow for the complex and unique nature of each person.

GENDER PRONOUNS

Throughout this book, you may sometimes see gender pronouns used to describe adults and students. This is for ease of reading only. All the information discussed applies to females and males alike.

PARENTS AND FAMILIES

Students live in many kinds of families. They may live with one or two parents. They may live with a stepparent, a guardian, or an adult relative. This book usually uses the word *parents*. When you see this word, think of the adult or adults students live with who take care of them.

PART 2

. . . .

Mental Health and Learning Disorders

CHAPTER 8

Anxiety Disorders

"Some anxiety motivates us. It makes us better people. But there are some people where their anxiety interferes with their lives. And when it interferes with your life, that is when anxiety becomes a disorder."

—*Angela Neal-Barnett, Ph.D., psychology professor and author*

Children experience anxiety disorders more than any other mental health disorders. Students with anxiety disorders have excessive and irrational worries and fears. These worries and fears persist, occurring not just for a day or two, but for at least six months. Anxiety can interfere significantly with students' abilities to function at home and school, causing problems in their personal, social, or academic lives. When possible, children with anxiety tend to avoid situations that might provoke their anxiety. If avoidance isn't possible, they may experience distressing physical symptoms.

> About 13% of young people will experience an anxiety disorder at some point during childhood or adolescence. Children under twelve make up 6% of this group. Meanwhile, 25% to 33% of adolescents experience an anxiety disorder. Up to half of all students with an anxiety disorder may have at least one additional mental health disorder.[1]

Some students' anxieties may be obvious. A young child might cry and resist being separated from a parent when she is dropped off at school. A student who worries excessively about his behavior or grades may repeatedly ask you for assurance that he is doing an assignment correctly. Another student might refuse to answer questions or speak in front of the class. Each of these behaviors might be signs of excessive anxiety.

Other students may not outwardly show that they are anxious. A child who worries obsessively about performing well on tests won't necessarily share these feelings with you. A student with a fear of vomiting or of seeing another student throw up likely won't disclose this fear to you. It's common for teachers to misinterpret a student's reluctance or refusal to present a report to the class. Anxiety may underlie this refusal.

There are many different anxiety disorders, and some students may have more than one of these disorders. This chapter provides information to help you identify and understand students who experience anxiety disorders. It also offers many strategies you can use to help these children succeed in school.

Generalized Anxiety Disorder (GAD)

Studies have found a wide range for how many children are diagnosed with GAD. Estimates range from 1% to 10% of children and teens.[2] Younger children with GAD are more likely to also have separation anxiety disorder (page 78) and ADHD (page 102). Older students with GAD may be more likely to experience depressive disorders (see chapter 10).

Everyone worries. Most students struggle at times with new experiences that cause them to feel anxious. However, children with generalized anxiety disorder (GAD) have excessive, frequent, and uncontrollable worry about almost anything and everything in the present and future. Students with GAD often worry about things that most children don't worry about. They may have daily worries or fears about grades, friends, parents, sports, health, schedules, appearance, and other aspects of school and life. These worries can lead to restlessness, fatigue, difficulty concentrating, irritability, headaches, and sleep disturbances. Some of these symptoms interfere with a student's functioning. To qualify for a diagnosis of GAD, anxiety must be present a majority of the time for six months.

Behaviors and Symptoms to Look For

Worry can be very private and invisible, so students with GAD may be especially difficult to spot within your classroom. They often are the quietest and best-behaved children. Following are some signs to watch for.

Children with GAD may:

Express apprehension about tests, assignments, and grades. Concerns may center on the difficulty of material ("This is too hard"), the workload ("I'll never be able to get all of this done"), or evaluation ("If I don't get a B, my mom will punish me"). Children who are perfectionistic may worry about meeting higher standards than teachers or parents require.

Feel fatigued or restless. Excessive worries often keep children and adolescents from getting enough sleep. These students may appear to be exhausted or fidgety.

Have trouble concentrating. Anxiety can make it difficult for students to concentrate. They may be inattentive or easily distracted by noises or other students. Anxiety, not ADHD (page 102), may be a cause of inattention.

Be overly emotional. Excessive worry can cause children to be very sensitive. Crying and tantrums are common in younger students with GAD. Older students may be irritable and easily frustrated.

Experience frequent headaches, stomachaches, and other pains. The stress of constant worry often leads to muscle tension and physical pains. A young student may experience a stomachache on the first day of school. This is common and needn't cause concern. However, frequent physical complaints, especially if a physician has not found any cause for concern, may indicate an anxiety disorder.

Avoid participating in school activities. Students with GAD may try to get out of class activities because they fear they won't perform well. Such situations may include responding to questions, reading aloud, or solving problems on the board. Students also may be afraid to try a new activity. They often avoid participating in extracurricular activities.

Be absent frequently. Frequent absences not related to medical problems may suggest ongoing anxiety. Students (especially younger children) may feign sickness to stay at home. Older students—with or without parental consent—simply may not show up for school (see "School Refusal" on page 81). Absences often occur on days when students are unprepared or overwhelmed, such as test days and other times when school demands spike.

Use alcohol and other drugs. Some students—especially those in middle school and high school—may use alcohol, marijuana, and other drugs in an effort to reduce anxiety.

Classroom Strategies and Interventions

You'll likely observe a wide range of behaviors from students who worry excessively, regardless of whether these students meet the criteria for GAD. Your responses to and accommodations for these students will depend on the children's ages and the frequency and severity of their worries. Student accommodations also depend on the class size, your everyday activities, and other aspects specific to your classroom.

Following are some suggestions for helping students with GAD succeed at school:

Give lots of reassurance and genuine, specific praise. Provide students with ongoing reassurance to diminish their anxiety. Compliment them on specific areas in which they excel or are showing improvement. Sincere compliments are an effective way to promote desired behaviors. Be aware that students with GAD often deflect compliments and instead focus on what they fear may go wrong. Do your best to emphasize students' positive qualities and accomplishments.

Carefully monitor students. Because children with GAD often do not act in ways that attract attention, a student's worry may not be obvious. Pay special attention to students who seem especially shy or timid.

Empathize with a student's anxiety. Show concern while also suggesting a more rational way for students to think about their worries. ("I understand that you feel the speech wasn't your best, but I thought it was excellent. I learned a lot about black bears.")

Establish routines and clarify expectations. Students with anxiety may benefit from consistency and clear expectations. Consider posting a daily schedule and behavior guidelines so students know what to expect—and what is expected of them—in the classroom. For more information on establishing consistent classroom routines and expectations, see chapter 1.

Be patient with repetitive questions. Students with anxiety often worry about whether they've heard instructions or directions accurately because they're so concerned about doing things the right way. Right after you've given a direction, a student may ask you to repeat it. You may be tempted to ask, "Were you listening?" or say, "I just told you." Understand that these students may have anxiety and may simply want to make sure they've heard you correctly.

Allow flexibility regarding deadlines. Because students with GAD are often anxious about meeting a teacher's or parent's expectations, they may worry excessively about completing assignments or projects on time. These students may be perfectionists, so when appropriate, relax deadlines and give full credit for work that is turned in late.

Establish check-in points. Checking in with students enables you to verify that they are on schedule with assignments and projects. Check-in points are also opportunities to provide guidance and encouragement. Emphasize progress students have made on assignments.

Establish provisions for times when students feel overwhelmed. You may choose to set up a "safe space" or a "quiet place" in your classroom (or a room nearby) where students can go to calm down. Also allow students to leave the classroom without asking permission, so they can visit the office or a school counselor as necessary. Consider setting up a coping plan for students who feel overwhelmed. The reproducible "Student Coping Plan" on page 20 can help you do this.

Facilitate social relationships during unstructured time. Some students worry because they eat lunch alone or because no one wants to play with them at recess. Try to create "buddy" relationships for these students during these times. Teachers can ask a kind, empathetic student to be a buddy to a student who may be shy or isolated. For example, a teacher might explain to the buddy that she would like someone to play, sit, or eat with Jonas because he always seems to be alone. She would tell Jonas that this other student will be his buddy.

Monitor and intervene if bullying occurs. Students who are bullied are justifiably anxious about going to school. Encourage your students to report bullying situations, and act to protect bullied students.

Speak with the school counselor, parents, and outside professionals working with the child. Students with GAD don't worry exclusively at school. This disorder is pervasive and occurs at home, too. These students may have trouble sleeping, which causes fatigue in school. GAD also affects children at home. Parents and mental health professionals, such as a school counselor or psychologist, can be valuable sources of information for anxiety-reducing strategies you might use in the classroom.

HOW TO SAY IT . . .

How you speak with students who have GAD is very important. The following scenarios show how you can acknowledge students' anxiety while helping diminish their fears. In every scenario, notice this important message for children who worry: There is always a solution to their worries.

Elementary school student (starting to cry toward the end of school): "I'm scared my mommy is going to forget me."
You (kneeling and taking the student's hand): "That must be awfully scary to think that your mom would forget you. But no mommy has ever forgotten her child at our school. And I have my cell phone right here. If she's late, I'll call her."

Middle school student: "I'm afraid I'll get carsick on that long field trip."
You: "I don't blame you for worrying about getting carsick. That's an awful feeling. Would it be helpful if we make sure you can sit up front? Can we ask your dad what he's done in the past to make sure you don't get sick?"

High school student (with a worried look): "I don't know if I can memorize all those algebra equations."
You: "Sounds like you're not sure you can do well on the math test. You've always done well before. Your score doesn't have to be perfect, you know. If you get a couple of answers wrong, your grade will still be very good."

What Not to Say . . .
Students with GAD may have worries that you can't really understand. With these students, it's often best not to say what you might be thinking. Asking a question like, "Why in the world would you be worried about something like that?" could make a student feel *more* anxious because of your astonishment. Keep in mind that anxiety often is not rational, but the feelings kids have are real nevertheless.

It's also important to avoid discounting or criticizing a student's concerns ("There's nothing to worry about," "That's silly," "That will never happen"). Such responses can cause students to believe you aren't taking them seriously or that you're minimizing their worries. They may choose to keep future concerns private.

ADJUSTMENT DISORDER WITH ANXIETY

One type of anxiety disorder begins within three months of experiencing an identifiable stressful event and ends within six months if the stressor is removed. The anxiety is either out of proportion to the severity or intensity of the stressor, the distress causes impairment in an important area of functioning, or both. This is called an adjustment disorder with anxiety. Treatment may vary depending on the specific stressful event.

PROFESSIONAL TREATMENTS

Two psychotherapies are particularly effective for GAD: cognitive-behavioral therapy (CBT) and dialectical behavior therapy (DBT). These therapies help students become aware of exaggerated or unrealistic fears and teach them to think more rationally and objectively. In addition, DBT teaches students to be "in the moment" and to tolerate distress through relaxation training, meditation, and breathing exercises. Young children who cannot fully verbalize their thoughts and feelings may find success working with a play therapist.

Medication also is a helpful treatment for anxiety disorders in students. A psychiatrist or another physician may prescribe medication when a child's anxiety is severe. The most common medications used for anxiety disorders are selective serotonin reuptake inhibitors (SSRIs). Students need close monitoring during the initial days and weeks of taking these medications. A small percentage may experience heightened symptoms or depression. Other possible side effects of medication can include drowsiness, insomnia, stomachaches, headaches, nervousness, and weight gain. If you observe any troubling symptoms in a child taking medication, immediately share your observations with your school nurse and the child's parents.

Social Anxiety Disorder (SAD)

Social anxiety disorder (SAD), sometimes called *social phobia,* is the perception of being negatively evaluated by others. This perception can occur in conversations or other social situations or while performing in front of others. Students with SAD fear they will act in some way that is embarrassing or humiliating. This fear is out of proportion to the likelihood of being negatively evaluated.

Students who have SAD are more than shy. Although shyness is a form of anxiety, it is also a common personality trait. Children with SAD either endure the situations they fear while experiencing intense anxiety or avoid these situations altogether. Very young children may cry, throw tantrums, or cling to a parent. In order for a student to qualify for a SAD diagnosis, anxiety or avoidance must occur routinely over a six-month period, and it must cause significant distress or impairment in social or educational settings.

> SAD is a common anxiety disorder, affecting about 7% to 8% of students.[3] Up to 60% of these young people may have an additional mental health disorder. Most commonly, these additional disorders include specific phobia (page 73), panic disorder (page 75), or depressive disorders (chapter 10).[4]

Some shyness or performance anxiety isn't necessarily unusual or bad, but extreme anxiety can lead to avoidance of many situations, which can negatively affect a student's life. Students who feel anxious around others may be so anxious in social situations that they don't speak. Fear of performing in front of others or answering a question in class may cause multiple physical symptoms as well as internal feelings of anxiety. SAD is one of the most common reasons why students refuse to attend school (see "School Refusal" on page 81).[5]

Some students who endure intense anxiety and are visibly anxious in social or performance situations will be obvious to teachers. Teachers may misinterpret the behaviors of other students who, because of social anxiety, refuse to perform in expected ways. Teachers may mistakenly identify these students as oppositional. It is important not to jump to conclusions about the meaning of a student's behavior. A small percentage of young children have such severe anxiety that they don't speak to anyone outside their immediate families. This anxiety disorder is called *selective mutism.*

Behaviors and Symptoms to Look For

Many students feel anxious in new social situations. It's also common for students to worry before a performance, whether it's a concert, a class speech, or a sporting event. In most cases, students are able to overcome their fears and perform capably. With repetition, they gain confidence in their growing abilities.

Children with SAD, however, typically feel overwhelming dread at the mere thought of socializing with or performing in front of others. They sit in the classroom and in other situations enduring significant fear that they might have to speak or perform in some way. They are deliberately quiet and well behaved because they don't want to draw negative evaluation of their behavior. It's important to carefully monitor extremely shy or quiet students.

Students with SAD may:

Act in an extremely shy manner. Shyness is a form of social anxiety that occurs in varying degrees.[6] Interacting with peers, particularly in new situations, can cause some shy children great anxiety. Because they fear humiliation, these students often will isolate themselves and speak as little as possible. The importance of social relationships in adolescence makes this a particular problem for older students. Students with SAD may respond to social overtures by blushing, sweating profusely, looking away, stuttering, or not speaking for fear of saying something stupid. Sometimes, signs of SAD are not visible, but invisibility doesn't lessen the intensity of symptoms.

Avoid participating in school activities. Students with SAD often fear making mistakes and feeling embarrassed. These students are unlikely to respond to questions you ask the class. Reading aloud or solving math problems in front of others may terrify them. During group work, students with SAD may stay on the periphery of the activity. These students may also limit their participation in extracurricular activities.

Act in a distracted or confused way. Social anxiety can be all consuming. Students with SAD frequently are very self-conscious, constantly vigilant, and may appear distracted or inattentive.

Experience intense anxiety about being looked at. When a student comes to class late, opens the door, and walks to a seat, usually all the other students briefly glance at the late student. Students with SAD would be extremely anxious walking into a classroom late, because they would believe that other students were negatively evaluating them.

Be overly emotional. Constant social anxiety can cause students to be emotionally sensitive. Fits of crying and tantrums are common, especially in younger students. Older students can be moody, irritable, or oppositional.

Experience frequent physical signs of anxiety in social or performance situations. These students may become lightheaded, have butterflies, sweat, shake, or stutter. While many people experience these sensations at times, students with SAD experience them often and intensely.

Frequently miss school. Frequent absences may suggest that a student feels social anxiety. Students (especially younger children) may pretend to be sick so they can stay home. Students who feel performance anxiety are often absent on days when they have to present a report or project.

Classroom Strategies and Interventions

Symptoms of SAD vary among students. Some children may approach unfamiliar situations with obvious signs of fear or apprehension. Others will not show visible effects. Some students overcome anxiety as an activity progresses while others do not. Young people who experience extreme fear may refuse to participate at all. The strategies you use to help students will depend in part upon the severity of their social anxiety and upon the classroom situation.

Following are some suggestions for helping students with social anxiety in the classroom:

Provide a warm and encouraging environment. Show students, especially those who are socially anxious, consistent empathy and support. Do not tolerate bullying or teasing, and promote positive behavior in peers.

Work to improve children's social skills. The primary emotion affecting socially anxious students is fear. Help diminish a student's fears by teaching socials skills at a pace comfortable to the student. (See chapter 5.)

Foster friendships and joint activities through curriculum. Pair up a socially anxious student with another student who is kind and pleasant. When students choose partners, make sure a shy student is chosen (or facilitate an appropriate choice for her). Keep in mind that socially anxious students may need coaching, even in basic conversation skills.

Give high, genuine praise for social behaviors. Compliment students on specific social skills they show. If a student gives the wrong answer after raising his hand, you might say, "That's an interesting idea. Thanks for answering the question." For the child who reluctantly joins a small-group project for the first time, say, "It was terrific to see you join the group!"

Show sensitivity when speaking about a socially anxious student. Avoid referring to a student by using a label such as "shy." Students with SAD do not feel good about their social fears, and labels tend to have connotations that make them feel worse. Instead use phrases like, "Sometimes Kim doesn't feel like talking" or, "Rohan is just feeling quiet today."

Create a place where overwhelmed students can go to avoid large groups. You may choose to establish an "alone place" where students with SAD can go to calm themselves when anxiety overwhelms them. They might also visit the school counselor. On page 20, you'll find a reproducible "Student Coping Plan" you can use to set up accommodations for students with SAD.

Facilitate lunch with another student. Invite a shy student who eats lunch alone to eat with another student. You might ask the shy student to identify a preferred student. Then invite the other student to eat with the shy student one day.

Give students plenty of time to prepare for class discussion questions. Prepare socially anxious students so they know you intend to call on them. Prior to calling on them, have a private conversation and say, "I'd like to call on you in class today. Do you mind answering a question about the Civil War?"

Share or talk about a socially anxious student's work or contribution. Make a point to acknowledge the student's work before the entire class. Be sure to seek the student's permission before you do this. For example, you might say, "I really like your project on Iceland. Do you mind if I share it with the class tomorrow?" If students resist, talk about how much you like their work and why you'd like to show it to the class, but ultimately respect students' decisions to have their work publicly acknowledged or not.

Minimize students' oral reading requirements and oral reports. Consider assigning written work or projects to replace oral reports. Modify curriculum in any other appropriate ways.

Speak with others involved in the care and development of a student with SAD. Consult parents and mental health professionals working with the child to learn about other social anxieties you may not be aware of, as well as interventions that have work well for the student when he or she is outside of school. Consult with your school counselors and other staff.

 CAUTION! Some people believe forcing socially anxious students to interact with others will help them overcome anxiety. This doesn't respect the enormous fear children have and may lead them to believe that you aren't taking their experience seriously. People rarely overcome anxiety by being forced to confront or experience the feared situation. This can make a student's symptoms worse instead of better.

PROFESSIONAL TREATMENTS

Students with SAD often worry that their behavior will humiliate them and that others are judging them critically. Cognitive-behavioral therapy (CBT) can help these children think more objectively. Relaxation, breathing techniques, and meditation may also help students manage anxiety.

Psychiatrists or other physicians may prescribe medications to complement therapy, especially when SAD is severe. Selective serotonin reuptake inhibitors (SSRIs) are typically prescribed in these situations. Students need close monitoring during the initial days and weeks of taking these medications. A small percentage may experience heightened symptoms or depression. Other possible side effects of medication can include drowsiness, insomnia, stomachaches, headaches, nervousness, and weight gain. If you observe any troubling symptoms in a child taking medication, immediately share your observations with your school nurse and the child's parents.

Specific Phobia

A phobia is severe fear about a specific object or situation. This fear is out of proportion to any actual danger. To qualify as a phobia, fear or avoidance of the object or situation must last for at least six months and cause impairment in important areas of functioning. An example might be a child who refuses to go outdoors because of a fear of dogs. Specific phobia is a very common anxiety disorder, affecting 5 percent of children and up to 19 percent of adolescents.[7]

COMMON PHOBIAS

Common categories of phobias are animals (insects, dogs), natural environment (weather, heights), blood (injections, medical or dental procedures), or situational (planes, elevators). It is common for children with phobias to have multiple phobias and other mental health disorders.[8]

Behaviors and Symptoms to Look For

Sometimes students will tell you about a specific phobia ahead of time. They might ask if there will be dogs near the school playground. A fear of vomiting on a long car or bus ride might cause a child to avoid a field trip.

Other students may not tell you anything, but you'll see them react with great anxiety at the sight—or even the prospect—of a feared object or situation. This might be another student vomiting or bleeding or a bee flying into the classroom. While it is not unusual for people to move away from these situations, students with phobias might scream and run.

Classroom Strategies and Interventions

Following are some suggestions for helping students with phobias in the classroom:

Don't require students to face their fears. Telling students they'll "get used to it" if they stay near feared objects or situations will likely increase students' fear.

Always respect students' phobias. Don't attempt to minimize students' fears. Accept their fears and quickly take action to reassure students or remove them from feared objects or situations.

Anticipate future situations. Once you know a student's phobia, you can be proactive in the future by helping the student avoid the feared object or situation.

Allow for some calming time after a student's phobic reaction. Severe anxiety created by exposure to a phobia trigger does not go away quickly. You might suggest the student engage in some slow, deep breaths or allow the student to visit the school nurse or counselor.

PROFESSIONAL TREATMENTS

Exposure therapy is the most effective treatment for phobias. A therapist may first teach relaxation methods. The therapist then exposes the individual in very gradual steps to the feared object or situation. The therapist can do this through imagery or with live exposures. Individuals then calm themselves at each step before moving to the next one.

Panic Disorder

A panic attack is an abrupt surge of intense fear or discomfort that includes physical symptoms (such as chest pain, nausea, sweatiness, and dizziness) as well as mental effects (such as a feeling of unreality or doom). These feelings last several minutes or longer. Some people feel like they're going to pass out or die during a panic attack. Panic disorder is diagnosed when recurrent panic attacks occur. A panic attack is a frightening experience. After an initial attack, individuals begin to fear anticipated attacks or avoid situations where they think attacks might occur.

> Panic disorder does not occur often in young children. It is much more prevalent in adolescents, especially among girls. As many as 16% of adolescents may have experienced at least one panic attack.[9] A majority of adolescents with panic disorder qualify for diagnosis with another mental health disorder.[10]

Panic attacks are related to the fight-or-flight response people experience when they feel they are in danger. In this normal stress response, adrenaline and other chemicals flood the body to help people escape potentially harmful situations. Panic attacks are fight-or-flight false alarms. The response occurs even when there is no real danger. The increase of panic attacks in adolescence may be related to the hormonal changes that occur during puberty.

The mental and physical effects of panic attacks are frightening, and so is their unpredictability. After a first attack, other attacks may occur in random situations, and the unpredictability of these attacks creates more fear. In extreme cases, individuals may be afraid to leave their homes or the company of their parents. These people may have *agoraphobia*—anxiety about not being able to escape or get help in a situation where panic might occur.

Behaviors and Symptoms to Look For

It's important for you to be knowledgeable about panic disorder symptoms so you can help students who experience panic attacks. Children experiencing their first panic attack will be frightened and bewildered by the experience. You can help by suggesting that they may be experiencing a surge of anxiety. Reassure students that you will stay with them until additional action can be taken.

Possible signs of panic attacks and panic disorder include:

Visible physical changes. Physical symptoms of panic attacks can include sweating, shaking, rapid breathing, shortness of breath, dizziness, or unsteadiness.

Private, invisible sensations. Students may experience heart palpitations, a feeling of choking, nausea, stomachaches, numbness, feelings of unreality, or fears of losing control, "going crazy," or dying.

Avoidance of certain places, activities, and people. Students may associate panic attacks with certain classrooms, activities, or people. Fear of another attack may cause students to avoid any situation that makes them feel uncomfortable.

Inattention. Students worrying about having a panic attack are constantly monitoring their physical sensations. With so much attention focused inwardly, students may not be able to focus on your lessons or instructions. Students may appear distracted and may be unable to remember something that was just said.

Slow, inadequate work production. Constant self-monitoring for signs of anxiety can make it difficult for students to complete work. Students may fail to finish tests, classroom assignments, or homework within expected time frames.

Abuse of alcohol and drugs. Some adolescents attempt to prevent panic attacks by "calming" themselves with chemicals.

Classroom Strategies and Interventions

It's important to respond right away to a student who is experiencing a panic attack. What looks like intense anxiety could be a medical emergency. Immediately consult with your school nurse. Provide calming reassurance to the student. Following the incident, it's also a good idea to work with parents and mental health professionals who are involved with the child. They may be able to offer ideas that you, counselors, and other staff can use to ease a student's fears.

Following are ideas for helping students with panic attacks or panic disorder:

Respond to a panic attack with reassurance and calming suggestions. Stay brief, calm, and reassuring in your response to panic attacks. For students with known panic disorder, remind them that their bodies are sending false alarm signals again and there's no real danger. Suggest slow, deep breaths. Take your lead from the students. If they want to be alone, let them be alone—but stay close by. If they want someone to stay with them, make sure someone does—whether inside or outside the classroom.[11]

Don't make assumptions or minimize the anxiety. Ask only once if the student knows what caused the panic attack. Frequently there is no obvious trigger. Don't minimize the student's anxiety by saying there's nothing to worry about.[12]

Minimize attention from other students. Other students may be startled or frightened by a child experiencing a visible panic attack. Do your best to deflect students' attention toward some other activity. As you help a student having a panic attack, you might calmly say to the class, "I'd like you all to turn to page sixteen and begin reading."

Establish provisions for students experiencing panic. Students who have suffered a panic attack will not return to normal immediately after the attack. These attacks are physically exhausting. Create a "safe space" or "quiet place" in your classroom (or one nearby) where students can calm down, or allow students to visit the office or a school counselor without asking permission. Some students may want to walk around. Consider setting up a coping plan for when students feel panic. (See the reproducible "Student Coping Plan" on page 20.)

Allow for accommodations to address panic and constant worries of an attack. A student with panic disorder may require extended time and a separate room for tests. A workload reduction and other curricular accommodations may also be appropriate. If a coping plan allows a student to leave the classroom at the onset of panic, you may choose to seat that student near the door.

Excuse students from panic-triggering activities and situations. A student may anticipate panic at the thought of being in a situation where a previous attack occurred. When possible, provide an alternative for this situation or others that might cause significant anxiety.

HOW A PANIC ATTACK CAN LEAD TO SCHOOL REFUSAL

The most challenging student I've encountered was an eleven-year-old girl who experienced a panic attack one day at school. Students were getting ready to line up for buses at the end of the day, and it was pouring rain outside. This student couldn't identify her bus, and she had a panic attack. Eventually, someone helped her go to the correct bus.

She got on the bus the next day to go to school, but as she got off the bus and walked toward the school door, the panic recurred. A teacher walked toward the student and asked her to come inside, but the student refused to accompany the teacher. She was crying, shaking, and saying she wanted to go home. The staff called her mother to come get her.

In the following days, the student began to panic upon waking up. She refused to go to school. We attempted many strategies, including graduated exposure (see "Separation Anxiety Disorder" on page 78) along with counseling, but we had no success. Eventually, the student's doctor prescribed medication, but the refusal continued. The student would not consider attending any other school either. Her teachers sent home her homework for almost a month, and her parents got approval for a homebound program with a part-time teacher and virtual learning.

This girl's family history included multiple people with anxiety disorders, and it's likely that she inherited a predisposition to anxiety. This probably made her more vulnerable to a panic attack when it first occurred in school. The recurrence of panic and the student's avoidance of the triggering situation was a classic example of panic disorder. Six months later, she was still attending virtual school at home and had achieved the necessary credits to advance to the next grade.

PROFESSIONAL TREATMENTS

Cognitive-behavioral therapy (CBT) can be effective in treating students with panic disorder. In CBT, therapists first teach children that the effects of a panic attack—although frightening—are not dangerous. Therapy then focuses on realistic thinking, breathing, relaxation exercises, or meditation. For students whose attacks are predictable and limited to one situation, gradual exposure to that situation, along with calming techniques, is helpful.

Depending upon the intensity of panic attacks, treatment may also include medication. Selective serotonin reuptake inhibitors (SSRIs) are commonly used to control panic. SSRIs may take several weeks to take effect, so other medications may be used initially to reduce anxiety. Students need close monitoring during the initial days and weeks of taking these medications. A small percentage may experience heightened symptoms or depression. Other possible side effects of medication can include drowsiness, insomnia, stomachaches, headaches, nervousness, and weight gain. If you observe any troubling symptoms in a child taking medication, immediately share your observations with your school nurse and the child's parents.

Separation Anxiety Disorder

Some children—especially young kids—may worry excessively about being away from their parents. They may resist going to school and get upset when their parents leave them with a babysitter. Separation anxiety disorder is one of the most common causes of school refusal (page 81). Students with this disorder feel intense anxiety when they are separated from parents or caregivers. Approximately 1 to 4 percent of all children experience separation anxiety disorder.[13]

Preschool and kindergarten teachers are most likely to observe separation anxiety disorder, since it is during the early school years that children and caregivers are first separated for long periods of time.

If symptoms of separation anxiety last longer than four weeks and cause significant distress in some important area of functioning, the student may qualify for a diagnosis of separation anxiety disorder. Briefer disturbances resolved within four weeks might be diagnosed as adjustment disorder with anxiety.

Behaviors and Symptoms to Look For

Common signs of separation anxiety disorder are:

Statements about not wanting to go to school. Students with separation anxiety will say they don't want to go to school. There may be problems at school that cause this resistance. However, in many cases the primary problem is that the student does not want to be separated from a parent.

Crying, tantrums, and clinging behavior. These can be especially intense before a child boards the school bus or is dropped off at school.

Stomachaches, headaches, nausea, and other physical complaints. Aches and pains may be real (caused by anxiety) or feigned (an excuse to return to the parent).

Excessive questioning of a parent. Questions might include, "Where are you going?" "When will you be back?" "Is your phone going to be on?" "What if something happens to you?"

Excessive fears. Children may refuse to sleep alone or go anywhere without a parent or caregiver. They may ask a lot of questions about the possibility of a parent being injured, kidnapped, or killed. Children with an ill parent or a parent who is being abused are more likely to want to stay near the parent to provide care or protection.

Parent Interventions

Modifications in parents' behaviors might be helpful for a student exhibiting separation anxiety or school refusal. Teachers might offer these suggestions to parents:

Send something comforting with the child. Parents can send their picture, a love note, or a favorite small stuffed animal in the child's lunch box or backpack.

Create a goodbye ritual. Parents can say or do the same thing every day with their child when saying goodbye. Encourage parents to make their goodbyes short and sweet.

Make home boring. If a child stays home, encourage parents to remove most rewarding activities for the day to decrease the incentive for staying home.

PROFESSIONAL TREATMENTS

Treatment for separation anxiety disorder usually includes slowly exposing students to graduated increases in separation. Parents are advised to separate quickly and confidently from children. This reduces the parents' anxiety, which may have provided the fuel for a child's fears. Treatment is more effective if it begins as soon as possible after symptoms develop.

FELIPE

Seven-year-old Felipe and his mother were in a minor car accident. Although not injured seriously, both were taken to the hospital for observation and then released. Felipe seemed fine upon arriving home. He looked forward to returning to school and telling his friends about the excellent ice cream he had at the hospital.

The following Saturday, Felipe spent the day with his grandparents. Though he knew his mother was working, he tried to call her. When she didn't answer her phone, Felipe began to panic. Even as his grandparents did their best to reassure him that his mother was okay, Felipe grew more and more upset.

It was not until she was on her way to pick up Felipe that his mother received the tearful messages and was able to call the grandparents. When she arrived, she found Felipe asleep after many hours of crying. He woke up briefly and said that he never wanted her to leave again.

Felipe refused to return to school on Monday morning. He cried and protested when his mother tried to force him to go. This persisted for a few days until Felipe's mother took him to a therapist. After a conversation with Felipe, the source of his anxiety became clear. He now associated being separated from his mother with the car accident. The thought of her leaving filled him with terror because he feared that she'd be hurt.

After another session with the therapist, Felipe was able to accept being separated from his mother for a shortened day of school. This period of time was incrementally expanded. Within a week, Felipe was back in school full-time. He still experienced occasional fears about his mother's safety, but reassurance from his teacher helped him realize his fears were not rational.

GRADUATED EXPOSURE PLANS FOR STUDENTS EXHIBITING SEPARATION ANXIETY DISORDER OR SCHOOL REFUSAL

One effective way to help a student who has fears about school or about separating from parents is to use a graduated exposure plan. This collaboration between parents and school officials helps students adjust to separation. A child's time at school expands over several days or weeks.

The following steps can be practiced multiple times on the same day, depending upon how a child responds. It's important for students to be comfortable with each exposure step before moving on to a more difficult one. Also, prior to beginning the graduated exposure, it's essential that children learn and practice breathing exercises and other calming techniques. When anxiety occurs after each exposure, the student uses a calming technique to decrease the anxiety before moving on to the next exposure step.

Example Graduated Exposure Plan
Step 1: After school has started for the day, the student and parent sit in the parking lot for fifteen minutes. If they take a bus or train, the student and parent may remain together at the transit stop for fifteen minutes.

Step 2: Repeat Step 1. Next the parent and student walk ten steps toward the school building and stand for five minutes.

Step 3: Repeat Step 2. Next the parent and student walk up to the school sidewalk and stand for five minutes.

Step 4: Next the parent and student walk up to the front door of the school and stand for five minutes.

Step 5: The parent and student enter the school together and then exit quickly.

Step 6: The parent accompanies the student to the school entrance. The student enters alone and exits quickly.

Step 7: The parent accompanies the student to the school entrance. The student enters alone and stands for five minutes.

Step 8: The parent accompanies the student to the school entrance. The student enters and walks the halls with the school counselor for five minutes. The parent waits at the school entrance.

Step 9: The parent accompanies the student to the school entrance. The counselor walks the student to the classroom door, and they stand there for five minutes. The parent waits at the school entrance.

Step 10: The student walks into school alone while the parent waits outside. The student walks to class with the counselor, and they stand outside the door for ten minutes.

Step 11: The student walks into school alone and walks to class with the counselor. Then the student enters the classroom alone.

Step 12: The student walks into school alone, then walks to class and enters the classroom alone.

Another exposure plan might involve a parent entering a classroom with the child and remaining in class as a "helper." The parent then gradually spends more and more time away from the classroom—periodically returning to reassure the student before leaving again—until the student is comfortable being separated from the parent.

School Refusal

Some children refuse to attend school. School refusal itself is not a mental health disorder. Instead, the term refers to a student's fear of school or unwillingness to attend school. Possible causes for school refusal include:

Between 2% and 4% of children and adolescents refuse to attend school at some point.[16]

A mental health disorder. Many students who are afraid to go to school—especially younger children—have separation anxiety disorder (page 78).[14] Panic disorder (page 75), depression (page 91), and social anxiety disorder (SAD) (page 69) are three other common reasons for school absences. Up to 75 percent of students with SAD may refuse to go to school.[15]

Anxiety about performance. Pressure to get A's or B's and test anxiety cause some students great stress and can lead them to miss school. This is especially true for students who have learning difficulties.

Fear for their safety and well-being. Many children are teased, bullied, or ostracized by peers. When students don't feel safe or accepted at school, they may choose not to attend. It's estimated that 160,000 students miss school each day due to fear of being teased, attacked, or intimidated by others.[17] Harassment by other children can also lead to the development of mental health disorders.

Difficulties at home. Some students have a legitimate concern about a family member or a situation at home. They feel more comfortable if they can be home to monitor what is happening. These children may have separation anxiety disorder.

Disengagement or defiance. Some students would simply rather stay home and watch TV or play video games than attend school. Others struggle with learning difficulties and behavior problems. Students who experience only failure or punishment at school are more likely to avoid school.

Behaviors and Symptoms to Look For

Frequent absence not due to illness may be a sign that a student is afraid of attending school or is unwilling to attend. Other children make it to school only after some resistance. Young children, especially preschool and kindergarten students, often protest when they are dropped off in the morning. Older students may oversleep or be tardy for another reason. Some children readily go to school, but report sickness or physical complaints once there so they may return home.

Classroom Strategies and Interventions

There are many reasons for school refusal. It's important to understand why students are resisting or missing school so you can design appropriate interventions. A team approach can help. Talk with students and their parents. Check in with counselors, other teachers, and administrators for any insight they may have on students' struggles. Consult a mental health professional if children can't (or won't) say why they don't want to go to school. These professionals can be helpful if school refusal continues for more than a few days and collaborative parent and school interventions fail.

In extreme cases of school refusal, you may not be able to do anything to address the problem—a child simply may be absent for long periods of time. When students *are* at school, use these strategies to encourage their continued presence:

Eliminate bullying and create safe learning environments. Many students stay home because they don't feel safe at school. It's important to prevent bullying at the schoolwide level (including in classrooms, hallways, gymnasiums, lunchrooms, and locker rooms and on playgrounds and buses) so students feel safe.

Avoid criticizing students' anxiety. Questions like, "You're not a baby, are you?" or, "What are your classmates going to think if they see you crying?" can make students feel worse about school. Empathize with children's feelings and remain positive about their abilities to overcome anxiety.

Modify instruction to reach reluctant learners. Motivating tuned-out students through learning can increase their enjoyment of school as well as their motivation to achieve. Consider adapting the curriculum if a student's avoidance of school is due to apprehension about a particular subject or activity.

Adjust classroom expectations. Depending on the reasons for (and severity of) a student's school refusal, it may be important to adjust expectations. This could include modifying assignments or relaxing deadlines.

Praise student successes and applaud progress. Compliment students on specific areas in which they excel or are showing improvement. Help them perceive school as a place where they are succeeding, and let them know you are glad they are in your classroom.

Build students' social skills. Students who refuse to attend school often feel anxious or overwhelmed by the social expectations there. Help diminish a student's trepidation about other students and school staff by providing social skills instruction or facilitating social interaction. You'll find some social skills building activities and resources in chapter 5.

Use a graduated exposure plan with parental cooperation. If school refusal is due to anxiety, learn about this process in the section on separation anxiety disorder (page 78).

Speak with a school counselor, parents, and outside professionals working with the child. Speak with other school staff who are addressing attendance issues. Parents and mental health professionals also can provide helpful information. If a student begins experiencing problems after initially adjusting to the classroom, a parent may be able to explain the change.

CHAPTER 9

Obsessive-Compulsive and Related Disorders

Including Hairpulling (Trichotillomania) and Skin Picking (Excoriation)

· ·

"OCD focuses on the negative. I didn't think to myself, my praying will save my grandma. Instead, I thought, if I don't pray, my grandma will die for sure."

—*J.J. Keeler, author*

· ·

Students with obsessive-compulsive disorder (OCD) experience obsessions, compulsions, or both. Obsessions are frequent unwanted thoughts, images, urges, or sensations that a person tries to ignore or suppress. Compulsions are repetitive behaviors or mental acts that an individual feels driven to perform in order to decrease the anxiety of obsessive thoughts. Obsessions and compulsions must occur more than one hour a day and cause considerable distress or impairment in functioning to qualify for a diagnosis of OCD.[1]

Obsessions and compulsions may wax, wane, and change throughout childhood and adulthood. For example, students who feel they must go through the contents of their backpacks three times an hour may eventually replace that compulsion with the need to check a clock every minute. With both behaviors, students fear something bad will happen if they do not perform the behavior.

> Between 1% and 3% of children have OCD.[2] Children with a parent who has OCD are much more likely to have the disorder.[3] Stressful life events sometimes precede the onset of OCD, and highly responsible people seem to be more vulnerable.[4] Brain imaging has revealed several abnormalities and chemical differences associated with OCD.[5] Tics (page 110) and ADHD (page 102) are also common in children with OCD.[6] Up to 40% of children with OCD may not experience the disorder in adulthood.[7]

Common obsessions involve fears of being contaminated (by germs), excessive doubt (something has not been done correctly), disturbing images (violent scenes), sudden urges to harm someone (stabbing a sibling), a need for symmetry (lining up pictures precisely), and the fear that oneself or others might be harmed. Common compulsive behaviors to reduce anxiety caused by obsessions include excessive washing to relieve fear of contamination, repetitive checking to reduce uncertainty of task completion, mental rituals to prevent disturbing images, hiding kitchen knives to prevent harming someone, or constant rearranging to address lack of symmetry. Some OCD sufferers have obsessive thoughts without compulsive behaviors.

Some individuals perform compulsive rituals without a specific obsessive fear. They just feel uncomfortable or anxious if they don't perform a compulsive ritual. They believe that their compulsive behavior will prevent something bad, and they experience relief after they perform the ritual. For example, one person may feel compelled to turn doorknobs from right to left. Another person may arrange food on a plate in a very particular way. Compulsions may have no connection to the obsessions they're meant to minimize. People with OCD may or may not realize that their obsessions are unrealistic. OCD is an illogical disorder.

COMMON OBSESSIONS

- fear of illness, death, or contamination
- fear that something has not been done correctly
- fear of harm to oneself or others
- fear of committing a sin
- fear of a frightening image
- distress with asymmetry or disorder

COMMON COMPULSIONS

- avoidance of germs or dirt
- excessive handwashing or showering
- repeated requests for reassurance that something is right
- frequent prayer or confessions
- repeated checking of locks or appliances
- extreme perfectionism
- seeking balance by ordering, straightening, or arranging objects
- doing activities only an odd or even number of times

Behaviors and Symptoms to Look For

Students with OCD can have many obsessions and compulsions. Some of these, such as frequent requests to wash hands in the bathroom, may be very obvious. Other obsessions and compulsions, such as frequent mental images of being harmed or always having to choose items with an even number, may be difficult for you to observe in the classroom.

Children with OCD may:

Be indecisive and slow to accomplish tasks. Students may believe they cannot be absolutely sure of a correct answer or decision. As a result of this doubt and perfectionism, they get stuck trying to complete tests or work, erase excessively, count and recount items, or check and recheck written answers.

Avoid some classroom materials. Children who worry obsessively about their health and safety may refuse to use scissors and other sharp objects, paint, glue, paste, clay, tape, ink, or other classroom materials they perceive as dangerous.

Wash hands excessively. Students who frequently ask to use the bathroom may be fulfilling a compulsion to wash their hands. Red, chapped fingers and hands may be signs of excessive handwashing.

Be stubborn, argumentative, and demanding. Defiance may often result from a student's need to get something just right. When others interfere with this need, students often feel anxious and may react with a negative or hostile attitude.

Act in a distracted or an inattentive way. Students' intense preoccupation with their obsessions can make it difficult for them to focus on work or classroom activities. These students may miss instructions and be inefficient in completing work.

Require or avoid certain numbers or words. Students may insist on having an even number of pencils. They may avoid doing a math worksheet with an odd number of problems. They may avoid reading or saying words like *kill* because they think they may kill a loved one.

Excessively request reassurance or explanations. Students may doubt their perception or recollection of something you have said. In order to make sure they've heard or done something correctly, they may ask repeatedly for reassurance or clarification. "Are you sure?" is a frequent question students may ask.

Be irritable or have erratic mood swings. Constant anxiety related to an obsession can make students very emotionally sensitive. Impatience, a quick temper, and outbursts can result, especially if students have not been able to perform the compulsive behaviors that reduce their anxiety. Depression is also common in individuals with OCD.

Be ostracized by peers. Peers may bully or ostracize children whose compulsive behaviors are obvious and seem "strange." Pay close attention to students whom others tease or exclude.

A NUMBER NIGHTMARE

A few years ago, a seventeen-year-old girl consulted me for treatment for OCD. She had recently developed an obsessive fear of the number six or any multiple of it. Several months earlier, she had learned that some followers of Christianity associate this number with the devil. She began avoiding everything she could that contained a six or a multiple of the number. She could not go to a home address or call a phone number containing any multiple of six. She was terrified about turning eighteen years old. If she wrote a paper for school that was six pages long, she had to reduce it to five pages or increase it to seven. When she was computing math problems and one calculation yielded a multiple of six, she quickly had to calculate the next step. Sometimes she could not avoid the number. If the answer to a math problem was six or a multiple of six, she would leave it—but it made her very nervous until she turned in the paper or test.

During our consultation, she told me that when she arrived at my office with her mother and saw that I was in suite 218, she couldn't open the door. Her mother persuaded her to come in. At the end of our session, I handed her a card with her next appointment date. As I handed it to her, I announced that we'd meet again on the twelfth of that month. She dropped the card on the floor like a hot potato and said she wouldn't come on the twelfth. We scheduled another session, but she did not show up and didn't respond to my phone call. One possibility is that confronting her disorder was too uncomfortable for her. Treatment of OCD requires that an individual be willing to temporarily experience intense anxiety while gradually decreasing the ritual behavior that usually eases the anxiety.

Classroom Strategies and Interventions

Your reaction to obsessive and compulsive behaviors will vary depending on a given situation. Sometimes a student's compulsive behavior has little impact on others and may be acceptable in class. In other situations, compulsions interfere with your ability to teach or a student's ability to produce academic work, and the compulsions need to be addressed.

The general approach to helping students with OCD is to minimize their anxiety while not enabling their OCD behaviors. This balance can be difficult to achieve. It's helpful to work with parents, outside mental health professionals, and school staff in a team approach to address a student's needs.

Following are suggestions for helping children with OCD in the classroom:

Reassure students that they don't have to be perfect. When appropriate, assure students that it isn't necessary (or expected) for every aspect of a project, assignment, or test to be exactly correct. Talk about how it is acceptable to make mistakes and how fear of making mistakes can slow progress (for example, through repeated erasing of answers). Being good enough—meeting or exceeding standards for performance—is all that's necessary. In situations where students are struggling, reinforce positive steps they've accomplished to encourage continued progress. Finally, discuss mistakes you make and talk about how perfection is an impossible goal.

Be patient with repeated requests for clarification. You might become impatient with students who keep asking you to repeat something. It may seem as if they have not been listening. Your first reaction might be to ask, "What did I just say?" or to declare, "You weren't listening." You might even ignore these requests. Students with OCD have heard you, but they doubt they heard you accurately. They fear they won't do what you requested correctly or perfectly. They are simply asking for clarification in order to be certain.

Consider decreasing a student's overall workload. OCD can interfere substantially with schoolwork. Think about ways you can reduce students' workloads while still allowing students to show what they know. For example, for students who compulsively check and recheck their work, assign fewer questions on math or reading assignments.

Allow flexibility in deadlines and testing. Students with OCD often obsess about completing assignments, tests, and projects perfectly. They also may procrastinate due to uncertainty about the right way to complete an assignment. To accommodate these students, relax the deadlines, give full credit for work that is turned in late, and allow additional time to take tests.

Closely monitor students' progress with classwork. Watch students to ensure they are progressing consistently (not erasing, checking and rechecking, or starting over on work). When you're reviewing a student's progress, reinforce the importance of moving ahead instead of making sure the work is perfect.

Avoid grading students on the neatness of their work. Students with OCD can become obsessed with writing perfectly and become stalled as they write and rewrite answers. Young students may repeatedly erase their work until there are holes in the paper because of an imperfectly written letter. Stress that neatness will not be part of students' grades and place emphasis on completion of the work.

Allow for breaks and create a place where students can go to calm down when they're frustrated. For example, allow students who are upset to sit in a quiet area of the classroom and do some deep breathing or engage in another anxiety-relieving strategy they've learned. A visit to the office or the school counselor also may help. See page 20 for a reproducible "Student Coping Plan" you can use to establish provisions for students who are overwhelmed.

Eliminate teasing. Children with OCD may have strange compulsions that draw negative attention from peers. These may involve physical gestures. Institute anti-bullying interventions to protect students with OCD from abuse or exclusion by peers.

COMMON TYPES OF OCD

These are not formal diagnostic categories or labels. Rather, they are informal monikers you can use to understand how OCD might look in different students:

The Reassurance Seeker
A student might worry that the topic he chose for a paper is not the right one. He may question you repeatedly. After you reassure him a couple of times, it's probably best to say something like, "I told you the topic you chose will be okay. I wouldn't have said it if I didn't mean it. Please stay with that topic, and it will be just fine." Another student might worry that she won't get a good enough grade on a paper because she didn't finish it in class. This student spends too much time perfecting her work and takes far too long to complete it. When you urge her to turn in her work, she may resist or reluctantly comply. She may express concern multiple times during the remainder of class that her work was bad. After your second reassuring response, tell this student that her work was definitely good enough and that it's not worth worrying or talking about anymore. Give her feedback that her paper was fine after you've looked at or graded the paper.

The Bathroom's Best Friend
Young people with OCD may ask for excessive trips to the bathroom to perform a cleaning or washing ritual. Sometimes their fingers and hands will look dry, red, or chapped. They might also overuse hand sanitizer. When you first notice this behavior in a student, it's best to check with his parents to find out if he has a medical problem. If he has no medical problem and you have reason to suspect he is excessively washing or sanitizing his hands, it's important to inform his parents of this behavior.

The Eraser or the Cross-Out Queen

A student whose written work or drawing always has to be just right may erase and cross out letters and words excessively. This student may also be very cautious, careful, and slow in completing work. Emphasize to this student that you won't penalize her penmanship or artwork as long as it's legible and understandable. You might also consider providing her a copy of another student's notes. This will allow a student who struggles with note-taking to stay on top of information presented during class. Reducing the quantity of required writing and offering alternative methods of evaluation in place of written tests also might help.

The King of Questions

This student asks repeatedly for clarification in an attempt to be sure he's heard something correctly. His questions are a checking compulsion performed in response to his doubt that he understands directions accurately. Reassuring this student more than once will only perpetuate the problem. Privately tell this student that you'll repeat something for him once, then he's to do his best at what he thinks he's supposed to do. If he continues to ask, arrange a hand signal, such as holding up your index finger, to indicate he's already used his one request for assurance. This signal allows you to acknowledge him while also saying that you are sticking to the one-question plan. When this student successfully completes an assignment after only one clarification, reinforce the fact that he didn't need excessive clarifications.

The Snail

Imagine the student whose work has to be perfect, who doubts if it's perfect, who has to recheck to see if it's perfect, who has to correct the "imperfections," who has to start over on the paper because it's not perfect . . . You and the rest of the class are moving on while this student is stuck. This is a student whom you'll perceive as very slow and unproductive. Until you can make progress in reducing her anxiety, you may decide to shorten her assignments or allow her extended time on tests.

The Checker

Imagine a middle school student who worries constantly that he didn't lock his locker. After he locks it and walks away, he's struck by doubt. This makes him anxious, so he goes back and locks his locker again. He walks away, and the doubt recurs. He goes back again. He may experience this doubt every time he locks his locker. When he finally makes it to class, he may worry the locker is not locked through the entire class period. Do not penalize this student for being late to class if you know his OCD was the reason. Reassure him that it's highly unlikely that another student will be looking for open lockers, so no one will know his locker is not locked.

Obsessive-Compulsive–Related Disorders: Hairpulling and Skin Picking

These disorders are similar to compulsive rituals of OCD. People feel a strong urge to pull hair or pick at skin, and they feel a relief after the behavior. To qualify for a diagnosis, these behaviors must cause significant distress or impairment in functioning and people must have tried unsuccessfully to stop them.[8]

HAIRPULLING (TRICHOTILLOMANIA)

Trichotillomania is a disorder that causes people to compulsively pull hair from the scalp, eyebrows, and eyelashes. A person feels a tension or need to pull out hair, and the pulling relieves the tension. Bald patches sometimes result. (Bald patches can also be caused by an autoimmune disorder called *alopecia*.)

About 1 percent of children and adolescents have this disorder. It affects many more girls than boys. Depression and other anxiety disorders commonly accompany trichotillomania.

With students who have trichotillomania, you may see them in your classroom twirling or stroking their hair before pulling it—or you may see only evidence of it in the form of thinning eyelashes, eyebrows, or hair on the scalp. If you observe hairpulling, privately ask students if they're aware that they pull their hair and whether there's anything you can do to reduce stress related to hairpulling.

If students are undergoing therapy for trichotillomania, it can be helpful to speak with the involved professionals so that strategies are consistent across settings. Some students take medication to address compulsive hairpulling.

SKIN PICKING (EXCORIATION)

People with excoriation pick at their own skin, nails, scabs, or pimples and may spend at least one hour per day doing this. Embarrassing physical signs and medical problems can result. There are many similarities between skin picking and hairpulling. Both disorders run in families, are more common in girls, and sometimes coexist with OCD and depression. For guidance on responding to these students, see the preceding section, "Hairpulling (Trichotillomania)."

PROFESSIONAL TREATMENTS

The most effective treatment for OCD is a type of cognitive-behavioral therapy (CBT) called exposure and response prevention (ERP). First, the student who doubts his locker is locked learns different ways of thinking about not locking his locker. Rather than imagining that this would result in some catastrophe, he learns that a theft from his locker would be an inconvenient but solvable problem. Next he learns breathing and other relaxation techniques that he must practice. He uses these calming techniques to respond to anxiety when he's prevented from checking his locker.

Next, a hierarchy is established with behaviors that come closer, step by step, to locking the locker. The student and therapist begin the procedure with the student imagining or actually engaging in a behavior at the lowest end of the hierarchy. This creates some anxiety, which the student works to decrease with relaxation techniques. After the student has become comfortable at one level of the hierarchy, he moves up to the next level. A student could go through the procedure by imagining these situations in a psychologist's office. Alternatively, and ideally, a psychologist could gain access to the school and do the procedure with the student after school. This procedure can take from several weeks to many months to complete.

ERP stops the student from engaging in his compulsive ritual of checking and rechecking that his locker is secured. The student usually becomes quite anxious when unable to complete his compulsion. As he calms his anxiety, he becomes better able to endure the anxiety, which tends to dissipate by itself over time. Each time he returns to his locker and sees that it's locked, he's reassured that he does, in fact, lock his locker the first time. Gradually, the student feels increasingly safe, stops obsessing about this concern, and gives up the related ritual.

Depending upon the severity of OCD, a physician may prescribe medication to complement behavior therapy. Medications in the family of selective serotonin reuptake inhibitors (SSRIs) are commonly used for OCD. Students should be carefully monitored during the initial stages of starting medication, since side effects can occur. A very small percentage may experience depression. Other possible side effects of medication can include drowsiness, insomnia, stomachaches, headaches, nervousness, and weight gain. If you observe any troubling symptoms in a child taking medication, immediately share your observations with your school nurse and the child's parents.

ACCOMMODATIONS CAN BE HELPFUL

Thirteen-year-old Johanna had developed a reluctance to go to school because of her fear of germs and illness. When she was in school, she would visit the restroom multiple times a day to wash her hands.

The school psychologist and Johanna's parents developed a plan. Johanna entered the school after classes began and when not many students were in the hallways. Johanna's parents opened all doors, and the psychologist waited in her office with hand sanitizer on her desk. With this plan, Johanna saw that the school staff understood her problem. The plan included the following accommodations:

- Johanna came to school fifteen minutes after classes started and entered through a side door.

- She was allowed to go to the bathroom only twice in the morning and twice in the afternoon.

- Her school day was shortened.

- She had a designated desk and chair slightly set apart from other students.

- She received extra time for classwork with frequent check-ins from the teacher.

- Teachers did not touch her or her desk.

- Johanna's mother brought her lunch to school and ate with her.

These accommodations helped minimize Johanna's anxiety throughout the school day. Over several months, as she realized that she was not getting sicker than other students, she realized that her precautions were unnecessary. Ultimately, she needed fewer and fewer accommodations.

CHAPTER 10

Depressive Disorders

. . . .

"Our mental health seriously affects our physical health—studies suggest that
people living with depression are more likely to die from heart disease."

—Michelle Obama, attorney, children's health advocate, and former US first lady

. . . .

Everyone experiences temporary mood changes. Students with depressive disorders, however, exhibit significant changes and problems with mood and behavior. These changes impair children's functioning at school and at home.

It is natural for students to feel unhappiness or a decreased interest in activities at times. Many experiences at home or school can cause these feelings for a brief period of time. Major life changes, such as the loss of a loved one, may also cause major changes in mood. Most children—with help from adults—can overcome challenges and tragic life events and adjust to new circumstances.

Other children experience extreme feelings of unhappiness that can last for long periods of time. These feelings may or may not be triggered by a particular event. When students experience symptoms of unhappiness or irritability, sometimes accompanied by physical complaints, for many months—or for just two weeks if symptoms are severe—they may have a depressive disorder.

About 1% to 3% of children and between 11% and 18% of adolescents experience depressive disorders.[1] Up to two-thirds of these young people may have at least one additional mental disorder.[2]

The more time teens—especially girls—spend on smartphones and social media, the more likely they are to experience loneliness, depression, sleep deprivation, and suicidal thinking. Teens are spending much less time in face-to-face social interaction, sports, and religious activities, all of which are known to reduce the likelihood of these problems.[3]

Students with depressive disorders experience low moods or loss of interest in usual activities. They may also have ongoing feelings of sadness, irritability, guilt, or hopelessness. Low self-esteem, lack of energy, difficulty concentrating, and loss of interest in daily activities are common. So are physical symptoms such as insomnia, changes in appetite, and body aches and pains. Some mood problems lead to severe tantrums and verbal or physical aggression. Students who are depressed are at a greater risk of poor school performance and of becoming socially isolated. Depressed teens are more likely to use drugs and alcohol. They are also at greater risk for suicide.

CAUTION! Depressive disorders can be very serious. Depression is the most common reason for attempted suicide. More teens and young adults die from suicide than from cancer, heart disease, AIDS, birth defects, stroke, pneumonia, influenza, and chronic lung disease combined.[4] It is important to take suicidal wishes and threats seriously and to respond immediately. Any students suspected of being dangerous to themselves or others should always be supervised. Most states require teachers to report these students.[5] For a full list of suicide warning signs and appropriate responses, see chapter 14.

Approximately 1% of children and between 2% and 8% of adolescents experience persistent depressive disorder (PDD).[6] About 3% of children and more than 10% of adolescents with PDD will have at least one episode of major depression. A majority of teens with depression are female.[7] Between one-half to two-thirds of young people with major depression have at least one other mental disorder. It is estimated that between 2% and 5% of children and adolescents may exhibit disruptive mood dysregulation disorder.[8]

Four diagnoses exist for depressive disorders:

Persistent depressive disorder (PDD). This is the new diagnostic label for what was previously labeled dysthymia. Children with PDD have a depressed mood a majority of the time for at least one year. They also may have appetite or sleep problems, low energy and self-esteem, poor concentration, and feelings of hopelessness. PDD is a chronic, low-grade depression that can prevent people from enjoying much of what life has to offer. The symptoms are not necessarily severe, so observing them in young people can be difficult. Children with PDD have a 70 percent risk of developing major depression within five years.[9]

Major depressive disorder (MDD). This is a serious mood disorder in which depressed mood and loss of interest or pleasure exist along with at least three of the following symptoms for two weeks:

- significant weight loss or decrease or increase in appetite nearly every day
- insomnia or sleeping too much
- feeling agitated or slowed down
- fatigue and loss of energy
- feelings of worthlessness or excessive guilt
- difficulty concentrating or indecisiveness
- recurrent thoughts of death

Some children with this disorder are at risk for suicide. Depression has a tendency to recur if it is not treated. Up to one-half of adolescents who experience one episode of depression will experience another within the next four years.[10]

Disruptive mood dysregulation disorder (DMDD). Children with DMDD have chronic, long-standing, severe irritability along with frequent temper outbursts that are out of proportion to the situation. The irritable, angry mood must be present almost every day at home and school to qualify for this diagnosis. Outbursts can be verbal or behavioral. They sometimes are referred to as aggressive rages.[11]

The American Psychiatric Association (APA) created this new diagnosis in response to increasing numbers of children being diagnosed with bipolar disorder, which is often treated with powerful medications that have serious side effects. Many of these children had severe irritability but did not exhibit the mania required for a bipolar diagnosis. The new DMDD diagnosis allows for children with intense mood and behavior issues *without* manic episodes to be diagnosed and treated. As increasing numbers of children receive this diagnosis, the numbers receiving a bipolar disorder diagnosis are expected to decrease.

Adjustment disorder with depressed mood. This type of depressive disorder begins within three months of an identifiable stressful event. Changes in mood are out of proportion to the severity or intensity of the stressor. The depressed mood also creates impairment in an important area of functioning. An example might be a student who exhibits many signs of depression because she got a B instead of an A on her report card. If the stressor is removed and the depressed mood terminates after six months, it is called an adjustment disorder with depressed mood.

Behaviors and Symptoms to Look For

Look for symptoms of depression when a student shows a change in attitude or behavior. A once enthusiastic and outgoing boy may suddenly seem sullen and may withdraw from friends and activities he likes. A high-achieving girl may no longer care about schoolwork. A previously confident student may make many self-deprecating comments. If a student is typically soft-spoken, shy, or withdrawn, it may be more difficult to observe changes in attitude and symptoms of depression.

Following are common symptoms that may occur with any of the depressive disorders covered in this chapter:

A generally unhappy mood with sadness, anxiety, or irritability. Depressed children often appear sad or worried. They may interact less with peers. They may become more quiet or unproductive in class due to decreased energy or lack of interest.

Social withdrawal. Alienation from peers can be the result of, or a partial cause for, depression. Be particularly observant of students who seem isolated from peers.

Academic failure or marked changes in achievement. Children who are depressed may suddenly appear to lose interest in schoolwork, and their grades may drop. This can include students who once performed at a high level.

Loss of interest or pleasure in usual activities. A student's general loss of enthusiasm may indicate depression. Students might continue to participate in activities, but seem not to enjoy them.

Frequent absences. Depression and lower grades can lead to a decrease in homework productivity and studying for tests, which in turn can lead to distaste for school. Students may avoid going to school.

Lethargy or a sudden decrease in energy. Consistent fatigue or a change in a student's energy can suggest a depressed mood. Less energy can lead to poor work production and falling grades.

Sleepiness. Children with depression often have disrupted sleep patterns. These students may be late to school often, may appear drowsy, or may even fall asleep in school.

Feelings of worthlessness or guilt. Low self-esteem is a common characteristic of depression. It often can be observed in a student's words, demeanor, and behavior. Students may criticize their abilities in the classroom ("I'm no good at math") and other settings ("I shouldn't play; I always strike out"). Feelings of inferiority ("I'm fat") can lead to withdrawal because students don't feel they are worthy of peers' acceptance.

Problems concentrating or indecisiveness. Students with depression are commonly inattentive and have difficulty making decisions. Inattention caused by depression can be confused with ADHD (see page 102).

Significant weight gain or loss. Students' eating patterns may change in reaction to emotional distress. Some students will eat more and gain weight when they are depressed. Others will lose their appetites or deliberately limit how much they eat. Eating disorders may accompany depression, especially among adolescents. (See chapter 15.)

Oppositional and defiant behavior. Children—particularly young children—who are depressed may show aggression, irritability, and social withdrawal. (They may also complain of aches and pains.)[12]

Recurrent thoughts of death. One sign of severe depression is suicidal thinking. If a student expresses any thoughts or threats of self-harm (or harm to others), take these threats seriously and respond to them right away. Different states have different reporting requirements for teachers, so check your state's requirements. For more information on suicide warning signs and appropriate responses, see chapter 14.

Classroom Strategies and Interventions

Only a qualified mental health professional should diagnose a depressive disorder, as with all mental health disorders. If a student has not been diagnosed but you observe symptoms that might represent depression, it's important to inform parents, counselors, and other school staff of any behaviors that concern you.

Following are some suggestions for helping students whom you suspect or know are experiencing depression:

Give students compassion and empathy. Show students you are genuinely interested in their lives and well-being. Ask about their families, friends, interests, and other aspects of their lives. An educator's genuine, sustained interest can have a strong positive impact on the life of a depressed student.

Provide additional encouragement and genuine praise. Students with depression are likely lacking confidence and feeling pessimistic. Encourage effort and perseverance with schoolwork and offer more praise for the effort than the outcome.

Show flexibility with school policies, including those for absences and tardiness. Students with depression are likely to experience significant sleep disturbances, which can affect their attendance. A depressed mood may also lead to school refusal. Attending appointments for therapy might also cause some absenteeism. Provide accommodations for these students in your classroom schedule and rules.

Allow for flexibility in workload. Adjust course work to accommodate a student's mood as well as any extended absences. To avoid overwhelming a student, break large assignments or projects into smaller steps. Consider extended time for exams to help ease a student's difficulties with concentration, decreased energy, and slower processing speed.

Provide a safe and caring classroom. Bullying may be a partial cause for depression, and bullying can make students who are already depressed feel worse. Ensure that your classroom does not tolerate harassment. You can find strategies for creating supportive school environments in chapter 2.

Offer a place where depressed students can take a break or talk. Students who are overwhelmed by their feelings should be allowed to visit a safe place or to speak with a school counselor.

Plan for gradually reintroducing a student to school. After a hospitalization or lengthy homebound period, a child might need to be slowly reintroduced to school. Work with counselors and other school staff to establish a plan for a student's return to the classroom.

Carefully observe all students. The signs of depression are not always readily apparent and may not emerge in an obvious way in the classroom. It's important to know your students and to note any changes you see in their behavior.

PROFESSIONAL TREATMENTS

Cognitive-behavioral therapy (CBT) and dialectical behavior therapy (DBT) are effective treatments for depressive disorders. These therapies teach students how to think more logically as a way of helping themselves feel better. Students learn to view their moods as feelings that can be accepted and that will pass when they stay in the moment and engage in calming techniques. For young children who cannot yet fully verbalize their thoughts and feelings, working with a play therapist may be best.

Several studies have found certain types of exercise to be an effective antidepressant treatment for children and adolescents.[13] Physicians may prescribe antidepressant medication for moderate to severe depression, but this is effective only for a minority of children and teens.[14]

The most common medications prescribed for depression are selective serotonin reuptake inhibitors (SSRIs) and serotonin and norepinephrine reuptake inhibitors (SNRIs). Students must be monitored very closely during the early days and weeks of taking these medications. A very small percentage of young people become more depressed, agitated, and even suicidal in the initial stages of taking medication. Other possible side effects include drowsiness, insomnia, stomachaches, headaches, nervousness, and weight gain. If you observe any troubling symptoms in a child taking medication, immediately share them with the school nurse and the child's parents.

LUCIANA

Luciana was an outgoing high school cheerleader who suddenly quit cheerleading because she had gained ten pounds. On weekends, she used to hang out with friends. Lately, she was staying in her room. She didn't seem to care when her grades began dropping. She missed a couple of days of school because she couldn't get out of bed in the morning. Her mother read Luciana's diary, in which Luciana said she didn't know what the purpose was for anything. She may have been experiencing a major depressive episode. Luciana's comment worried her mother, who made an appointment for Luciana to see a psychologist.

MICHAEL

Michael was a bright thirteen-year-old with a lot of heart. He was a popular kid among his classmates and always had a joke for his teachers. But all of this changed after the winter break. Michael came back to school a different person. He wouldn't speak to others unless he was forced to. His work began to fall off, and it didn't seem to bother him. In the halls, Michael would pull the hood of his sweatshirt over his head as if to become invisible. Teachers knew something was wrong, but Michael wouldn't talk to anyone.

Michael's teachers asked the school counselor to intervene. She brought Michael to her office. They spent a few sessions in silence, with Michael avoiding eye contact, until he finally revealed that his father had left home abruptly over the holidays. The counselor recommended to Michael's mother that she take him to see a psychotherapist. With professional help, Michael was able to adjust to his new home situation within a couple of months. When Michael started seeing the therapist, the therapist diagnosed him with an adjustment disorder with depressed mood.

CHAPTER 11

Bipolar Disorder

....

"One of the most common scenarios I encounter in practice is the child
diagnosed with severe ADHD and oppositional defiant disorder who is not
getting better with current treatment and who probably has bipolar disorder."

—Linda Jo Volness, psychiatric clinical nurse specialist

....

Bipolar disorder—the term for what was once called manic depression—is a brain disorder that causes major changes in mood and energy. The *Diagnostic and Statistical Manual of Mental Disorders: Fifth Edition* (*DSM-5*) has removed this disorder from the category of mood disorders because bipolar disorder is now thought to be an illness that is between a mood disorder and schizophrenia.[1]

Children with bipolar disorder have rapid changes in mood, sometimes within the same day. Their behavior may be manic for a few hours and shift to depression for the remainder of the day. Manic symptoms include abnormally elevated mood, boundless energy, grandiosity, severe irritability, agitation, or defiance. Children in a manic phase also exhibit unexpected, frequent, and inappropriate happiness, silliness, or goofiness. Depressive symptoms include lethargy, sadness, and a lack of interest in usual activities.

Estimates suggest that up to 1% of adolescents and less than 0.5% of children experience bipolar disorder.[2] Children who have one parent with bipolar disorder are five to ten times more likely to inherit the disorder.[3] In the 1990s, the diagnosis of bipolar disorder increased dramatically. One reason for this spike was that children with severe irritable moods but without clear manic episodes were receiving bipolar diagnoses. The criteria for diagnosis have changed in the *DSM-5*. A diagnosis of bipolar disorder now requires manic or hypomanic episodes. The *DSM-5* introduces a new diagnosis, disruptive mood dysregulation disorder, or DMDD (page 92), for children with severe irritability and explosiveness who do not exhibit manic or hypomanic episodes. As increasing numbers of children are given a DMDD diagnosis, the numbers receiving a bipolar disorder diagnosis will likely decrease.

ADHD is the most common disorder to coexist with bipolar disorder.[4] It is also common for children with bipolar disorder to have one or more anxiety disorders. It is up to a mental health professional to diagnose these disorders. The educator's responsibility is to accurately report behaviors to parents, school staff, and other professionals involved in a student's care.

Behaviors and Symptoms to Look For

Students with bipolar disorder are more frequently observed to be depressed or in a "normal" mood. (For information on the symptoms of depression, see page 93 in chapter 10.) Manic behavior typically lasts for a short time—such as a few hours, a few days, or one week—between longer periods of depression. Changes in mood and energy during transitions are so unusual, striking, and troubling that they are typically easy to recognize.

Manic behaviors in children include:

An unrealistically euphoric mood. A student may exhibit an exaggerated mood of elation or giddiness, which may last from a few minutes to a few hours. This euphoric mood does not appear to be justified by real-life events. For example, a child may be unable to stop laughing and giggling during class for no apparent reason.

Excessive energy and activity. Students may use their boundless energy in productive or unproductive ways. One student might suddenly begin completing previously ignored classwork. Another might be unable to stop moving or talking and may cause classroom disruptions.

Need for less sleep. Someone in a manic phase of bipolar disorder will sleep much less than usual. The student may not appear tired and may even be overly active in class.

Fast speech. A student experiencing a manic mood may talk very fast. It can be difficult to understand the student or get in a word of your own.

Racing thoughts. A student in a manic episode may have many racing thoughts and may not be able to express them clearly. These ideas may be unrelated to one another and difficult to suppress. Students may frequently interrupt class to share these thoughts.

Distractibility. Students may attend to many irrelevant external stimuli.

Plans for or attempts at unrealistic, risky, or illegal activities. Students may lack good judgment and may be very impulsive, which can lead them to endanger themselves and others. Substance abuse and reckless driving are common among teens.

Grandiose thinking. Students may have a very unrealistic self-image. They may view themselves as the smartest student or the best athlete when they are actually average in these areas. Grandiosity can be associated with risk-taking tendencies. ("I'm much smarter than my teachers, so I'm going to tell them how to teach today.")

Irritability, severe rage, and verbal or physical abuse. Students' mood changes can be rapid and extreme. Aggressive, violent behavior can occur with bouts of explosiveness that last for long periods of time.

Cognitive deficits. Bipolar disorder affects many aspects of brain functioning. Students may show problems with processing speed, working memory, and executive functions[5] (see chapter 6).

Hypersexual thoughts and behavior. Children (even young children) may talk about sexual topics or act out sexually in inappropriate ways. Adolescents may engage in promiscuous sexual behavior.

Suicidal thoughts and behaviors. Young people with bipolar disorder are at very high risk for suicide.[6] (See page 93 in chapter 10 for symptoms of depression.)

Classroom Strategies and Interventions

For suggestions on responding to students with depressed mood, see page 94. To address manic moods, you can use the following strategies. Check with counselors, other school staff, parents, and any mental health professionals involved in the care of a student for insight into the child's behavior and helpful interventions.

Be prepared for extreme mood swings and grandiosity. Students with bipolar disorder often experience extreme fluctuations in mood—from sadness to giddiness, from anxiety to anger, and many other emotions. Some students may also express delusional thinking. Accept a student's views as true rather than arguing about them. For example, if a student claims to be smarter than all the teachers in the school, it's probably better just to say "okay" than to dispute this opinion with a more realistic statement.

Avoid verbally engaging a student experiencing strong emotions. When students' emotions are overwhelming, they can't think or speak logically. Respond to outbursts in a low voice and with a calm demeanor. Anger or criticism can fuel children's emotions.

Let students leave the classroom to talk with someone. Students may experience feelings or behave in ways that are very disruptive. Have a school-approved plan in place that allows students diagnosed with bipolar disorder to leave the classroom to talk with a counselor or psychologist.

Allow for flexibility in workload to accommodate the student's energy level. Students with bipolar disorder may experience wide variations in their energy levels and may have cognitive deficits. Adjust classwork and homework requirements to accommodate a student's ability to function in the classroom and at home.

Identify situations that trigger a child's heightened moods. Note events that seem to cause or aggravate a student's mood disturbances, and take steps to avoid these triggers.

Note: Children with bipolar disorder often have academic and behavior problems similar to those of children with other disorders. Many strategies and accommodations listed for students with ADHD (page 102), DMDD (page 92), oppositional defiant disorder (page 157), depressive disorders (page 91), and anxiety disorders (page 63) can also be useful with students who have bipolar disorder.

 GET HELP! If a student is behaviorally explosive, make sure you have a plan in place to call your school's crisis team or personnel designated to respond to such emergencies.

PROFESSIONAL TREATMENTS

Medication is essential for students with bipolar disorder. Mood stabilizers—which steady a person's mood between two extremes—are the most commonly prescribed medications. For some students with bipolar disorder, physicians prescribe an antidepressant or an atypical antipsychotic medication in addition to a mood stabilizer. Side effects of medications include excessive thirst and urination, drowsiness, diarrhea, stomachaches, weight gain, and headaches. It's important to allow students on these medications unrestricted access to fluids and use of the restroom. Check with students' parents about any medications being taken and ask them to inform you of any changes in medication as they happen. Be observant of side effects, especially during the initial stages of medication use, and immediately report any concerns to a school nurse and the child's parents.

Psychotherapy can also be helpful to teach students and their families how to cope with bipolar disorder. A child who becomes destructive with rage might be taught healthier ways, such as relaxation and breathing exercises, to deal with intense anger.

CHAPTER 12

Neurodevelopmental Disorders

....

"If the human brain were so simple that we could understand it,
we would be so simple that we couldn't."

—*Emerson M. Pugh, physicist*

....

The disorders discussed in this chapter involve "how the brain wires itself during development, how the end result can vary in different people, and what happens when it goes wrong."[1] The first edition of this book listed these disorders in separate chapters, because the *DSM-4* categorized them separately. The *DSM-5* classifies all these disorders as neurodevelopmental disorders since they are all caused by differences in the development of brain functions, which in turn can cause problems whose symptoms are first seen in early childhood. Challenges in personal, social, or academic functioning continue at least through childhood. Some students outgrow these disorders. For other individuals, functioning improves.

Attention Deficit Hyperactivity Disorder (ADHD)

Students with ADHD have difficulty sustaining attention to uninteresting tasks and controlling their impulses. They may struggle to concentrate on lessons and complete schoolwork. These problems often lead to academic underachievement. Children with ADHD are more likely to get into trouble for inappropriate behavior caused by difficulty controlling impulses. These students tend to act or speak before they think. They may also have difficulty with peer relationships.

Between 5% and 10% of young people have ADHD.[2] Boys are diagnosed with the disorder more than twice as often as girls are. Among children with ADHD, 44% qualify for one other mental health or learning disorder, while another 43% qualify for two other diagnoses.[3] Developmental coordination disorder (very poor handwriting or dysgraphia) may be diagnosed in up to 50% of students with ADHD.[4] (See "Specific Learning Disorder with Impairment in Written Expression" page 134.)

Despite its name, ADHD is not primarily a disorder of attention. It's an impulse-control disorder that makes it difficult for students to delay immediate gratification. Immediate rewards typically have a greater influence on students with ADHD than they have on those without ADHD. Because watching television or playing video games offers immediate rewards, children with ADHD may show very few signs of the disorder during these activities. Symptoms show when these students are required to do things they find unrewarding. These tasks are sometimes described as "cognitively effortful." During class time, it's hard for students with ADHD to avoid doing things they'd enjoy more—such as moving around, talking with others, daydreaming, or having fun. For the same reason, it's difficult for them to resist playing until after their homework is done.

ADHD is sometimes considered a mental or behavioral disorder, but it is caused by differences in five areas of the brain.[5] Medication can be effective in controlling symptoms because it helps normalize chemicals in the brains of students with ADHD. Behavior management strategies and accommodations in school are also important in helping these students succeed.

Behaviors and Symptoms to Look For

Students who have ADHD show different symptoms. Some students are mainly inattentive and struggle primarily with schoolwork and homework. They are not generally disruptive, and they may do well academically in the lower grades. Other students with ADHD primarily struggle to control their impulses. This leads to excessive activity levels, difficulty complying with rules, and difficulty sustaining attention to schoolwork and homework. It may seem that the majority of your time is spent reminding these students to remain seated, silent, and on task. By the time they reach the upper elementary grades, these students may be underachieving and may continue to have difficulties controlling their behavior. In middle school, organizational and planning requirements, in addition to more homework assignments, make school increasingly frustrating for students with ADHD.

WHAT'S YOUR ADHD IQ?

For questions 1 through 9, choose *T* for if the statement is true or *F* if the statement is false.

1. ADHD is a relatively new disorder, unknown until the 1970s.   T   F

2. ADHD is overdiagnosed.   T   F

3. ADHD is a learning disability.   T   F

4. Sugar causes hyperactivity.   T   F

5. There are tests to diagnose ADHD.   T   F

6. Pediatricians conduct comprehensive evaluations of ADHD.   T   F

7. Students with ADHD often have reading comprehension problems.   T   F

8. Many ADHD medications are stimulants. They are effective because they work in an opposite way in students with ADHD, calming them down.   T   F

9. ADHD medications are addictive.   T   F

10. A student with ADHD is likely to do which of the following with a pencil? (Choose only one answer.)

    a. Blow it across the desk.
    b. Hold it high in the air and drop it.
    c. Thread it through belt loops.
    d. Lose it.
    e. Forget it.
    f. Poke a neighbor with it.
    g. Sharpen it, break it, sharpen it, break it, and so on.
    h. None of the above.
    i. All of the above.

Answers:

1. **F.** The name of the disorder has changed over the years, but a hyperactive boy, Fidgety Phil, was described in a medical journal in 1902.

2. **T and F.** ADHD may be overdiagnosed in families with higher socioeconomic status, but it's underdiagnosed in minority populations and in people at lower socioeconomic levels due to lack of knowledge and less access to healthcare.

3. **F.** A learning disability refers to reading, math, or writing skills that are unexpectedly poor despite adequate academic instruction. However, students with ADHD are more likely than other students to have learning disabilities.

4. **F.** This is a myth refuted by more than twenty-five studies.

5. **F.** There are no diagnostic tests for ADHD. It can be diagnosed only by a thorough evaluation from a mental health professional or pediatrician. A thorough evaluation includes a parent interview providing a developmental and family history and parent and teacher rating scales. Other conditions that could be causing symptoms (such as a learning disability or anxiety) should be assessed and ruled out. Since almost 50 percent of children with ADHD have at least one other disorder, an appropriate question in an evaluation is "ADHD and what else?"

6. **F.** In 2011, the American Academy of Pediatrics published updated guidelines for the diagnosis, evaluation, and treatment of ADHD by clinicians and other healthcare providers. However, research finds that pediatrician office visits often don't comply with these guidelines. In addition, if an office visit does not meet these standards for ADHD, it's also unlikely that coexisting disorders would be evaluated.[6]

7. **T.** Because their concentration is limited, students with ADHD frequently need to reread material in order to understand it.

8. **F.** Some ADHD medications are in the stimulant family. However, they work by stimulating more availability of a certain chemical in the brain.

9. **F.** ADHD medications are not addictive if taken in prescribed doses. Adolescents and adults can become addicted if medications are taken in much higher doses, not as prescribed, or without a prescription.

10. **i.** These behaviors are all examples of lack of attention, impulsivity, and hyperactivity.

It is very important not to oversimplify ADHD as a problem with attention and impulse control only. Most children and adolescents with ADHD also have executive function weaknesses (see chapter 6), including problems with self-control, starting and finishing work, planning, organizing, self-monitoring, and working memory.

INTERNET GAMING DISORDER

First mentioned in 1983, video game addiction is now formally being recognized as a mental health problem.[7] The *DSM-5* proposes that internet gaming disorder is a condition for further study. In 2018, the World Health Organization (WHO) announced that it will include internet gaming disorder in its next diagnostic manual. The disorder is characterized by persistent or recurring gaming behavior including impaired control over gaming, increasing priority given to gaming to the extent that gaming takes precedence over other interests and activities, and continuation of or increase in gaming despite negative consequences. This behavior must exist for one year and must significantly interfere with personal, family, or educational functioning.[8]

The mental health community is split on whether this problem is a habit or an addiction. Some feel the name of the disorder should include all internet use, including social media use. A large study showed that males and people with ADHD, obsessive-compulsive disorder (OCD), and depression are more likely to engage in this behavior.[9]

There are three types of ADHD. Only a qualified mental health professional or physician can diagnose a student with the disorder.

ADHD, PREDOMINANTLY HYPERACTIVE-IMPULSIVE PRESENTATION

This type of ADHD is usually diagnosed in preschool or kindergarten children who have problems primarily with self-control and following rules. These students do not necessarily have difficulty with attention, though they may face challenges in this area as they grow older and are required to focus and stay on task for longer periods of time.

A student is diagnosed with this type of ADHD when six or more of the following behaviors interfere with or reduce the child's functioning in at least two settings (at home and at school, for example):

- often fidgets, taps hands or feet, or squirms in seat
- often leaves seat in situations where remaining seated is expected
- often runs or climbs excessively in situations where it's inappropriate; feels restless (adolescent)
- often is unable to play or engage in leisure activities quietly
- often acts as if driven by a motor; unable to be comfortable being still for extended periods of time
- often talks excessively
- often blurts out an answer before a question has been completed (or before raising hand in school)
- often has difficulty waiting or taking turns
- often interrupts or intrudes on others

ADHD, PREDOMINANTLY INATTENTIVE PRESENTATION

This form of ADHD was once referred to as attention deficit disorder (ADD). Young people with this type of ADHD have little or no impulsivity or hyperactivity. They mainly have difficulty with attention, alertness, organization, memory, and planning. Some of these children may be described as slow-moving, spacey, or lethargic. These students are often misinterpreted as being lazy, unmotivated, or irresponsible because they have difficulty initiating, remembering, and following through on tasks.

Many people believe that the inattentive presentation of ADHD is underdiagnosed, since its symptoms do not include highly visible, disruptive behaviors. As a result, many children who struggle with concentration may not be getting the academic support they need.

A student is diagnosed with ADHD, predominantly inattentive presentation, when six or more of the following behaviors interfere with or reduce the child's functioning in at least two settings:

- often fails to give close attention to details or makes careless errors in schoolwork
- often has difficulty sustaining attention in tasks or play activities
- often does not seem to listen when spoken to directly
- often does not follow through on instructions or finish schoolwork or chores
- often has difficulty organizing tasks and activities

- often avoids, dislikes, or is reluctant to engage in tasks that require sustained mental effort (schoolwork or homework)
- often loses things necessary for tasks and activities
- often easily distracted by extraneous stimuli
- often is forgetful in daily activities

ADHD, Combined Presentation

Children with this form of ADHD struggle with impulsivity, hyperactivity, and inattention. They often get plenty of attention from teachers, because they experience a wide variety of challenges in the classroom related to both behavior and academic performance.

A student is diagnosed with ADHD, combined presentation, when a combination of six or more inattentive and hyperactive-impulsive behaviors negatively affect the child's social and academic activities.

AN ADHD CHILD'S BILL OF RIGHTS

In 1991 Ruth E. Harris created a "Bill of Rights" for students who have ADHD,* and its advice and wisdom still ring true today:

"Help me to focus." Please teach me through my sense of touch. I need hands-on and body movement.

"I need to know what comes next." Please give me a structured environment where there is a dependable routine. Give me an advance warning if there will be changes.

"Wait for me, I'm still thinking." Please allow me to go at my own pace. If I rush, I get confused and upset.

"I'm stuck, I can't do it!" Please offer me options for problem-solving. I need to know the detours when the road is blocked.

"Is it right? I need to know NOW!" Please give me rich and immediate feedback on how I'm doing.

"I didn't forget, I didn't 'hear' it in the first place." Please give me directions one step at a time and ask me to say back what I think you said.

"I didn't know I WASN'T in my seat!" Please remind me to stop, think, and act.

"Am I almost done now?" Please give me short work periods with short-term goals.

"What? Please don't say, 'I already told you that.'" Tell me again in different words. Give me a signal. Draw me a symbol.

"I know, it's ALL wrong, isn't it?" Please give me praise for partial success. Reward me for self-improvement, not just for perfection.

"But why do I always get yelled at?" Please catch me doing something right and praise me for my specific positive behavior. Remind me (and yourself) about my good points when I'm having a bad day.

"Reward me for my effort." Please remember to say, "Thanks for trying so hard." It takes extra effort to stay on task.

*From "An ADHD Child's Bill of Rights" by Ruth E. Harris (Eau Claire, WI: Northwest Reading Clinic, 1991). Used with permission.

Classroom Strategies and Interventions

Many educators believe that helping students with ADHD is one of the biggest challenges facing today's schools. It is important to remember that ADHD is a neurobiological condition. That is, students with ADHD are not willfully defiant or uninterested in schoolwork. As Russell A. Barkley, psychologist and ADHD expert, points out, "People with ADHD know what to do, but they can't do what they know."[10] You can address students' performance and behavior difficulties and help them be more successful by working with school counselors, other staff, parents, and any mental health professionals who work with the student. The strategies in this section will help you support students with ADHD.

Because students with ADHD have diverse challenges, there is no one-size-fits-all approach for helping them. For example, a student who benefits from interventions for organizing work and planning ahead won't necessarily need reminders to show appropriate classroom behavior. You'll find classroom strategies, accommodations, and interventions for ADHD in chapter 6, since students with ADHD may also have executive function difficulties.

Some behavior management strategies are effective for all students with ADHD. Russell A. Barkley emphasizes the following strategies:[11]

- Classroom rules and instructions must be delivered *clearly, briefly, and frequently.*
- Positive consequences must be implemented prior to punishments. It's unlikely punishment will work in an environment with little positive reinforcement.
- Consequences must be delivered more *frequently* and *swiftly* and must be *more powerful* than they are for students without ADHD.
- Consequences need to be changed or rotated more frequently for children with ADHD.
- Anticipation is the key to preventing problems. Remind students with ADHD of rules more frequently, especially before transitions.
- Behavioral interventions may need to remain in place indefinitely and be modified periodically to maintain effectiveness.

When you see a student struggling, match your approach to the specific needs you observe. Teach, model, and encourage the continued use of the strategies that benefit specific children. Often, students are able to wean themselves gradually from teacher support and require fewer classroom accommodations as they get older. It is also important to know that children with ADHD are "consistently inconsistent." They will know something or behave appropriately one day, and then forget what they knew and misbehave the following day.

THE IDEAL TEACHER (AND PARENT) FOR AN ADHD CHILD*

- thoroughly knowledgeable about ADHD and accepts the legitimacy of the disorder
- tough as nails about rules but always calm and positive

- ingenious about modifying teaching strategies and materials in order to match the child's learning style

- tailors academic material to suit child's abilities and skills

- creates assignments that require as much activity on the child's part as possible—hates dittos and endless seatwork

- mixes high- and low-interest tasks in tune with child's predilections

- isn't into homework in a major way

- knows to back off when student's level of frustration begins to peak

- knows to back off when a teacher's level of frustration begins to peak

- speaks clearly in brief, understandable sentences

- looks the child straight in the eye when communicating

- runs an absolutely predictable and organized classroom

- controls the classroom without being controlling

- provides immediate and consistent feedback (consequences) regarding behavior

- develops a private signal system with child to gently notify him when he's off task or acting inappropriately

- maintains close physical proximity without being intrusive

- ignores minor disruptions—knows how to choose battles

- has no problem acting as an "auxiliary organizer" when appropriate and necessary

- makes sure the child is organized for homework and parents are notified about school events

- maintains interest in the child as a person with interests, fears, and joys—even after a trying day

- more than willing to call or meet with parents frequently to keep in step with other efforts

- has a sense of humor you wouldn't believe

*From *ADHD/Hyperactivity: A Consumer's Guide* by Michael Gordon (DeWitt, NY: Gordon Systems Inc., 1991). Used with permission.

PROFESSIONAL TREATMENTS

A few different approaches may reduce symptoms of ADHD. Medication has been shown to be very effective. It helps primarily with concentration and impulse control. It is not as helpful in improving memory, planning, and organization. Some students with ADHD may take more than one medication due to an additional mental health disorder. Possible side effects of medication for ADHD are loss of appetite, headaches, stomachaches, fatigue, irritability, tics, nervousness, and sadness. If you observe any troubling symptoms in a child taking medication, immediately share your observations with the school nurse and the child's parents.

Two books published in 2017 emphasize the role of supplements, such as magnesium and omega-3, in the treatment of ADHD. These books also describe the effects of food allergies and sensitivities, sleep, exercise, and environmental chemicals on the development and treatment of ADHD. Neurofeedback, an expensive intervention and a form of computerized cognitive training, has not been shown to result in significant improvement in children with ADHD.[12] Mindfulness meditation has shown some potential for reducing ADHD symptoms in adults and teens.[13] Training parents to modify their behavior management strategies can be quite helpful, too. Effective behavior management strategies for children with ADHD provide very clear rules with a consistent system of consequences. Working with learning strategists, tutors, or educational coaches can help students improve executive functions. Traditional counseling or psychotherapy may be useful to treat a mental health disorder accompanying ADHD.

WHAT IT'S LIKE . . .

Chris—ADHD, Predominantly Hyperactive-Impulsive Presentation

A preschool teacher writes: "Chris is having trouble following rules. He doesn't sit in the circle with other children, and he doesn't want to listen to stories—he seems to want to do 'only what Chris wants to do.' When we use crayons, Chris scribbles and doesn't seem to try to stay inside the lines. On the playground, he pushes, kicks, and takes toys from other children. When we're lined up for snack or for lunch, he can't stay in the line and he wants to run instead of walk. Chris doesn't listen well and isn't learning his letters and numbers as well as other children are. I'm concerned Chris might not be ready for kindergarten in the fall."

Mai—ADHD, Predominantly Inattentive Presentation

An eighth-grade teacher writes: "Mai is the sweetest girl. She's never a behavior problem. I do see her doodling in her notebook more often than other students do. And while she appears to be listening to me most of the time, when I call on her, she sometimes hasn't heard a question. She also seems to get confused easily about where we are in our books—that is, if she remembers to bring hers to class. I've spoken with other teachers, and they've seen similar behavior from Mai. Her grade in my class is suffering because of incomplete homework. She often forgets to write assignments down or bring her book home to complete work. At other times, she's completed her homework (according to Mai and her parents) but somehow it doesn't make it to class!"

Anthony—ADHD, Combined Presentation

A third-grade teacher writes: "Anthony is easily distracted by sounds. He can't stay on task for more than five minutes at a time. Another thing is that he doesn't actually sit at his desk—he either stands or sits on one leg. His work is careless, with answers that are very brief and lack detail. Anthony has trouble calming down after recess. He also has difficulty working in a group without getting loud and physical. He's impulsive and blurts out answers, too. In PE, Anthony's too rough and is quick to complain about 'injustices.' His behavior makes him the last one chosen for team sports. Anthony's grades are bad, mostly because he doesn't give school enough attention. When he decides to do his best, the quality of his work is good. I have to be very conscientious about engaging him and helping him develop social skills."

Tic Disorders

Students with tic disorders experience repeated, sudden, and involuntary movements or sounds. Tics can occur with varying frequency, in combinations, and over different periods of time. They can also disappear and come back. Many people mistakenly believe tics are a sign of anxiety. While tics can increase when students are anxious, they are not caused by anxiety. Tics are caused by neurological dysfunctions that lead to involuntary movements or sounds.

> Between 6% and 20% of young people may exhibit one or more tics. Tics usually emerge around age six. Boys are more likely than girls to exhibit tic disorders. Many young people with a tic disorder also have ADHD (page 102) and/or OCD (page 83).[14]

Some tics resemble behaviors that are not commonly thought of as tics. As a result, you may overlook them. For example, you might think that students who sniff or clear their throats often have allergies or colds. If the child does not have respiratory problems and the behavior continues over a long period of time, these behaviors could be vocal tics.

The frequency and severity of tics determine the degree to which a student is affected. Tics may become more frequent or pronounced when a student feels stressed or fatigued. Students can temporarily suppress tics, but this causes discomfort. Tics that go unnoticed by most people are not likely to cause a child any significant problems. Obvious and frequent tics put students at greater risk for teasing and bullying.

Behaviors and Symptoms to Look For

Tics are considered provisional or transient when they last for less than one year. They are considered persistent or chronic when they have existed for more than one year. There are two different kinds of tics:

Motor tics. Simple motor tics include repetitive muscle movements, such as eye blinking, facial twitching, tooth clicking, neck jerking, shoulder shrugging, nose twitching, head turning, lip licking, mouth twisting, jaw snapping, finger movements, or any other jerking part of the body.

Complex motor tics seem more purposeful and longer lasting. They can include sustained looks, licking, jerking one's shoulder, clapping, tapping, tensing certain muscles, or any other body movements.

> Tourette syndrome (sometimes called *Tourette disorder*) is a tic disorder diagnosed in children who exhibit multiple motor tics and one or more vocal tics. These tics may occur at the same time or at different times over the course of at least one year. Fewer than 1% of children are diagnosed with Tourette syndrome.[15]

Vocal tics. Simple vocal tics are sounds made with the nose, mouth, or throat. These include throat clearing, coughing, spitting, grunting, gurgling, whistling, hissing, sucking, snorting, and sniffing.

Complex vocal tics may include spoken words or phrases. Most often, these words seem random or out of context. (For example, in the middle of class a student says—and keeps repeating—"I want the blue bike.")

AN UNUSUAL MOTOR TIC

I was sitting across a desk from Olivia, an eight-year-old girl doing psychoeducational testing. She kept slowly turning her head every few minutes to look at the clock on the wall behind her. After about ten minutes, it occurred to me that she was looking much too frequently. Could she not remember the time since she last looked? I then suspected that this might be a very unusual motor tic, and I asked Olivia whether she had been looking at the clock. She confirmed my suspicion and told me she wasn't looking at the clock. Turning her head was a habit she did all the time, without thinking about it. Tics are frequently treated by a specialized behavior therapist using a technique called *habit reversal training (HRT)*.

Classroom Strategies and Interventions

Tic disorders can cause significant difficulties with learning, as well as negative effects on a child's social development and emotional health. Following are some strategies you can use to address tic disorders in the classroom:

Avoid commenting on tics. Students often are very self-conscious about tics—especially those that are severe and draw negative attention from peers. Avoid commenting on a student's tic—or worse—asking the student to stop. These comments can make self-conscious students feel even worse and can increase their stress as well as their tics.

If a student and family approve, educate your whole class about tic disorders. Studies have found that learning about tics creates more positive attitudes and behaviors toward students with tics. Make sure you get written student and parent permission and involve a guidance counselor or school psychologist if possible.

Provide accommodations for testing. Stress can make tics more pronounced. As appropriate, allow extra time and provide a separate room where a student with tics can take tests. This also keeps a child's tic from distracting other students.

Provide accommodations for writing difficulties. Students with tics often struggle with writing. As necessary, reduce written work and allow students to show their knowledge in content areas in other ways. Teachers report that use of a computer is one of the most useful accommodations.[17] You'll find additional accommodations later in this chapter in the section "Specific Learning Disorder with Impairment in Written Expression" (page 134).

Allow students extra time to complete work. Tics can interrupt a student's workflow, so students with tic disorders may be slow in completing work and tests. As necessary, relax deadlines, shorten class and homework assignments, and provide other accommodations to address this slow place.

Repeat instructions and give reminders as necessary. Tics can interrupt children's thoughts, so students with tics may miss something you say. Write instructions on the board or hand out an instruction sheet. Students with tics occasionally get stuck on tasks. Gently remind them to move on.

Create a special time outside of class when a student may speak with you. Students with tics may be reluctant to ask questions or participate in class discussions. Invite them to meet with you outside of class time to address any concerns they might have. Set up a daily or weekly appointment (such as during recess or lunch).

Emphasize social and emotional support. (See chapter 5.) Students with tic disorders are among the most vulnerable for experiencing peer relationship problems, teasing, and bullying. These students do best in the most socially and emotionally supportive classrooms.[18] Request that other students ignore tics. Immediately address teasing and bullying throughout the school (including in classrooms, hallways, gymnasiums, lunchrooms, and locker rooms and on playgrounds and buses) so students feel safe. Minimize stress and criticism toward students with tics.

Allow students with tic disorders to leave the classroom. Students with tics may become very uncomfortable when tics increase. They may try very hard to suppress their tics. Let these students leave the classroom temporarily to relieve their tension.

Note: Many of the strategies for helping students with ADHD (page 102) and OCD (page 83) may also be helpful with students who have tic disorders.

MOST COMMON SCHOOL PROBLEMS FOR STUDENTS WITH TICS[16]

Some students with tics may also report problems with:

- writing in class (25%)
- homework (22%)
- concentrating (22%)
- being prepared for class (19%)
- being teased (18%)

PROFESSIONAL TREATMENTS

Many parents take children to a physician for tic behaviors to rule out other medical problems. A physician may refer a child to a psychologist for behavior therapy treatment if tics are causing a significant problem in the child's life. Comprehensive behavioral intervention for tics (CBIT) is the most effective therapy for tics.[19] It is based on a procedure called *habit reversal training (HRT)*. Some school psychologists may be trained in this procedure. A physician may prescribe medication to suppress more serious tics. Medication can cause side effects such as sleepiness, dizziness, and low blood pressure. Teachers should inform the school nurse and the child's parents about any concerning behaviors they observe after a student begins taking medication.

TOURETTE SYNDROME: WHAT IT'S LIKE . . .

From a father about his son:

"My son Scott has Tourette syndrome, a strange, little-known, and less understood neurological disorder. He suffers every day because his body does things he doesn't want it to do—shake his head, blink his eyes, make faces, twitch and jerk his arms or legs, hop when he tries to walk, squeak, cough, or shout. They call these symptoms 'tics.' He can't stop them.

"When he was four years old, we noticed him making strange sounds—little squeaking noises—continual, annoying squeaking noises. We asked him to stop. He said he couldn't. We said, 'Sure you can—just don't make those noises!' He said he couldn't stop. We sent him to his room. This was before we knew about Tourette syndrome. Sure enough, after a few months of pressuring him, he stopped making the squeaking noises. We said, 'See, we knew you could stop those annoying noises! But why are you shaking your head like that all the time?' Thinking his hair must be in his eyes, we took him for a haircut. He still shook his head all the time. We didn't know why. He said he couldn't stop it.

"When we thought we had him cured of the head shaking, we noticed he was blinking his eyes. Not a regular eye blink like we all do; he was squashing his eyelids down and sometimes squinting. We took him to an eye doctor—nothing wrong with his eyes. He kept blinking. We took him to more eye doctors. 'His eyes are fine,' they'd say. 'Must be a nervous habit he picked up. He'll grow out of it.' When we asked Scott, he would say, 'I can't stop it.' By the age of six, Scott had seen several different eye doctors. Finally, one suggested a neurological specialist. The neurologist diagnosed Scott's problems as Tourette syndrome."

Autism Spectrum Disorder (ASD)

In the *DSM-5*, autism is now considered to be a neurodevelopmental disorder. It is also now considered to be on a spectrum. That means that children with autism may have different types and degrees of symptoms. Large differences in cognitive and social skills differentiate children with low- and high-functioning autism. Students with low-functioning autism (LFA) have IEPs and are taught by special education teachers. Students with high-functioning autism (HFA) are frequently in general education classes with a resource teacher occasionally providing support. If you are a general education teacher, you will likely have students with HFA in your class. This section will focus on these students.

WHAT HAPPENED TO ASPERGER'S SYNDROME?

Students once diagnosed with Asperger's syndrome were considered to have a type of HFA. There was little reason to have two different terms to describe these children, so the American Psychiatric Association (APA) decided to discard the diagnosis of Asperger's syndrome and refer to these individuals as having HFA. All the literature you may have read and strategies you may have learned regarding Asperger's syndrome apply to students with HFA. It is difficult to determine how many children have HFA, since they are classified and counted with all other children on the autism spectrum.

Students with HFA are identified primarily by their deficits in social communication and social interaction skills and by their limited, repetitive behaviors, interests, or activities. Problems in both areas cause impairments in these students' educational and social functioning.

Socializing is often the greatest difficulty for young people with HFA. Social communication and interaction difficulties cause problems in understanding and developing social relationships. These students may not know what to say in social situations. They may struggle with taking turns in conversation and may frequently interrupt others or talk exclusively about themselves or their own interests. Often, these students also have difficulty understanding facial expressions, body language, and other nonverbal communication.

Students with HFA frequently require certain routines that, if changed, create anxiety. They typically have difficulty with transitions, and they may be preoccupied with certain areas of interest or objects. Ordinary sensory stimuli can cause very strong negative reactions in these students. These stimuli include sounds, lights, smells, tastes, textures, and touch.

Behaviors and Symptoms to Look For

As a result of limited social ability, students with HFA tend to have difficulty relating to peers and forming friendships. These children often want friends but have underdeveloped social skills.

Behavioral differences in children with HFA affect many areas of functioning. These students may:

Use formal language. Students with HFA often use words such as *frankly, typically, in fact,* or *ordinarily.* They may begin most of their sentences with *well.* Children with HFA often seem "book smart" but lack common sense. Their speech may have an unusual tone or inflection.

Interpret language literally. Literal interpretation can make it difficult for students with HFA to understand jokes, sarcasm, idioms, or nuances of speech. As a result, they may respond strangely to questions. For example, if you ask a child with HFA, "Will you give me a hand with these books?" the student may look confused and extend a hand.

Have poor ability to understand abstract concepts. While students with HFA may have a strong understanding of concrete language and factual information, their ability to think abstractly is often limited. This leads to difficulty in language arts and other subjects that require abstract thinking. They may understand a story's plot but not its theme. They tend to see issues in black or white and view behavior rigidly as right or wrong. Students with HFA may tattle on other students for rule violations.

Be preoccupied or obsessed with one or two areas of interest. Interests often include video or computer games, works of art, fiction books (frequently science fiction), or TV programs. Strong rote memory can make these children seem like walking encyclopedias.

Show poor conversational ability. Students may not know when to speak or may say irrelevant things. They may begin, end, and interrupt conversations inappropriately. Children with HFA often have little regard for other people's reactions, feelings, or interests. They go on at length about their own interests, not realizing when others are bored with a topic of conversation. Poor social skills can result in these children being isolated or bullied.

Have problems understanding nonverbal communication. An inability to read facial expressions, body language, and other social cues further hampers social ability in children with HFA. They often misinterpret others' expressions and react with inappropriate behavior. For example, a student may not realize that someone's expression indicates anger or irritation and may continue the problematic behavior.

Be tactless. Students have little knowledge or understanding of social etiquette. They are very honest and may be extremely rude without realizing it. (For example, "It's obvious you have a weight problem. I wouldn't lean on that shelf if I were you.") Children with HFA also have difficulty judging personal space and may ask invasive personal questions that violate another person's privacy.

Show differences in sensory reactions. Students with HFA may be especially sensitive to sound, movement, light, temperature, and other classroom conditions. Their senses of touch, taste, and smell may also be strong.

Have difficulty understanding and discussing feelings. While these children are highly verbal, they have a limited ability to discuss how they are feeling. As a result, they become very upset (or even explosive) with no warning and little indication as to what is bothering them. This can make it especially challenging to address a student's difficulty. In addition, students with HFA have little ability to empathize with or attribute feelings to others.

Have difficulty coping with changes in routines. These students often feel the need to engage in repetitive routines. Students may become upset or defiant when routines are changed.

Have difficulties with attention and organization. Students may appear to be listening, but instead be thinking about something else—often one of their favorite interests. Staying on top of schoolwork can be difficult for these students because of their poor organizational skills. ADHD is also common among students with HFA.

Have poor motor skills. Students may walk or move in peculiar ways that draw attention (or ridicule) from others. Children may perform poorly in physical education classes, sports, and other activities. Because extracurricular activities are a way for students to socialize, motor difficulties can further separate children with HFA from peers. Weak fine motor skills can create handwriting challenges for these students.

Have other psychological problems. Anxiety is common among students with HFA. In adolescence, they are also prone to depression because they have few of the social relationships that are so important to teens.

 CAUTION! At times, students with HFA may have meltdowns. They may scream, cry, run out of the room, or become aggressive. It is important to know how to respond to these students before meltdowns occur. Consult with your school psychologist or counselor for some strategies. If a situation gets out of control, immediately get help from someone else on staff.

Classroom Strategies and Interventions

Students with HFA show a variety of behaviors that call for multiple interventions. Social development is often a higher priority than academic achievement.

The following strategies and accommodations can be helpful:

Work together with school staff, parents, and any outside professionals. It's important to align your efforts with those of classroom aides, counselors, and other school staff. HFA also affects students at home. Parents and mental health professionals can provide valuable insight to guide classroom coping strategies.

Use precise and literal language. Clear, specific directions are important for students who interpret language literally. Students with HFA might miss or misinterpret a nonverbal signal or facial expression that would seem obvious to other students.

Teach rules in a step-by-step manner. Students may need to be taught rules and social behavior in specific detail. A written tip sheet can be helpful.

EXAMPLES OF TIP SHEETS FOR STUDENTS WITH HFA

Answering a Question in Class

1. Raise your hand if you want to ask or answer a question.

2. Wait until a teacher calls on you before you speak.

3. Put your hand down if the teacher asks another student to answer a question.

Walking in the Hallway

1. Walk the same speed as other students are walking.

2. Walk on the same side of the hallway as the students going in the same direction as you.

3. Try not to touch or bump into other students.

4. Speak in a voice that's only loud enough to be heard by a person next to you.

Establish a structured environment and minimize surprises. Students with HFA thrive on predictability, structure, and routine. They may become anxious when they don't know what to expect or when plans change suddenly. Prepare these students in advance for any anticipated changes in routine. Explain contingency plans. (For example, "This afternoon we're going to watch a video about the solar system. But if for some reason the video isn't available, we'll be doing our regular science work.") When the schedule changes in the future, preface the announcement of the change with "schedule change!" Visual schedules are useful, so students can refer to them throughout the day to know what's coming next.

Explain classroom rules. Students may acknowledge a rule but not understand why it exists. Without this understanding, they may not recognize situations in which the rule applies. (An example of an explanation might be, "You must raise your hand and be called on if you want to answer a question. If you answer out loud when you haven't been asked, you might be interrupting the teacher and not letting other students have the chance to answer a question.") Be cautious with explanations, though, since students may wish to engage in extended debates about rules.

Modify instruction to match student strengths. Students with HFA have difficulty with abstract and critical thinking. As you work to develop these skills in students, match content work to their strengths. Rather than compositions or essay tests, for example, these students will benefit from assignments and tests that require short, factual answers. They're more comfortable with topics that are fact-based and involve data. Also consider curriculum that incorporates a student's interests.

Monitor sensory hypersensitivity. Students with HFA may be particularly sensitive to sound, light, touch, taste, and smells. Noisy, crowded environments (such as the cafeteria or playground) can overstimulate and upset students with HFA. Work to minimize students' exposure to stimuli that aggravate their particular sensory sensitivities. Examples might be minimizing fluorescent lighting, allowing the student to eat lunch in a quiet area, and taking the student outside the building just before a fire drill. Students' sensory needs may require that you get help from an occupational therapist to eliminate environmental stressors (such as glaring light) in your classroom.

Establish provisions for times when students are emotionally upset. Make sure students have a private place to go and a person (such as a school counselor or psychologist) they can see when they are having emotional difficulties. The reproducible "Student Coping Plan" on page 20 can help you set up provisions.

Teach and model social skills. Students with HFA often need to be taught basic or obvious social skills. Emphasize turn taking, tact, manners, nonverbal communication, and rules of conversation.

Closely monitor children at unstructured times. For students with HFA, their lack of social skills can be painfully apparent during unstructured periods, such as recess and lunch. Observe students closely during these times to make sure others are not teasing or bullying them.

Assign a student buddy. Choose an empathetic student who likes to help others to give a child with HFA quiet classroom guidance and aid in social situations.

Gently discourage inappropriate classroom commentary. Students with HFA may talk endlessly about something that is off-topic or interesting only to themselves. Not only can this create classroom disruptions, but it may also alienate other students. Tell students that they can talk with you further about the topic after class.

Appreciate students' difficulties. Realize that students aren't acting or speaking inappropriately to deliberately upset you or other children. Students' behavior is often due to a lack of social understanding. Don't take inappropriate comments personally.

If the student and family approve, educate your whole class about HFA. Classmates are less likely to tease (and more likely to befriend or help) a student with HFA when they understand the reasons for the student's actions. Make sure you have written student and parent permission, and involve a guidance counselor or school psychologist if possible.

   Note: Some of the strategies and interventions for helping students with ADHD (page 102) and social communication disorder (page 154) may also be helpful with students who have HFA.

From a thirteen-year-old who has HFA:

"Apparently I am very pedantic and speak slowly and monotonously. I am also told that I have a problem with communication, because I do not know when I am boring someone. I like to talk about computers and don't usually realize that others don't want to. Well, actually I do, but when I am thinking about computers, I am not thinking about anyone else. Sometimes—well, most of the time—my mind is so full of computers that I don't stop to think about myself or other people at all. It is very difficult for me to recognize that I may go on too intensely about my special subject, as I am me and cannot imagine myself as any different.

"For any kid, whether they enjoy it or not, school is a whole minefield of challenges and new experiences. For kids on the autism spectrum, it seems as if we spend all our time stepping on these mines (don't worry, kids reading this, there are no mines really—I am just using metaphors), and the whole school experience becomes a very difficult one. School is one place where children are expected to be sociable and have friends. It is very difficult for kids with autism to have these expectations pushed on them as well as having all the hassles of school to contend with.

"People with autism have a great difficulty with social stuff. There seem to be lots of hidden rules and subtle ways of speaking and behaving that are just impossible to fathom. Most kids with autism don't usually even bother. Difficulties with facial expressions, the use of language, and body language all make us targets for ridicule."

*From *Freaks, Geeks & Asperger Syndrome* by Luke Jackson (Philadelphia: Jessica Kingsley, 2002). Used with permission.

PROFESSIONAL TREATMENTS

Treatment for children with HFA varies a great deal, depending upon the pattern and severity of behaviors. Most students benefit from social skills development in individual or group counseling settings (see chapter 2). Many work with someone to strengthen executive functions (see chapter 6). Others may get help from an occupational therapist, who can address sensory problems and difficulty with motor skills. Students with HFA who also experience anxiety, depression, or ADHD may take medication to address these problems. Students should be very closely monitored when taking medications—especially early on. Possible side effects of medications include increased feelings of depression, drowsiness, insomnia, stomachaches, headaches, nervousness, and weight gain or loss. If you observe any troubling symptoms in a child taking medication, immediately share your observations with the school nurse and the child's parents.

Specific Learning Disorders (SLD)

Students with specific learning disorders (SLD)—frequently called *learning disabilities (LD)*—have neurodevelopmental disorders that interfere with their reading, spelling, math, and writing skills. These students generally have average to above average intelligence, but differences in brain functions cause them to perform poorly at school. These students usually perform well below their peers in reading, math, or writing. These difficulties cannot be explained by intelligence, lack of adequate instruction, or other factors.

> Students with LD compose the largest category in special education in the United States. Five percent of all US students, totaling almost 2.5 million children, are designated as having LD.[20] Schools used to segregate these students in special classes with special education teachers. Today, many of these students are in inclusion classes with resource teachers assisting them.

Because LD has been redefined multiple times over the years in different reauthorizations of the Individuals with Disabilities Education Act (IDEA), there is currently no consensus on how to define LD. Most school districts now use failure to respond to interventions (see "Response to Intervention (RTI)" on page 24) as the primary criterion for defining LD.

Alternatively, the *DSM-5* definition gives "low achievement" as a primary criterion. This definition requires the following:

- academic skills that have not responded to interventions and are well below expected levels for a student's chronological age
- skill deficits that interfere significantly with academic performance
- deficits that are not caused by any other cognitive or physical disabilities, lack of instruction, or inadequate proficiency in the language of academic instruction

Still others argue that LD requires the existence of cognitive processing deficits that cause the student's academic weaknesses. These deficits are found through a psychoeducational battery of tests. School districts require a comprehensive evaluation using many assessment tools and strategies before a student is eligible for special education.

This section provides information on types of LD and offers advice on understanding and helping students with LD in the general education classroom. These strategies can help you raise academic achievement and foster positive self-esteem in these children. "Learning disabilities are not a prescription for failure," points out Sheldon Horowitz, senior director of learning resources and research at the National Center for Learning Disabilities. "With the right kinds of instruction, guidance, and support, there are no limits to what individuals with LD can achieve."[21]

DISORDERS COVERED IN THIS SECTION

Specific Learning Disorder with Impairment in Reading
(Including Dyslexia)

Students with a reading disorder or reading disability (RD) may have difficulty sounding out new words, identifying words automatically, reading fluently (with adequate speed), and comprehending text.

Dyslexia is a specific type of reading disability that can be identified in early elementary school. Dyslexia is a pattern of reading difficulties affecting phonetic decoding (the sounding out of words), automatic word recognition, and spelling. The brain of a person with dyslexia processes these tasks in a different and inefficient way. Some older students with dyslexia may read somewhat well, despite their disability. More often, these students read with reduced speed and comprehension, because difficulty reading words hinders fluency and understanding.

DYSLEXIA FACTS

- As many as 17% of people may have a reading disability.[22]
- Dyslexia is the most common learning disability.[22]
- Dyslexia has nothing to do with intelligence.[22, 23, 24]
- Dyslexia is often inherited.[22, 24]
- ADHD is more common in students with dyslexia.[22]
- Slightly more boys than girls have dyslexia.[23]

Because reading is essential in all school subjects, poor readers struggle in multiple content areas. Reading disabilities often affect handwriting and spelling as well as the ability to understand word problems in math.

Types and severity of reading disabilities vary among children. Some students are strong in one area of reading and weak in others. Others may benefit from additional help in all areas of reading. This section is designed to identify and address different aspects of reading disabilities.

Behaviors and Symptoms to Look For

Difficulties with reading can occur in three major areas: decoding and automatic word recognition (dyslexia), fluency, and comprehension.

Decoding and Automatic Word Recognition (Dyslexia)

If students have had adequate instruction, signs of possible dyslexia are identifiable by the end of kindergarten or first grade.

Students with dyslexia may:

- Have poor ability to hear the sounds that make up words (such as the difference in vowel sound between *cat* and *cut*).
- Have difficulty naming letters and numbers rapidly.
- Guess at words that look similar to other more familiar words (reading *between* instead of *because*).
- Have difficulty decoding nonsense words or pseudowords. (An essential test for dyslexia is to give a student a pseudoword, such as *glap*, to see if he or she can read it. If the student is tested using only real words, he or she may have memorized the words.)
- Have difficulty reading single words accurately and fluently.
- Have poor spelling skills.
- Read aloud inaccurately or in a choppy way.

In middle and late elementary school, students with dyslexia may show additional difficulties. They may:

- Read silently at a very slow pace.
- Have weakness in reading comprehension, vocabulary, and written composition skills.
- Transpose words or letters (such as *b* for *d*, or *bog* for *dog*). However, it is a myth that this is one of the primary characteristics of dyslexia.
- Dislike reading.
- Struggle with other academic subjects.

Fluency

Students with fluency difficulties:

- Read only with a lot of effort.
- Stumble over reading some words.
- Read in monotone (with little expression).
- Read with inconsistent (and generally slow) speed and inappropriate pauses.

Comprehension

Students with comprehension difficulties:

- Have difficulty understanding text or recalling facts.
- May have a limited vocabulary.
- Have difficulty using strategies to understand what they are reading (such as thinking and asking questions about what they're reading, looking ahead or back in the text for facts, and understanding a piece of text before continuing to read).
- Frequently have to reread text to comprehend it.

Classroom Strategies and Interventions

If your school has implemented RTI, your Tier 1 assessments will identify students with reading disabilities in kindergarten or first grade. If you're not using RTI and you recognize a problem, don't wait to intervene, thinking a student's difficulty represents a developmental lag and the child will catch up. Children who have difficulty *learning to read* in the early years will have trouble *reading to learn* in later years. About three-quarters of poor readers at age nine will be weak readers in high school.[25]

The exact form of your literacy efforts will depend on your school's Tier 2 small-group interventions and the areas in which your students are struggling—whether with dyslexia, fluency, comprehension, or a combination of these.

USE THE TERM *DYSLEXIA*

Historically, school districts have been reluctant to use the term *dyslexia*. Several reasons have been suggested for this reluctance. First, to resolve the confusion between the terms *reading disability* and *dyslexia*, the National Association of School Psychologists recommended using *reading disability*.[26] Second, using the term *dyslexia* means a student may need substantial special education resources, which cost schools money.[27] Finally, the term *dyslexia* may scare parents and teachers who don't understand what it means.[28]

In 2015, the US Department of Education issued a letter to school districts titled "Dear Colleague: Dyslexia Guidance."[29] The letter points out that there is nothing in IDEA that prohibits the use of the term *dyslexia*. The definition of the term *specific learning disability* has always included dyslexia, and educators should not refrain from using *dyslexia* if it is accurate.

Despite your best efforts to build students' reading skills, some children will continue to experience difficulties and will require accommodations in the classroom. Like teaching strategies, these classroom accommodations are not one-size-fits-all. You will need to match interventions with your students' individual needs. The following strategies and accommodations are noted with the reading disability (in parentheses) they may most successfully address, though the suggestions may prove effective with students who have other challenges as well.

Provide reading and vocabulary instruction accompanied by images. Pictures from books, magazines, or other media can help children associate words with concrete images. Ask students to visualize a given word as you provide a visual representation of it. (dyslexia)

Encourage children to use kinesthetic or tactile learning methods where students engage in physical activities. Ask students to say new words while also tracing them with their fingers on their arms or desks. Incorporating multiple senses can aid memorization. (dyslexia)

Use already acquired word knowledge. When students struggle phonetically with particular words, bring to their attention similar words they are able to pronounce. This can help them recognize how a given letter or letter pattern sounds and how it should be spoken. For example, a student who is able to say the *o* sound in *rock* can apply that knowledge to the word *clock*. (dyslexia)

Provide visual cues and tools to reinforce language instruction. Consider posting new or difficult words in a prominent place in the classroom. You might do this by using markers on a whiteboard or creating a bulletin board display specifically for vocabulary. You might also use this technique to display common words that weak readers often misidentify or misunderstand. Encourage students to create flash cards for use outside of class. (dyslexia)

Use music and rhythm in language instruction. Most children enjoy music and rhythm. Songs, raps, and rhymes can reinforce word sounds and meanings. (dyslexia)

Teach specific skills for finding the main idea, finding facts, and drawing conclusions. When you're discussing a reading assignment, ask *who, what, when, where,* and *why* questions. ("Who was the main character? What was the big problem she had to solve? When did the story take place? Where did the character live? Why did the character have this problem?") Teach students to think about the facts of a story in a logical sequence, so they can verbalize or write a summary. In class discussions, call on students who have comprehension difficulties only if you're reasonably certain they might provide the right answer. (comprehension)

Ask students to make predictions. Provide consistent breaks in reading to ensure that everyone understands the themes of a story or book. At important points, ask students to predict what will occur next in a story. ("Okay, so we know that George has just found out where the dragon lives. What do you think will happen next?") Predictions can help prepare weaker readers for upcoming content in reading assignments. (dyslexia, comprehension)

Model fluent reading. Read out loud to students frequently. Teach students how to read smoothly and with expression. ("Did you hear how I said, 'up on the roof'? These words go together. That's how we know where the cat went. Then, when I read that the girl was asking how the cat got up on the roof, I raised my voice at the end because she was asking a question, and there is a question mark (pointing to it) after 'How did he get up there?'") Also encourage students to practice reading out loud with an adult at home. (dyslexia, fluency, comprehension)

Provide repeated practice in oral reading. Having students repeat the same text multiple times will improve their fluency, especially if you offer feedback. The text should be relatively short and should contain words a student knows so that word recognition problems don't interfere. (dyslexia, fluency)

Practice reading in unison. Ask students to read aloud as a class or in groups. This strategy allows students to work on reading aloud without exposing an individual student's reading weaknesses. (dyslexia, fluency)

Teach reading comprehension strategies. Give students tools they can use to focus on particular elements of a story and visually organize information. For example, students might use a Venn diagram (see page 126) to compare and contrast two concepts from a nonfiction text. Semantic and graphic organizers may also be helpful. You may suggest that students create story maps as they read. You can teach older students to use the SQ3R method (survey, question, read, recite, and review) to organize and reinforce ideas from a given text. (comprehension)

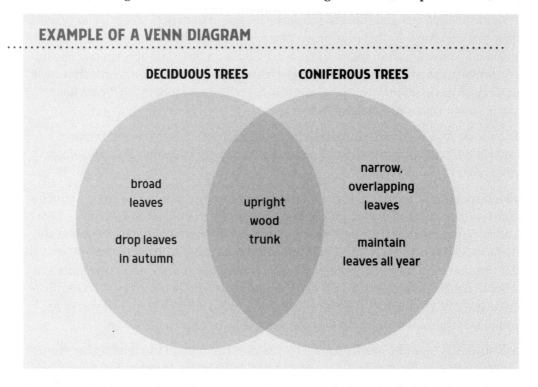

EXAMPLE OF A VENN DIAGRAM

DECIDUOUS TREES   CONIFEROUS TREES

broad leaves

drop leaves in autumn

upright wood trunk

narrow, overlapping leaves

maintain leaves all year

Use recording-assisted reading. Ask students to read along in their books as they listen to a recording of another reader. This can help students read more smoothly and with expression. (dyslexia, fluency, comprehension)

Emphasize vocabulary instruction. Reading is a primary contributor to vocabulary development, but students with reading difficulties tend to avoid reading. Consequently, their vocabularies may be limited. This further hinders their reading fluency and comprehension. Digital tools, media, and the internet have shown impressive results in increasing students' vocabularies.[30] You also can preview a text by explaining certain vocabulary words before reading it. Show students the same word in multiple contexts, and show them how to use a dictionary to look up meanings. (fluency, comprehension)

Shorten reading assignments. Children may be very slow readers. As appropriate, reduce the amount of reading you assign to students to accommodate this pace, and emphasize comprehension of the material they are able to complete. Encourage students and provide genuine praise on their progress. (dyslexia, fluency, comprehension)

Read written instructions aloud. Students often make mistakes on assignments and tests because they don't fully comprehend written instructions. Help avoid this by reading aloud all instructions, including those posted on the board. (dyslexia, fluency, comprehension)

Be cautious in requiring oral reading. Many students with reading disabilities feel self-conscious or ashamed of their difficulties. To avoid aggravating these feelings, choose small parts of a text you know students can manage. Reduce classroom pressure by reassuring students that you will call on them only when you know they're able to answer the question or read the text. (dyslexia, fluency)

Assign a reading buddy. Reading buddies are students who sit near children with reading disabilities. When children begin to struggle, they may quietly solicit the help of their buddies to sound out words or clarify meaning. (dyslexia, fluency, comprehension)

Avoid grading a student's spelling. Poor spelling is a primary characteristic of dyslexia. When appropriate (such as on creative writing assignments), assure students they will not be graded on their spelling but on the overall content of their work. (dyslexia)

Allow students to demonstrate knowledge in alternative ways. When appropriate, allow students who struggle with reading to show what they know in ways that don't involve excessive reading or writing. These students might give oral reports or create art projects in place of reading lengthy books or writing reports. Consider administering tests orally to students who have reading or writing difficulties. (dyslexia, fluency, comprehension)

Allow extra time for assignments and tests involving reading. Students with weak literacy skills may need more time to show they understand and can answer questions based on reading material. Relax deadlines and time constraints on assignments and tests. (dyslexia, fluency, comprehension)

Monitor student progress on assignments. Verify that a student is on schedule with a reading assignment. Ask if the student has any questions and encourage any progress made. (dyslexia, fluency, comprehension)

Provide background information on assignments and tests. When assigning stories or books for students to read, give weaker readers copies of notes, story summaries, outlines, lists of key vocabulary words, and other tools that can help prepare them for what they will read. (dyslexia, fluency, comprehension)

Consider using multimedia formats in the classroom. Recorded texts are available through Learning Ally (www.learningally.org). Recordings can help students understand a text that may be too difficult or lengthy for them to read independently. Following along in a book while listening to a recording can help students recognize words and improve reading speed. Encourage the use of other technology, such as pens that scan and read words aloud. Big books—large, illustrated editions of texts—and audiobooks are available from many publishers. (dyslexia, fluency, comprehension)

Make accommodations or exemptions for learning a foreign language. Students with dyslexia will likely have difficulty learning a foreign language. Consider accommodations for or exemptions from a foreign language requirement. (dyslexia, fluency, comprehension)

Increase student interest and engagement. Poor readers often don't like to read. They experience reading as boring or too difficult, and they tune out or give up. Counteract this disengagement by including reading materials for a wide range of ability levels and interests in your classroom and curriculum. If you know a particular student likes animals, for example, suggest reading a book about them in place of a text the student found too boring or difficult. (dyslexia, fluency, comprehension)

Promote an attitude of enthusiasm for reading. Talk about all the benefits of reading and how it can be a lot of fun. You may want to mention some of the books that have excited you. Ask students to talk about books they're interested in and why. Avoid judging students' reading preferences. For example, if a student loves reading comic books or a particular website, reinforce the act of reading without offering any opinion about the content. (dyslexia, fluency, comprehension)

Build students' self-esteem as you teach reading skills. Children who have difficulty reading often think of themselves as "stupid" and may choose to give up on reading efforts because they feel they'll "never learn." Emphasize that reading difficulty is not a sign of low intelligence. Rather, some students simply haven't found the right reading strategies to succeed. Talk about how you are teaching them tools they can use to read better. Tell students some doctors, lawyers, and celebrities have reading difficulties. (dyslexia, fluency, comprehension)

Eliminate mistreatment and bullying. Many children who struggle with reading may be singled out for teasing. Immediately stop any harassment you observe. For ideas on creating supportive school environments, see chapter 2. (dyslexia, fluency, comprehension)

Coordinate literacy efforts with other teachers, special education services, and parents. Work with other school staff to improve students' reading abilities in multiple settings and across content areas. This may involve making others aware of student accommodations you have found helpful or setting up a cross-disciplinary project. Also engage adults at home to encourage and support students as they work to improve their reading abilities. (dyslexia, fluency, comprehension)

> ### PROFESSIONAL TREATMENTS
> Some students may require more individual reading instruction or remediation than is available in school. They may require the help of reading specialists who are trained in research-based reading instruction methods.

ELEMENTS OF CLASSROOM READING INSTRUCTION

Reading instruction may vary a great deal from school to school. Following are some key elements that all reading programs should include.

- Instruction must be *explicit*. Learning the fundamental reading skills of letter-sound relationships cannot be left to chance. Educators cannot assume a student knows that the letter *t* makes a certain sound, that the letter *a* can make multiple sounds, or that the letter combination *au* sounds different from *ae*. Educators must teach, repeat, and help students practice these skills.

- Instruction must be *systematic*. Phonics instruction should happen in a logical sequence. For example, students should master all single letters before learning letter combinations.

- Instruction must be *intensive*. Students with weak reading skills should receive considerably more reading instruction than other students beginning as early as first grade.

- Instruction must be *sequential* and *gradual*. Students should learn, practice, and master one skill before tackling another skill.

- Instruction must happen in the *context of academic content*, not in isolation. Teachers should also emphasize fluency and comprehension.

- Instruction must be paired with *positive emotional support* and *reinforcement*, which are crucial for students with learning difficulties. Teachers should be cheerleaders for these students.

For more information on specific reading strategies and programs, see the resources on page 222.

Specific Learning Disorder with Impairment in Math
(Dyscalculia)

About 7% of students may have a math disability.[32]

Children with a math disability (sometimes called *dyscalculia*) may struggle in many different areas of mathematics. These challenges involve understanding the meaning of numbers and their relationships to one another, memorizing math facts, calculating number problems, and solving math word problems (math reasoning).[31]

Behaviors and Symptoms to Look For

Students have difficulties performing math due to a number of possible skill deficits. These may include:

Memory. Some students have trouble memorizing basic facts of math. Addition, subtraction, multiplication, and division facts need to be learned and stored in memory, or they won't be available for subsequent recall. Other students can learn and store facts initially, but they have difficulty retrieving the facts quickly from memory. Still other students have difficulty remembering sequences for solving calculation problems. This type of difficulty involves working memory, which is the ability to hold certain information in memory while performing some other task. For example, solving a long division or algebra problem requires recalling a number of steps in the correct order while simultaneously working on one step in the sequence. Any or all of these memory difficulties can interfere with a student's ability to solve math problems successfully.

Comprehension and problem-solving. Some students have difficulty understanding various aspects of math problems. For example, young children just beginning to learn math may have difficulty understanding math symbols. Some students may have difficulty mastering the concepts of counting or place value. Language processing or reading problems can interfere with a student's ability to understand and solve word problems. Other students have difficulty with systematically solving a math problem. These students may also have little understanding of patterns and relationships between objects or numbers' real-world significance or application. In lower grades, they may have difficulty telling time or counting money.

Visuospatial organization. Organizational difficulties can interfere with students' abilities to solve a problem on paper in a way that they and their teachers can understand. Difficulty lining up numbers in columns can confuse students and interfere with calculation. This visuospatial disorganization can lead children to lose track of what step they're completing and make reviewing their work difficult.

Attention and impulse control. Problems paying careful attention or an impulsive, hurried response style can lead to excessive errors in math. Students may forget or confuse procedural steps. These students' preference for solving problems in their heads instead of writing down numbers also contributes to careless errors.

Slow speed. Students may be very slow to retrieve facts or procedures from memory. Their problem may be with processing speed (speed of information retrieval from memory) rather than absence of information or understanding. Slow processing speed also makes it difficult for students to turn in work or tests on time.

Anxiety. Math seems to evoke more anxiety than any other academic subject. Girls have considerably more math anxiety than boys do.[33] Students who worry about math typically have some weaknesses in math, and their anxiety compounds their difficulties.

Classroom Strategies and Interventions

Choose strategies for helping students in the classroom based on the specific math skills students need to develop. Instructional strategies for building math ability follow. In parentheses you'll find the area of weakness a strategy best addresses. Keep in mind, however, that any strategy may be relevant at some point for a particular student.

Even with consistent efforts to build students' math skills, some children may require curriculum accommodations. As with strategies, match appropriate accommodations with the needs of individual students.

Model step-by-step problem-solving methods for students. When you're solving problems in front of the class, clearly state the steps you are performing. Have students restate the steps as they solve their own problems. (memory, comprehension and problem-solving)

Have students estimate answers or evaluate potential solutions before they begin computing. This step checks for a basic understanding of the problem and the mathematical procedure. It may prevent students from arriving at answers that make no logical sense. (comprehension and problem-solving)

Use real-world problems to demonstrate math concepts. This strategy is particularly relevant when you're teaching word problems, but you also can use it with number problems. Real-world applications illustrate math's relevance and are great opportunities to add interest to a subject many students feel is boring. (attention and impulse control)

Ask students to explain or teach a solution to the class. Talking about math procedures helps integrate these procedures into students' memories. Check with students in advance to ensure they can complete a given problem. ("Do you think you might be able to do number ten in front of the class tomorrow?") (memory, comprehension and problem-solving)

Monitor students' progress on class assignments. Check in frequently with students to ensure they're on task. Offer guidance and encouragement as a student works on tasks. (attention and impulse control)

Consider small-group work. Students with a math disability often will benefit more from group brainstorming than from working alone. (comprehension and problem-solving)

Introduce new skills using concrete examples. It is important that students understand math in the context of real objects and shapes. When possible, ground concepts in the physical world by using concrete manipulatives. Hands-on learning is very effective in teaching concepts to kinesthetic learners. (memory, comprehension and problem-solving, attention and impulse control)

Allow students to quietly talk to themselves at their desks. Quietly repeating problem-solving steps and mathematical procedures can help students execute math equations. (comprehension and problem-solving, attention and impulse control)

Allow time for questions. Conclude each teaching period with time for students to ask about anything they may have missed or not fully understood. (memory, comprehension and problem-solving, attention and impulse control, anxiety)

Allow the use of calculators. When appropriate, allow students to solve problems or check their answers with a calculator. (memory, slow speed, anxiety)

Adjust deadlines and workload as necessary. Give students who are struggling the time they need to complete an assignment or a test. For classwork or homework, reduce the number of problems required to demonstrate skill mastery. (attention and impulse control, memory, slow speed, anxiety)

Practice high-frequency, low-intensity repetition. For example, give two ten-minute practice assignments each day instead of one twenty-minute assignment. (memory, attention and impulse control)

Encourage students to check their answers. Students who have difficulty sitting still or paying attention may rush through a test or an assignment, making many careless errors along the way. Address this problem by telling these students you will not accept their test or work until at least half of the class has finished and guide them to use this time to check their work. (attention and impulse control)

Slow down lesson presentations. Summarize concepts at key points to reinforce them and check in with students frequently for understanding. (memory, comprehension and problem-solving, attention and impulse control, anxiety)

Use verbal explanations alongside visual ones. Some students have visuospatial deficits that make it difficult for them to understand concepts by looking at pictures or diagrams alone. Your verbal explanation will be important to these children. (visuospatial organization)

Have students use graph paper. Children who have difficulty organizing math problems on blank paper or horizontally ruled paper may find it easier to line up numbers and equations on graph paper. An alternative is to turn ruled paper sideways. (visuospatial organization)

Be cautious when calling on struggling students. Difficulties with math can harm a child's self-esteem. Refrain from calling on students unless you are sure they have a reasonable probability of answering a question correctly. To encourage participation, prepare students by letting them know in advance that you'd like to call on them for a particular answer. (memory, comprehension and problem-solving, slow speed, anxiety)

Let students review corrected assignments and tests. This allows children to see what they are doing incorrectly and to learn from their mistakes. For a student who struggles with a particular type of problem, you might provide in the margins key information for solving that problem. (memory, comprehension and problem-solving, visuospatial organization, attention and impulse control, anxiety)

Let students arrive at answers using alternate methods. Shortcuts and alternative problem-solving techniques often are not allowed during math instruction. Let students with math disabilities solve problems in whatever way they can, provided they show their work and their methods. (comprehension and problem-solving, visuospatial organization)

Break up the curriculum into small parts. Provide frequent, shorter quizzes on single concepts rather than long tests that incorporate multiple math procedures. With less material to remember, students are likely to perform better. Frequent quizzes also help you monitor a child's progress and provide appropriate interventions. (memory, comprehension and problem-solving, attention and impulse control)

Emphasize the importance of sequence. Students may not understand (or remember) that they need to complete multistep problems in a specific sequence. Reaffirm this idea and provide helpful reference materials as necessary while the student completes an assignment or a test. (memory, comprehension and problem-solving, visuospatial organization)

Let students use procedure sheets or their own notes during tests. Students with weaknesses in math often forget important procedural steps or formulas they'll need to do well on exams. To counter this and ease anxiety, allow students to use reference sheets with equations and other information that will help them succeed. (memory, comprehension and problem-solving, visuospatial organization, attention and impulse control, anxiety)

Allow use of a multiplication table. Students who struggle with multiplication may use valuable test time figuring out basic problems. Allow them to reference a multiplication table if it means they'll be able to focus on the actual concept being tested. (memory, slow speed)

Build students' self-esteem. Children who have difficulties with math may worry that they'll never "get it." Talk about the progress students have shown and express optimism that they can improve even more. (anxiety)

Use math apps for computers and tablets. These programs can teach math skills in ways that some students find much more enjoyable than listening to a teacher. (all areas)

Work with other teachers, special education services, and parents to improve math skills. Work with colleagues and parents to build up student skills in targeted areas. Designate a student for a specific role in a cross-disciplinary project, or encourage parents to practice skills at home with their children. (all areas)

Specific Learning Disorder with Impairment in Written Expression

Writing is a complex process involving multiple cognitive and motor skills. A helpful distinction to keep in mind is that writers perform two functions: those of "author" and "secretary." The author thinks about the message, the organization of ideas, and the language in which to express the message. The secretary, on the other hand, focuses on mechanical concerns, such as spelling, punctuation, capitalization, spacing, and handwriting. Some students have problems being authors, others have difficulty with secretarial tasks, and some have weakness in both functions.[34]

Between 7% and 15% of students may have a writing disability, depending on how it is defined. It is a common learning disability among young people with ADHD[35] (see page 102). Many young people with reading disabilities (page 122) also have a writing disability.[36]

Sometimes deficits in mechanical aspects of writing are separated from the diagnosis of SLD with impairment in written expression and referred to as *dysgraphia* or *developmental coordination disorder.* At other times, dysgraphia and a disorder of written expression are considered to be the same.[37] The *DSM-5* and the following discussion separates these disorders.[38]

Behaviors and Symptoms to Look For

WRITTEN EXPRESSION
Students with written expression weaknesses may show the following problems:

- difficulty with the conceptual aspects of writing
- difficulty organizing and expressing their thoughts
- short compositions

DYSGRAPHIA
Students with dysgraphia, developmental coordination disorder, or disorder of written expression may show the following problems:[39]

- very poor or illegible handwriting
- poor spelling, punctuation, or capitalization
- unusual pencil grip or unusual wrist or paper position
- hand fatigue or sore hand
- omitted words in sentences
- inconsistencies in letter size, uppercase and lowercase, print and cursive
- inconsistent spacing between letters and words
- slow writing

- difficulty writing and thinking at the same time
- run-on sentences

Most students with either or both of these disorders dislike writing. The effects of a writing disability are far-reaching, because they compromise skills important in every academic area. Students in upper grades may fail to show their knowledge of subject matter on an essay test because of their weakness in written expression.

Classroom Strategies and Interventions

A student's writing ability depends on writing legibly; using proper spelling, grammar, punctuation, and capitalization; and expressing thoughts in an organized way. All these aspects are essential to writing and should be addressed by writing instruction programs. Even with intense efforts to build writing skills, however, some children will continue to experience challenges. While consistent efforts to build writing skills are important, accommodations may also be needed to allow students to show their knowledge in content areas.

Following are some strategies for building writing skills and accommodating students with writing difficulties. In parentheses you'll find the writing difficulty each strategy may most successfully target, though suggestions may prove effective with any student.

Model and reinforce proper pencil grip, posture, and paper position with young writers. Particularly with students in kindergarten and first grade, it's important to watch for the correct basic mechanics for writing. An incorrect method can be a difficult habit to break. (dysgraphia)

Use multisensory techniques to teach letters and numbers. Letter and number formation may be easier for some students when multiple senses are used during instruction. For example, struggling students might benefit from your placing your hand over theirs as they form letters. You might ask students to say a letter as they stand and trace its shape in the air with an index finger to improve motor memory. When students practice writing on their own, encourage them to whisper letters and numbers quietly as they form them. (dysgraphia)

Allow students to show what they know in the ways they work best. Let students with writing disabilities demonstrate content area knowledge in ways that do not require extensive writing. Consider replacing written reports with oral presentations. In place of essay tests, use short-answer or multiple-choice formats. (written expression)

Avoid criticizing any aspect of written language. Remove neatness, spelling, and punctuation from grading criteria so that poor writing does not undermine a student's grades. Emphasize the importance of understanding key concepts and evaluate writing mechanics separately from content areas. (written expression, dysgraphia)

Be cautious about asking students to write on the board. Many students with poor writing skills are self-conscious about their abilities. To encourage participation, select small portions of text you feel students can handle writing on the board. Prepare the students in advance so they can practice and feel confident in the task. (dysgraphia)

Reduce copying assignments from the board. The mere task of copying an assignment, a question, or a math problem can be very time consuming and difficult for students with writing disabilities. Address this by providing information on handouts. For example, you could provide a sheet of math problems on paper rather than asking students to copy the problems from the board. (dysgraphia)

Allow print or cursive. Some students struggle with printing, others with cursive. Encourage students to use whichever form of writing works best for them. (dysgraphia)

Encourage the use of pencil grips. Comfortable pencil grips can make handwriting easier for students and less painful for their hands and fingers. (dysgraphia)

Use multiple kinds of paper. Match a student's writing ability and preference to wide or narrow ruled paper. Encourage students to use graph paper in mathematics. Vertical lines help students line up problems and keep track of place values. (dysgraphia)

Provide class notes for students with writing difficulties. Students may have difficulty not only creating legible notes, but also focusing on main concepts from a given class period. Give these students your lecture notes (or those of an assigned notetaker) so they have reference material to study as you progress through the unit. You might also consider providing handouts that require students to write in a single word or short phrase while listening in class. This abbreviated note-taking process teaches students how to summarize lecture material—an essential skill in note-taking. Another strategy is to record lectures and have a student transcribe them on a computer at a later time. This way, students can first hear, then type, lecture material. Typing what they have heard gives them a second opportunity to learn the information. (written expression, dysgraphia)

Encourage the use of technology. Various technologies offer many possible benefits for students who struggle with writing. For example, typing may be easier for these students than writing is. Word-processing programs can check for correct spelling and grammar. Voice-recognition software can be useful for completing written assignments at home. (dysgraphia)

Stress one or two aspects of writing at a time. For earlier drafts of a report, tell students not to worry about spelling, punctuation, or legibility, but to make organizing and expressing ideas their priority. Students can review and improve language and mechanics prior to a final draft. (written expression, dysgraphia)

Modify curriculum and relax classroom deadlines. When appropriate, consider reducing the length and number of written assignments. Allow additional time for all written tasks, including note-taking, copying, and test taking. (written expression, dysgraphia)

Teach composition strategies. Help students get familiar with the different stages of writing a report or another assignment: outline the paper, organize its ideas, write a draft, edit the draft, and revise the draft to produce a final paper. (written expression)

Teach and encourage the use of diagrams and other visual tools to organize information. Visual outlining tools can help students plan writing projects, carry out research, and organize research into clear writing. Clustering is a diagrammatic activity that can help students generate ideas and see patterns in their thoughts. Story mapping can help students plot how they'd like a story to go. Venn diagrams can help students compare and contrast two items in preparation for an analytical essay. (written expression)

Teach prewriting strategies. The goal of prewriting is to help students come up with and evaluate ideas for specific writing assignments. Popular prewriting strategies include clustering, diagramming, using graphic organizers, and drawing. (written expression)

Ensure student interest. Poor writers often think of writing with displeasure. They may believe it is too difficult. Counteract a dislike of writing by incorporating high-interest topics into assignments. If you know a particular student likes sports, for example, suggest that the student write a script for a sports report. As much as possible, allow students to select their own writing topics. Also include journal writing as an option. (written expression, dysgraphia)

Teach and encourage use of assistive technology software. These programs help students organize thoughts, write legibly, spell correctly, and recognize errors while writing.[40] (written expression, dysgraphia)

> ## PROFESSIONAL TREATMENTS
> Some students with dysgraphia may need to work with a professional outside of the classroom to improve fine motor skills. For students with poor handwriting, recommend an evaluation by a children's occupational therapist.

Nonverbal Learning Disability (NVLD)

Less than 1% of the population has NVLD.[41] On IQ tests, people with NVLD have much higher verbal IQs than nonverbal IQs. Students with NVLD are frequently misidentified as having other conditions, including ADHD (page 102) and autism spectrum disorder (page 114).

Nonverbal learning disability (NVLD) is an uncommon neurodevelopmental disorder caused by abnormalities in the right hemisphere of the brain. It is not now—nor has it ever been—included as a diagnosis in the *DSM-5* because of ongoing debate over what constitutes this disorder. NVLD is different from other learning disabilities in that it is *not* language based. The disorder is often overlooked because students who experience it have some learning strengths (including rote memory) that allow them to perform well at school—especially in the younger grades. Social skills are these students' primary problem. Children with NVLD have many characteristics similar to those of students with autism spectrum disorder (see page 114). Strategies and accommodations for students with high-functioning autism are also appropriate for students with NVLD.

The effects of NVLD on students tend to grow more severe over time. Elementary students with the disorder often are good readers and have excellent memorization and vocabulary skills. As students get older, reading ability drops. Children in middle school and high school must learn to read for comprehension; the rote memory that allows students with NVLD to perform well in younger grades is no longer sufficient to help them maintain grade-level abilities. Other difficulties with visual-spatial-organizational skills, motor skills, and social communication also surface.

Visual-spatial-organizational skills. Students with NVLD may have limited skill for visualizing imaginary objects, poor memory for things they have seen, faulty spatial perception, and difficulty with spatial relationships.

Motor skills. Students may have poor coordination, problems with balance, and difficulties with handwriting.

Social skills. Students often have difficulty picking up on nonverbal cues, show poor social judgment, and have trouble forming and maintaining relationships. Difficulty with transitions and new situations also is common. Students' reasoning skills are much weaker than their verbal skills are.

NVLD can be a particularly frustrating disorder because often it is not identified and children struggle at school without understanding why. With no firm idea that NVLD is affecting children, teachers may not know how to effectively address students' learning weaknesses. Students are most commonly diagnosed with NVLD in middle school, by which time they may already be behind in many academic areas and feel frustrated at school. Peers often alienate students with NVLD by this time, due to these students' social and motor difficulties. Early identification is important for reducing the severity of this disorder's effects.

ACADEMIC STRENGTHS AND WEAKNESSES OF CHILDREN WITH NVLD

Strengths:

- word decoding and identification
- spelling
- rote memory
- auditory verbal learning

Weaknesses:

- reading comprehension
- mechanical computation and reasoning
- handwriting
- organization

Behaviors and Symptoms to Look For

In addition to a specific pattern of academic strengths and weaknesses, students with NVLD often experience behavioral and social problems related to the disability. Clumsiness, a tendency to become lost or disoriented, and marked social skills deficits can lead these children to be labeled as "odd" (or worse). For this reason, students' behavior and social skills require as much, if not more, attention as their areas of academic difficulty do.

Students with NVLD may:

Be easily disoriented or lost. Visual-spatial-organizational deficits cause children to have difficulty getting familiar with new physical locations. Even after students have attended a school for days or weeks, they may have trouble finding their way around.

Have difficulty coping with changes in routines. These students rely on routines and can become upset when a physical environment or set of procedures is modified.

Have difficulty generalizing previously learned information. Students with NVLD may be able to recall specific details about a story or a topic of class discussion. However, they often find it difficult to summarize the material in a general way.

Have difficulty following multistep directions. If you give students with NVLD directions or procedures involving several steps, they may forget one or more steps or confuse the order of the sequence.

Interpret speech literally. These students tend to think in concrete terms. They may have difficulty detecting sarcasm or understanding idioms. For example, I once asked a seventh grader with NVLD how she found sixth grade last year. She said she never lost it.

Have problems understanding nonverbal communication. Students with NVLD often have trouble reading facial expressions, body language, and other social cues, which hampers the development of social skills. Poor social skills often result in these students being isolated or bullied.

Ask excessive questions. Students with NVLD tend to be confused by both verbal and nonverbal communication—they sometimes "don't get it." They may ask lots of questions to clarify something that is obvious to others.

Become easily overwhelmed and anxious. If these students don't understand what or why something is happening around them, they can become upset.

Note: Students with NVLD also exhibit many behaviors similar to those of students with HFA (page 114) and social communication disorder (page 154). Yvonna Fast, a writer with NLDline, has written an excellent article describing the differences between HFA and NVLD (nldline.com/yvonna.htm).

Classroom Strategies and Interventions

NVLD affects students in a variety of academic and social areas. These students may perform well in some areas and poorly in others. You can match the following instructional strategies to an individual's particular difficulties.

Provide background information for lectures, assignments, and tests. Prepare students as much as possible for upcoming material and expectations. Outlines of lectures can help students follow along in class and process content. Study guides handed out prior to tests can help students focus on the key areas in which they will be evaluated.

Teach students strategies for organizing their ideas. Students with NVLD often struggle with summarizing information. Work to build these skills by teaching outlining and other strategies for organizing information.

Break curriculum and assignments into small parts. Long units can overwhelm students with NVLD because these students have trouble processing large amounts of information at a time. Long assignments also can present difficulties because of problems students experience with handwriting.

Monitor students' progress. Check in often with students to ensure they are on track with assignments, projects, and tests. Students with NVLD may seem to have understood directions, but may really have little idea of what's expected of them.

Be precise in communication. Use specific and concrete language with students who have NVLD. State directions and classroom expectations simply and clearly. Check in with students to ensure they have heard and processed what you said.

Adjust reading instruction and pacing. Allow students with NVLD to proceed at their advanced pace in the early grades. With older students, be prepared to provide additional assistance for reading comprehension tasks.

Allow for math accommodations. Explain math procedures verbally with a step-by-step approach—minimizing the use of drawings, diagrams, and other visual displays. Provide graph paper for students to help them organize and line up equations. Simplify word problems by omitting extraneous information. When appropriate, let students use a calculator to solve problems or check answers. You may wish to consider exempting these students from geometry due to its heavy focus on visual-spatial skills.

Avoid grading written language. Remove neatness from grading criteria so that poor handwriting does not sabotage a student's grades. Emphasize the importance of understanding the material and evaluate writing mechanics separately from content understanding.

Modify curriculum and relax classroom deadlines. When appropriate, consider reducing the length and number of assignments in areas where a student struggles. Allow additional time for tasks that may be difficult for the student.

Assign the student a buddy. A buddy should be compassionate and helpful. The buddy may sit next to the student with NVLD to help the student stay organized or understand what to do. A buddy may also help an easily disoriented or lost student navigate the school.

Monitor peer interactions, particularly during unstructured time. Students with NVLD may act in ways that seem odd to others, or they may lack social judgment when interacting with peers. Observe these students closely when they interact with other children and ensure they are not experiencing teasing or bullying. Chapter 2 provides some ways in which you can address inappropriate student behaviors.

Teach students strategies for staying organized. Familiarize students with organizational strategies, such as color-coding to coordinate materials. Encourage the use of binders, organizers (including electronic ones), and assignment notebooks.

Reduce visual stimuli. The strength of students with NVLD is their ability to process rote verbal information rather than visual directions and spatial concepts. Reduce your reliance on visual instructions and translate visual instructions into verbal directions. For example, instead of showing a student a school map while explaining how to get to another classroom, have the student remember to "take two right turns, one left, and one right."

Teach and model social skills. Students with NVLD often need to be taught basic or obvious social behaviors. Emphasize turn taking, social cues, nonverbal behavior, and rules of conversation. You can find social skills activities and resources in chapter 5.

   Note: Strategies and interventions for social communication disorder (page 154) and autism spectrum disorder (page 114) may be very helpful for students with NVLD.

PROFESSIONAL TREATMENTS

Students with NVLD benefit from working with speech-language therapists on voice tone and social skills. Students with NVLD may also work with occupational therapists to strengthen visual-motor and spatial skills.

Communication Disorders

> About 7% of children between ages three and seventeen have some type of communication disorder.[43] These disorders persist for different lengths of time depending on the type of disorder and its severity. Language disorders may persist into adulthood while mild to moderate speech sound disorders and stuttering usually diminish in childhood.[44]

Communication disorders include various differences in how individuals communicate. These can include the way students' speech sounds, how they understand language, or how they express themselves. Students with communication disorders have difficulties with speech, language, and communication. Speech refers to sound qualities including articulation, speed, and tone. Language involves using and understanding language. Communication includes understanding and following social rules for exchanging ideas. These disorders are not caused by hearing difficulties or unfamiliarity with a culture or language. Heredity, differences in how the brain develops, and chronic ear infections during the first two years of life are probable causes of communication disorders.[42]

Communication disorders create challenges for students in many areas. Due to the difficulty children have understanding or remembering instructions, adults may assume these children simply don't pay attention or behave appropriately. Poor vocabulary recall can lead to writing difficulties and leave students struggling for the right word. Finally, some students' speech differences (such as stuttering) seem odd to others and may lead to social isolation or teasing.

Speech Sound Disorder

Most children develop intelligible speech by age three or four, although some sounds may be mispronounced until age eight. The most difficult sounds are *k, g, f, v, ng, y, r, l, s, ch, sh, j, th,* and *zh.*[45] If a student's speech interferes with communication and causes problems in social or academic situations after age four, the student may have a speech sound disorder—sometimes referred to as an articulation disorder. Some problems with speech sounds are caused by apraxia, a brain problem limiting mouth and tongue movement.

Behaviors and Symptoms to Look For

Children with speech sound disorder may:

Substitute certain sounds. For example, they may say "wed" instead of "red."

Omit certain sounds. For example, they may say "pay" instead of "play."

Distort certain sounds. They may say "thun" instead of "sun." This is common in children who have a lisp.[46]

Classroom Strategies and Interventions

Speech sound disorders can make it difficult for students to communicate with teachers and peers. These students may be reluctant to participate in class. Many of these children would benefit from a consultation with your school's speech-language therapist.

> Prior to first grade, about 8% to 9% of children are diagnosed with a speech sound disorder. By first grade, this number drops to 5%.[47]

Following are suggestions for assisting these students in your classroom:

Accurately restate the student's inaccurate sound. For example, if a student has difficulty with the beginning *y* sound of the word *yellow* and says, "I want the wewo one," repeat the words slowly with greater enunciation and stretch out the targeted word: "Oh, you want the YELL-OW crayon. Here it is." **CAUTION!** Do this only when other students cannot overhear the conversation, since this might embarrass the student.

Read words containing the mispronounced sound. Sit across from the student and ask him or her to look at you while you read some words. As you read each word, show the student how you position your mouth, lips, and tongue to make the correct sound. Have the student repeat each word after you. Compliment the student on any progress you see.

Allow for flexibility in course work. Consider replacing oral presentations with written reports. Respect a student's decision not to volunteer as spokesperson for a group project.

Accept inaccurate word pronunciation from the student. Accept the student's mispronounced communication in front of others. Correcting a student publicly will cause embarrassment.

Monitor teasing and bullying. Students who have difficulties with speech are more likely to be teased, bullied, or excluded by peers. Keep a close eye on this inside and outside the classroom.

Compliment students' progress. Any time you hear a student say a word more clearly, privately compliment the student's progress: "You said the *r* sound correctly in that word."

PROFESSIONAL TREATMENTS

Speech therapy is very effective for speech sound disorders. Many of these students will benefit from a referral to your school's speech-language therapist.

Childhood-Onset Fluency Disorder (Stuttering)

Students who stutter have problems with speech fluency. They may omit sounds, repeat sounds or words, pause in the middle of words, substitute words, hesitate while speaking, or have broken speech. It is a myth that nervousness, stress, or other psychological problems cause stuttering. Instead, stuttering is caused by information-processing differences in the areas of the brain that are responsible for speech.

> About 1% of young people experience periods of stuttering at some point during childhood. Most of these children outgrow the disorder by age six or seven.[48]

Academic problems for children who stutter are generally limited to difficulty participating in class. These students often are extremely self-conscious about their speech and may be particularly reluctant to talk in front of a group—including classmates. These students are frequently anxious when they have to speak.

They also are more likely to be teased or bullied by other students. Sometimes a fear of stuttering in front of others will cause these students to be severely isolated socially.

Behaviors and Symptoms to Look For

The most obvious difficulty in school for children who stutter is participating in class.

Following are some behaviors you may observe at school.

Repeating sounds, words, and phrases. For example:

- sounds ("c-c-candy")
- one-syllable words ("I-I want more.")
- multisyllable words ("Swimming-swimming is fun.")
- phrases ("I want–I want to see that.")

Sound prolongations and drawn-out words. For example: "The water looks bluuuuue."

Substitution of simple words to avoid difficult ones. For example, saying "tinfoil" instead of "aluminum foil."

Audible or silent blocking. Filled or unfilled (silent) pauses in speech. Filled pauses include breaks in speech with filler words like *um, uh,* and *er.*

Abrupt changes of words or thoughts. For example, "I went to—where did you get that?"

Word substitutions to avoid problem words. For example, "After school, I'm going h-h-h-h—to my house." (The student couldn't say *home*.)

Physical expressions of tension. Children may grimace, blink, or contort their faces in expressions of discomfort.

Social isolation. Students who have difficulties with speech are more likely to be mocked or teased by peers. Students with these disorders may choose to isolate themselves, avoiding games and other group activities.

Classroom Strategies and Interventions

Stuttering can create many difficulties for children at school. Work with speech-language pathologists and other school staff to help children succeed academically. In addition, try to address any social problems students may be experiencing.

Following are some suggestions for helping students who stutter adjust in the classroom:

Show patience. Always wait for a student to finish speaking. Students often are sensitive about their speech difficulties. Showing impatience or irritation is likely to make students feel worse about these challenges.

Reduce your rate of speech while speaking to a student. Students who stutter frequently feel pressure to quickly finish what they are trying to say. If you model a slower rate of speech, students may copy your speed. Speaking at a slower rate may improve their speech fluency.

Try to maintain eye contact with students while they are stuttering, even if they resist looking at you. You may be tempted to look away when students are stuttering because you feel bad about the difficulty they're having. This may cause students to think you're uncomfortable with them personally. They may think you're impatient and tired of listening to them stutter. By maintaining eye contact, you're letting students know you're interested in what they have to say.

Make it clear to others that you're waiting for a student to finish. Don't acknowledge other students who are getting impatient, interrupting, or speaking for the student who is struggling. You might maintain an expectant gaze toward the student while holding up your index finger to discourage other children from talking.

Ask questions that students can answer simply. You might call on children who stutter when only brief responses are required. This might include single-word short answers or solutions to multiple-choice questions. You might wish to check in with students before calling on them so they feel confident in their replies.

Minimize students' oral reading requirements and oral presentations. Consider assigning written work or projects to replace oral presentations and avoid asking students who stutter to read long passages. Modify curriculum in any other appropriate ways. **Note:** Some children who stutter can read fluently when reading in unison with another child.

Create a special time outside of class when a student may speak with you. The regular class period may not be an appropriate time for a student who stutters to share concerns. Let students know they can speak with you outside of class when something is bothering them. You might set up a daily or weekly appointment with a student.

Take immediate action if a student mimics, laughs at, or teases a child who stutters. Students who stutter often suffer from taunting or bullying by peers. Put an immediate end to any teasing you observe.

Provide social skills instruction. Children who stutter are more likely to be teased by other students. Intense fear of embarrassment may lead to a child becoming withdrawn. Try to diminish this by teaching a student social skills and conflict resolution skills. You can find activities and resources for building social skills in chapter 5.

If the student and family approve, educate the class about a child's stuttering. Classmates are less likely to tease (and more likely to help) a student when they understand why people stutter. If you take this step, make sure you first get written student and parent permission and involve a guidance counselor or school psychologist if possible.

Avoid finishing students' statements for them. Students who stutter may be extremely sensitive. It's important that you're an ally to them. This means being someone who understands children's difficulties, empathizes with them, and shows respect. You also want to value their contributions to the class. Finally, reiterate to other students in your class the importance of allowing others to speak in their own time.

Avoid telling students to slow down or think about what they want to say. Asking students who are stuttering to slow down, take their time, and think about what they want to say seems sensible, but the reason students stutter is much more complicated than just trying to talk too fast. Students who stutter have probably been told to slow down many times before. This suggestion does not work, and it may make students feel worse by causing them to feel that they've failed again.

PROFESSIONAL TREATMENTS

A speech-language pathologist can help a student form initial speech sounds more easily. The therapist might model a breathier quality to initial sounds to reduce the severity and frequency of blocked speech. Speech is blocked when the lips or throat tighten or when the tongue doesn't move smoothly to the palate. The result is that not enough air comes out to produce sound and a student stutters.

EXPLAINING A STUDENT'S STUTTERING TO THE CLASS

Ms. Perez had the following discussion with her fourth-grade class about a student who stuttered after getting the student's and his parents' permission:

"You know we've all heard Sean repeat sounds when he speaks. His speech is a little bumpy. Sean is working on making his speech smoother without the bumps. How can you be a friend to Sean when he speaks?"

Ms. Perez waited for responses, but no one offered any. She went on, "You could wait for Sean to finish what he wants to say before you start talking. You could also look at Sean when he's speaking. You might think about what Sean is saying instead of how he's saying it. For example, we've all heard Sean say, 'Teeeeeacher,' and we know he's talking about me."

Ms. Perez concluded: "Thanks to each of you. You're a great class, and I know you'll help Sean do his best."

Language Disorder

Language disorder used to be diagnosed as two separate disorders: receptive language disorder and expressive language disorder. Both are currently included in the category of *language disorder* in the *DSM-5*. Receptive problems refer to understanding language messages. Expressive problems involve the production of spoken language, written language, or sign language.

Language disorders can create many academic, behavioral, and social challenges for students. Children may appear to be less intelligent because of these difficulties. The pattern of language delays (and the problems they cause) can vary a great deal among students.

Behaviors and Symptoms to Look For

Students with a receptive language problem may:

Have difficulty understanding others. These students may seem to lack intelligence when they may actually have a language disorder.

Have poor attention span—especially when listening to others speak. Difficulty understanding someone's speech can cause a student's attention to wander. This behavior can sometimes be misinterpreted as ADHD (page 102).

Have difficulty following directions. Students with language disorders often have difficulty understanding and remembering directions and therefore may not follow them. Children who appear irresponsible or defiant may simply not know or remember what they are supposed to do. Watch for students who seem to lean heavily on cues from others to participate in classroom activities or complete assignments.

Show poor ability to process and remember verbal information. Some students may not take a single line of notes during a lecture or class period—even when you have specifically asked them to do so. They often will have difficulty taking notes because they do not remember information long enough to write it down. Others will be able to repeat isolated facts, but they miss the main point or perspective you're trying to get across.

Have limited reading comprehension. These students often have difficulties with reading. Those who are able to decode (or sound out) words may have a limited understanding of what a book or passage is about. Poor comprehension is related to weak vocabulary skills.

Have trouble understanding words with multiple meanings. Due largely to limited vocabulary, students struggle to understand or remember the multiple meanings of a single word.

Have difficulty with basic *what, where, why, when,* and *who* questions. Children may understand parts of a question but not its entire intention. For example:

Teacher: "Where should your pencils be right now?"
Student: "I don't need to sharpen them."

Teacher: "Why did you like that story?"
Student: "You read it to us yesterday."

Students with an expressive language problem may:

Speak in words, phrases, or incomplete sentences. Children may speak in a way that makes little sense to listeners. For example, "Milk! He bad boy."

Use gestures and sound effects instead of words to express ideas and feelings. For example, "Last night my cat *(makes scratching gestures accompanied by hissing sound)*. She wants the *(points to object)*."

Use pronouns, plurals, and possessives incorrectly. For example, "Me go to bed. Us went there. I have three cat."

Have difficulty telling a story or describing an event. Students may place events out of sequence, neglecting some and repeating others.

Have limited expressive vocabulary. For example, "I have a new video game—you know, the one with cars and you pick one . . . like the purple one . . . and you go fast, and sometimes they *(makes crashing sound)* and then you have to get them back and go really fast."

Have difficulty finding the right words to express meaning. For example, "You know, the thing that puts fires out" (instead of "fire extinguisher").

Overuse filler words and imprecise language. Students may rely on the words *ah, um,* and *you know* when speaking. They may also use *thing, whatchamacallit,* or other nondescript terms when they can't think of a word.

Have trouble with written compositions. Students produce work that contains vague ideas, in which it is difficult to discover (or follow) the point or argument.

Classroom Strategies and Interventions

Students with language disorders can experience many different challenges. For this reason, a wide variety of strategies may be necessary to address behaviors. Work to match these interventions with the specific needs of a student.

Following are some strategies and accommodations helpful for students who have language disorders:

Repeat and clarify instructions as needed. A student's short attention span and potentially limited grasp of language may make it necessary for you to repeat instructions. It's important to demonstrate patience and to avoid criticizing students. When appropriate, it may help to have students restate or paraphrase directions.

Deliver information in more than one way. In addition to explaining a concept verbally, provide graphics to help demonstrate it. You might use Venn diagrams, illustrations, or images from magazines or the internet. Teach students to make simple diagrams to organize information and remind them of important concepts from class.

Simplify daily language use. For example, say, "Please hand me the pencil" instead of, "Please hand me the big black pencil in your hand."

Help students compare and contrast objects and ideas. Show how two items are related or different. For example, in comparing a pen and a pencil, you might say the following: "They're the same because you write with both of them. They're different because a pen has ink and a pencil has graphite. You can usually erase what you write with a pencil, but you usually can't erase when you write with a pen." You might also wish to show students how to use a Venn diagram to compare and contrast.

Be specific when giving instructions. Students can be overwhelmed by extensive directions and may be confused about what they are supposed to do. Break down assignments into small steps.

Provide written directions. In addition to verbal instructions, write directions on the board. You might also provide a handout on which the student can check off each step as it is completed. Such a checklist can encourage independence and responsibility.

SAMPLE DIRECTIONS FOR A WRITING ASSIGNMENT

1. Get your notebook from the bin.
2. Get a pencil from the cup.
3. Turn to the first blank page.
4. Write today's date on the first line.
5. Think about the writing topics for today.
6. Write about your topic.
7. Done?
8. Read what you wrote.
9. Does it make sense?
10. Are words missing?
11. Read it again.
12. Return your notebook to the basket and your pencil to the cup.

Provide a preview of a class or lesson. Preview a lesson or an assignment with an overview of what students will be expected to learn. Ask students to think about a few key questions or concepts when reading or working on a project.

Show a sample of the finished product you're assigning. Students may have a hard time picturing what is expected of them based solely on verbal instructions. A sample or another visual representation can help them understand what you'd like them to do.

Teach students how to draw conclusions. To model drawing inferences, you might use a picture and talk about what is happening in it. For example, "Oh, I see a man carrying a can of paint and a paintbrush. Hmm, there's a ladder leaning against the house. The man is walking away from the house with the paint and brush. I guess he just finished painting the house."

Preteach vocabulary. Explain vocabulary words to be used in a discussion or lesson before presenting the lesson.

Teach prewriting skills. Students with language disorders often have difficulty organizing and fluently expressing their thoughts. Counter this by teaching prewriting strategies such as mapping (or webbing).

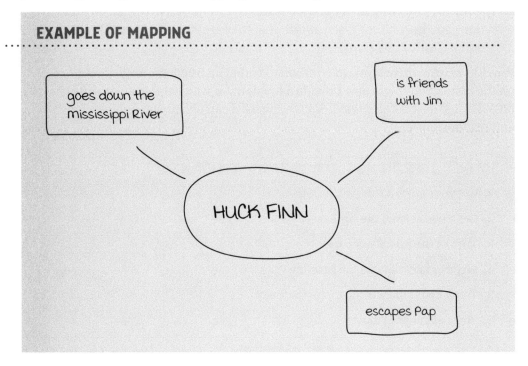

EXAMPLE OF MAPPING

goes down the mississippi River

is friends with Jim

HUCK FINN

escapes Pap

Allow for flexibility in course work. Adjust the work you assign based on a student's individual strengths and weaknesses. Replace tasks that are especially difficult for students with others that allow them to show their knowledge in content areas.

Eliminate bullying and create safe learning environments. Students who have difficulties with communication may be susceptible to teasing and bullying. Ensure that students are not harassed or excluded. For ideas on creating supportive school environments, see chapter 5.

Provide social skills instruction. Children who have language disorders may fear teasing by peers. Excessive fear of making mistakes in speech may cause children to become withdrawn. You may counter this by teaching social skills at a pace comfortable to the student. For activities and resources for building social skills, see chapter 5.

PROFESSIONAL TREATMENTS

It's important to make use of the speech-language pathologist at your school. Report concerning communication difficulties to this specialist so students can be evaluated and helpful strategies found.

JAZMIN

Fourteen-year-old Jazmin seemed to know a lot about history. She often raised her hand in class to answer Mr. Locke's questions. That's why Mr. Locke was surprised to read Jazmin's essay on the three branches of government. Jazmin had included some of the relevant details, but they were poorly organized and the paper was difficult to follow.

Mr. Locke decided to meet with Jazmin to discuss the essay. He learned that Jazmin has always had problems writing papers. "I'm good at remembering stuff," she said. "I just have a hard time getting it down on paper. I can't seem to get the words right."

Mr. Locke referred Jazmin for a language evaluation, which revealed she had a mild language disorder. (She may also be considered to have a specific learning disorder with impairment in written expression.) Jazmin was relieved to know why she struggled with writing. "No wonder I have trouble with papers!" Mr. Locke replaced written papers and essay tests with projects and multiple-choice tests for Jazmin. These accommodations were kept in place until Jazmin learned strategies she could use to improve her writing ability.

Social (Pragmatic) Communication Disorder

Students with social communication disorder may seem similar to those with autism spectrum disorder (see page 114). The important difference is that students with a social communication disorder do not have the restricted, repetitive patterns of behaviors, activities, or interests that exist in children with autism. In other words, children with autism spectrum disorder typically have social communication difficulties, but all students with social communication difficulties do not have autism.

Students who experience social communication disorder have difficulty communicating socially. This condition limits a child's ability to say the right things at the right times in the right ways. It causes students to have trouble understanding and interacting with others.

There have not been enough studies to determine the numbers of children who have social communication disorder. The majority of students with the disorder also have autism spectrum disorder (page 114) or NVLD (page 138).

Communication is a very complex system of spoken words, body language, and facial expressions. For most students, each of these aspects of communication comes fairly naturally as students develop socially. Children with social communication disorder have great difficulty with small talk and other social functions of language. They may not understand the nuances of another's speech or nonverbal cues (such as facial expressions), and they misinterpret meaning. They may not understand that communication is meant to be a shared experience. Instead of paying attention to what others are saying, they pursue their own agendas with a conversation.

Because of these difficulties, conversations with children who have social communication disorder may seem disconnected or awkward. Students may come across as self-centered or rude. It's common for children with social communication disorder to be considered odd by peers and to be socially isolated.

Behaviors and Symptoms to Look For

Students with social communication disorder behave very similarly to students with autism spectrum disorder (page 114) or NVLD (page 138). Refer to those sections for common behaviors students may display.

Classroom Strategies and Interventions

Strategies and interventions for these students will be the same as those for students with autism spectrum disorder (page 114) and NVLD (page 138).

PROFESSIONAL TREATMENTS

A referral to your school's speech therapist may be appropriate. Pragmatic language therapy can be helpful for these students.

CHAPTER 13

Disruptive and Conduct Disorders

Including Oppositional Defiant Disorder (ODD) and Conduct Disorder (CD)

. . . .

"The defiant child: 'I won't, and you can't make me!'"

—Mary-Elaine Jacobsen, psychologist

. . . .

Disruptive and conduct disorders involve problems with emotional and behavioral self-control. The most common diagnoses are oppositional defiant disorder (ODD) and conduct disorder (CD). Students with ODD are excessively argumentative, defiant, angry, irritable, or vindictive. They may break home and school rules and blame their behavior on others. Students with more severe oppositional behavior are at greater risk to develop CD compared to students with milder ODD or without ODD. For all children, interventions that reduce the severity of ODD reduce the likelihood of CD. CD occurs mostly in preteens and teens. Students with CD have more serious patterns of behavior that may include aggression toward people (or animals), destruction of property, lying, theft, running away, skipping school, or breaking the law.[1]

> About 3% of children and adolescents have disruptive or conduct disorders. These disorders are more common in boys than in girls.[2] Although the percentage is relatively small compared to numbers of children with other mental health disorders, children with disruptive or conduct disorders are among the most frequently referred for mental health treatment. About half of these young people have ADHD (page 102). Depressive (page 91) and anxiety disorders (page 63) also are common in these students.[3]

Identifying a disruptive or conduct disorder can be difficult since all children are angry or defiant at times. It's also natural for young people to test (or protest) parental limits and teacher directions. Some questioning of authority—especially during adolescence—can be a healthy sign of developing independence and assertiveness. If behaviors are frequent and persistent, however, students might qualify for a diagnosis of ODD or CD.

There are many reasons behind students' disruptive behaviors. Genetic, cognitive, and biological differences have been found in these children. Some children are born with certain temperaments that make them more susceptible to these disorders. The cause may also be related to dysfunctional parenting, family conflict, or low socioeconomic status.[4] Some of these students may have depressive or anxiety disorders. Students with ADHD who are diagnosed with ODD or CD may not misbehave intentionally, but their difficulty controlling impulses or hyperactivity can lead to behavior difficulties.

GET HELP! Children with disruptive and conduct disorders are among the most challenging students. They can be explosive or aggressive. It's important to respond immediately and alert other personnel at the first sign of out-of-control behavior. You may want to develop a plan for promptly taking this action if the need arises.

Behaviors and Symptoms to Look For

Students with disruptive and conduct disorders are likely quite visible in your classroom. These students argue, break rules, disrupt class, and take your attention away from teaching. They're probably the students who try your patience and require the most discipline.

Students with ODD may frequently:

- lose their tempers

- argue with adults

- defy or refuse to comply with adults' requests or rules

- deliberately annoy others

- blame others for their mistakes or misbehavior

- be easily annoyed by others

- be angry and resentful

- be spiteful or vindictive

Nearly every child shows some of these behaviors occasionally. Students qualify for a diagnosis of ODD if they engage in four or more of these behaviors within six months in ways that cause major problems in school, at home, or in relationships. Defer to the judgment of a mental health professional for classifying behaviors and their severity.

CD is more severe than ODD. In a child who has CD, defiant or angry behavior leads to serious violations of rules or the law. Students with CD may:

- show aggression toward people or animals—including bullying, threatening, or fighting others; using weapons; torturing animals; or stealing from others while physically threatening them

- destroy property—including committing arson and engaging in other destructive behaviors

- deceive or steal—including breaking and entering, conning people, or shoplifting

- break the law and other serious rules at school or home—including running away from home or skipping school

Some young people with CD show a lack of guilt, empathy, or concern about their behavior in school or at home.[5] However, not all students who violate rules or laws have CD. It's possible that children will break a serious rule once, realize their mistake, and amend their behavior. Students with CD show a pattern of repetitive and persistent misbehavior. Only a mental health professional can diagnose the condition.

Classroom Strategies and Interventions

The strategies and accommodations you choose to use with students who have ODD or CD will depend in large part upon the severity of the behavior problems. Check school and district policies to be certain your interventions fall within guidelines. Interventions should not embarrass or humiliate students but serve to keep students from continuing problem behaviors.

It's important to address students' behavior with the help of administrators, counselors, and other school staff. If your school has a Multi-Tiered System of Supports, or MTSS (see chapter 2), students with ODD or CD may be receiving Tier 3 interventions or be in special education classes. In severe cases—especially with older students—you might need to work with community agencies and law enforcement to effectively manage students' behavior.

Following are some ways to address difficulties with students' behavior in your classroom:

Build strong relationships with students. Students with disruptive and conduct disorders often resent teachers and other authority figures. These children may think you're only looking to punish them. Your best antidote to resentment is to care genuinely about your students. Research shows that caring is the most important factor in positive teacher-student relationships.[6] Caring also contributes to students' behavioral and academic success. Greet students by name as they enter class. Show genuine interest in them and talk about the ways in which you'd like to help them improve their behavior. Reaching out to challenging students can be very effective because they may not expect such a gesture. Your willingness to give them a chance to prove they can behave at school may help them do just that.

Establish clear rules and behavior expectations. Students must know classroom rules in order to follow them. Rules should be clear, consistent, and posted prominently in the classroom. Many schools and teachers involve students in creating rules to promote buy-in with children. For more information on establishing consistent classroom routines and expectations, see chapter 1.

Facilitate kind acts. Pair disruptive students with other children they can help in some way. For example, disruptive students who are good in math can feel good about themselves and receive positive reinforcement from helping other students with math. Feeling appreciated by peers might counteract some of the student's "bad kid" reputation.

Ignore minor undesired behaviors. Pick your battles with students who have ODD or CD. Ignore behaviors that don't have significant tangible effects on other individuals.

Use preventive cueing. To let students know they're starting to behave inappropriately, you can shake your head, make lengthy eye contact, or frown at them.

Provide positive reinforcement. Children with ODD and CD often receive more negative feedback than positive reinforcement. As a result, they know how *not* to act, but may not know what behaviors *are* appropriate. In the book *Lost at School*, Ross Greene asserts that "kids do well if they can." He believes that many students lack the skills to behave appropriately.[7] Subscribing to Greene's philosophy can help teachers reduce their criticism of students. As much as possible, teach and reinforce appropriate skills and behaviors. Help students see that you do not view them as troublemakers but as important individuals who can have a positive impact at school. You might reward positive behaviors by creating a "Certificate of Respectful Behavior" (page 16) or some other form of recognition students can bring home. When you acknowledge children's positive actions, children are less likely to seek attention by being disruptive.

Teach anger management and conflict resolution skills. Show children positive ways to deal with strong feelings and disagreements. Help build social skills and reinforce the benefits of resolving differences with others peacefully. You'll find activities and resources for helping students get along well with others in chapter 5.

Use a behavior contract to address misbehavior. Ask students to agree to appropriate behavior in writing, and tie positive behavior to rewards. You'll find a sample behavior contract on page 17. Parents should be aware of and involved in your efforts to improve behavior. Also check in with other staff for behavior management strategies they are using with a student.

Establish provisions for students to cool off. Work out a plan with students for times when they feel frustrated and about to act out. Let them go to a quiet place in the classroom or visit with a counselor to calm down. Your provisions may include a silent signal with which you indicate that it's okay for them to leave. You can use the reproducible "Student Coping Plan" on page 20 to create these classroom accommodations.

Remain calm. Many students with ODD or CD enjoy seeing teachers and other adults become upset. Regardless of how frustrated you may feel, do not allow these feelings to show. Instead, administer disciplinary action in a firm, detached way.

Give consequences for major inappropriate behavior. Immediately have a brief, private conversation with the student to provide feedback. A teacher or counselor can schedule another time that day or the next day to have a Collaborative and Proactive Solutions (CPS) session with the student (see page 163). A practice commonly used in elementary school is changing a student's color on a chart while saying something like, "Diego, that's a color change." However, avoid making a statement to or about Diego, because this is a public reprimand.[8] Diego's chart color can be changed without comment. In middle school and high school, teachers sometimes send students out of class or give them in-school suspension for disruptive behavior. This practice, too, should be avoided since it rewards students for misbehavior; they get to avoid a class they dislike and go to a more desirable environment.[9]

Be proactive: Anticipate and remind. Give reminders before an activity and describe the behavior that you expect.[10]

Use a timer to encourage positive behavior. Tell a student privately that you will give a sign when the student is engaging in some minor misbehavior or not doing the work. The student has a certain amount of time to correct this behavior before receiving a penalty. The next time the student misbehaves, walk to the timer and set it as you continue to teach. (An hourglass works well because it has minimal impact on other students.) The student will know that the behavior must be fixed, or the penalty you discussed privately will come next.

Teach children to self-monitor their behavior. In private, give students a behavior tracking form. Ask them to focus on decreasing one negative behavior (such as talking back to you). Develop a silent signal you can use during class to let students know when they have committed the behavior so they can mark it on the form. Set weekly goals with students (perhaps in conjunction with a behavior contract) and tie progress to rewards. As students become more aware of their behavior, they may no longer need a signal. Eventually their self-monitoring can make a behavior cease. You'll find a sample self-monitoring form on page 57.

Closely monitor behavior during transitions and unstructured activities. Children with disruptive and conduct disorders may have difficulty controlling themselves during lunch, recess, and other unstructured times. Reiterate rules for these periods and closely supervise students when activities are under way. Quickly step in to end any teasing, fighting, or bullying behaviors.

Consider asking parents to sit in on class. Many students will be embarrassed about behaving a certain way if a parent or caregiver is present. Asking a parent to join your class for part of the day may help address a student's difficult behavior.

Set up an Academy. Some students will repeatedly defy, protest, and refuse to change their behavior despite numerous interventions. Behavioral experts Ray Levy, Bill O'Hanlon, and Tyler Norris Goode describe an approach for these students called the *Academy*. There are four steps in an Academy:[11]

1. Privately explain to a child that repeated rule infractions are telling you the student needs more help to behave appropriately.

2. Ask the student to practice the desired behavior at a time that is inconvenient or undesirable for him or her (such as after school).

3. Ask the child to practice the appropriate behavior over and over again.

4. When a student successfully shows appropriate behavior, give praise and say you hope you don't have to go through additional Academies.

Example: A student refuses to clean up after a science lab. Instead of helping, the student complains and says that others should put away the equipment. Schedule an Academy with the student after school. Have the student get out typical lab equipment and supplies; then ask the student to clean up these items properly and put them back in their appropriate places. Thank the student and repeat the procedure. Repeat this procedure several times until the student is successful. This gives you the opportunity to offer praise for appropriate behavior. If the Academy is effective, the student will realize it's a lot easier to comply with your requests the first time than it is to participate in Academies.

Many young people with disruptive and conduct disorders thrive on confrontation. Levy, O'Hanlon, and Goode describe five communication strategies that can help end power struggles with these students. These communication strategies are often effective because they don't give students the satisfaction of upsetting adults.[12]

Use "brain-dead" phrases. These are responses that let a student know that you're not going to be manipulated by arguing and that you refuse to take responsibility for the child's behavior. These phrases follow a student's demand, protest, or mis-behavior. For example, a student says, "I didn't do it!" Your brain-dead response might be, "I understand" (said with sadness), "I'm sorry you feel that way," "I know that's what you think," or "Good try" (with a little smile).

Cool it. Anger from an adult can fuel an angry child. Don't feed the student's anger. Instead douse it with sadness. As you administer a consequence, respond as though you'd rather the situation weren't happening. (You may not actually feel sad, but it's important to act as if you do.) For example, instead of saying angrily, "Jessica, you will not go on our field trip," say sadly, "Jessica, I'm sorry you'll not be able to join us on tomorrow's field trip. I hope your behavior improves so you can come along next time."

Give more choices. Since control is what many defiant students want, give it to them by offering more than one choice. As much as possible, offer positive choices that teach instead of punish. For example, say, "I can give you a deten-tion, or we can talk about why what you did was wrong. Which would you like to do?" or, "I'll listen to you at lunch or after school. When would you like to share your side of the story?"

Zip it! If you must administer a penalty or consequence, name it and don't say another word about what's happened. Lecturing is not only a waste of time, it empowers a student by offering an opportunity to debate or argue.

Don't tell students what they just learned. Never say, "I told you so." It's coun-terproductive to rub a lesson into a child's face. The student has figured it out independently—but may not give you the satisfaction of telling you so.

Refer for alternative placement. Some students, especially those with CD, may not be able to function in the regular classroom. In cases of severe behavior problems, work with a school specialist to determine if outside placement (whether a special class or another school) is appropriate.

Note: Many strategies and accommodations listed for students with ADHD (page 107) can also be useful with students who have disruptive and conduct disorders.

AN ALTERNATIVE TO CONSEQUENCES

In *Lost at School*, Ross Greene says that consequences often don't work.[13] One rea-son is that consequences simply teach the difference between right and wrong. Kids know this already. Another reason is that some students do not know how to behave appropriately. They lack necessary thinking skills, or they may not think before they act. Some students have never learned alternative ways to behave.

Others haven't learned how to resolve conflicts. Still others may misunderstand peers' or teachers' comments or behaviors, so they respond inappropriately.

Greene suggests identifying a student's "lagging skills" in order to teach appropriate behaviors.[14] Misbehaving kids need to learn these skills in order to solve their behavior problems. Greene's Collaborative and Proactive Solutions (CPS) approach allows kids to partner with teachers to solve their problems.[15] This contrasts with traditional discipline methods, including most Positive Behavioral Interventions and Supports (PBIS) programs in which teachers create and impose solutions on students. Greene's procedure begins by identifying one or two "unsolved problems," along with the lagging skills that contribute to those problems. The goal of the CPS process is to teach the skills that will solve the problem. This procedure requires training and practice. Educators should not attempt CPS without this training.

STEPS IN THE CPS APPROACH

1. **Show empathy.** Gather information from the student to understand the student's concern. For example:

   Teacher: "I've noticed you're having trouble staying out of fights. What's going on?"

   Lucas: "Those guys bother me a lot."

   Teacher: "So you're really frustrated with kids annoying you."

   Lucas: "Yeah!"

2. **Define your concerns.** Explain how the student's behavior affects the student and others. For example:

   Teacher: "Well, the problem is that someone can get really hurt, and the fights cause a real commotion. They also interrupt my teaching and other students' learning."

   Lucas: "I don't care. If they keep bothering me, I'm going to get in their face."

3. **Invite the student to collaborate.** Brainstorm and evaluate possible realistic and mutually satisfying solutions. For example:

   Teacher: "I'm wondering if we could come up with some ideas that would help you react to these kids without fighting."

   Lucas: "I don't know."

   Teacher: "Well, let's figure it out together. How about if you tell a teacher when someone is bothering you?"

   Lucas: "No way. If I tell, they'll really get after me."

   Teacher: "Do you think you could say something to them instead of fighting?"

   Lucas: "Like what?"

   Teacher: "There's probably a bunch of different things to say. Let's brainstorm some ideas together."

DEALING WITH AGITATED STUDENTS

Some students with ODD or CD will become verbally or physically agitated. Here are some suggestions for responding to those students in the classroom:[16]

Ask the student to continue the discussion with you privately at the side of the room. Give the student some space, and move even farther away if the student asks you to.

Initially reassure the student. Ask calmly, "What's going on?" Say, "Let's talk about this." This says that you are ready to listen to the student's side of the story.

Maintain nonconfrontational body posture. Stand in an open, relaxed posture with your arms by your sides.

Keep communication brief. Students who are emotionally upset cannot process a lot of language.

Use empathetic responses and active listening. After the student has had a chance to speak, repeat back what you heard. For example, "So it sounds like you're really angry because you think Jijuan started the argument."

Agree with the student when appropriate. For example, "Yeah, I might be angry, too, if I thought I was being unfairly blamed for someone else's behavior."

PROFESSIONAL TREATMENTS

Students with ODD or CD can cause serious problems in a classroom, and there are no simple answers for teachers. The literature on the treatment of CD includes terms such as *intractable, highly resistant to treatment*, and *notoriously hard to treat*. Group treatment has advantages and disadvantages. Residential programs and boot camps have demonstrated some positive short-term outcomes, but worsening outcomes in the long run.

Teaching parents well-established principles of and strategies for child behavior management is the most effective therapeutic intervention for students with disruptive and conduct disorders. A mental health professional typically teaches parents over a period of months how to modify different aspects of their parenting. These modifications include how to communicate with children (especially adolescents), how to establish and communicate rules, how to pay more attention to positive behavior, how to establish and implement appropriate rewards and consequences, and how to respond to protests and noncompliance. Parents can also be trained in CPS.

CHAPTER 14

Self-Injury and Suicide

....

"I was sitting in my car and I knew the gas was coming,
when I had an image of my mother finding me."

—*Halle Berry, actress*

....

Self-injury, or self-harm, includes cutting, bruising, burning, and other acts designed to express emotional pain. Individuals who self-injure are not usually suicidal. Suicide is an act intended to end one's life. Both disorders have been increasing. Self-injury and suicide rates among adolescents have increased so much that the *DSM-5* proposes two new diagnoses for these behaviors. These suggested diagnoses hopefully will lead to more research and permanent inclusion in the next edition of the *DSM*.

Self-Injury

Between 15% and 25% of adolescents harm themselves by cutting, scratching, burning, or biting their bodies—sometimes to an extent requiring medical treatment.[4]

When people self-injure, they are not intending to commit suicide, although these individuals are at greater risk for later suicide attempts.[1] The proposed diagnosis for individuals who self-injure is non-suicidal self-injury (NSSI). Teens with a history of sexual abuse, sexual orientation confusion, bullying, and eating disorders have higher rates of self-injury.[2]

PROPOSED CRITERIA FOR NONSUICIDAL SELF-INJURY (NSSI)[3]

- In the past year, on five or more days an individual has intentionally self-inflicted bodily injury causing bleeding, bruising, or pain. Suicidal intent is absent.

- The individual engages in self-injury to escape from a negative feeling, to resolve an interpersonal problem, *or* to feel better.

- The self-injury is associated with relationship problems, negative emotions, preoccupation with self-injury that is difficult to control, *or* frequent thinking about self-injuring without acting.

- Self-injury causes major distress or interference in interpersonal, academic, or other important areas of life.

Self-injury serves many purposes. People who harm their bodies are usually releasing overwhelming negative emotions such as fear, anger, grief, and help-lessness. Young people who have difficulty expressing emotional pain may use self-injury as an outlet to express their emotional anguish.[5] They exchange their emotional pain for physical pain. Physical pain releases brain endorphins that relieve the pain and create a positive emotional state. Someone who self-injures begins to expect to feel much better after self-injuring, and the frequency of self-injury increases. Recent research suggests that certain abnormalities in brain chemistry may make some people more likely to engage in self-injury.[6]

Behaviors and Symptoms to Look For

It is unlikely you'll observe students in acts of self-harm. They usually are secretive about the behavior. It's more likely that you'll notice suspicious-looking scratches, scars, or burns, usually on a student's wrists or arms. Students may be quick to make excuses for these markings. They also might attempt to hide the markings by wearing long sleeves or pants—even in very warm weather.

Note: Alteration of the body for the purpose of decoration, such as by piercing or tattooing, is not considered self-injury. Family adults, of course, should be involved in a young person's decision to have these procedures done. Many states require this parental permission.

Classroom Strategies and Interventions

Students who self-injure need help from qualified health professionals. These students need to learn how to verbalize and resolve emotional problems. Students who self-injure may also be experiencing mental disorders, which need to be addressed. If you suspect a child of self-injury, it's important that you inform a counselor, school nurse, and other relevant school staff right away.

Following are some suggestions for supporting students who self-injure:

Give students compassion and empathy. Show students you are genuinely interested in their lives and well-being. Ask about their families, friends, interests, and other aspects of their lives. Genuine, sustained interest in a student can have a positive impact. Students are more likely to share their feelings when they regard you as someone who sincerely cares about them.

Respond to students calmly. Observing cuts, carvings, or scars on a student's skin can be shocking. Try your best to respond calmly to a child if you observe suspicious marks. Ask about any wounds you observe in a concerned, nonjudgmental way to try to determine what has caused them. If a student admits to self-injuring, say that sharing this information is an important first step toward getting help. Tell the student that you cannot keep this information confidential. (For guidelines on informing parents, see the sidebar about confidentiality on page 178.)

Show sensitivity. Avoid responding to self-injury with shock or disgust—which a student may perceive as negative judgment. Also avoid invasive questions. ("Why would you want to do that to yourself?") Offer your support and talk about how you will need to involve a counselor in getting help.

Educate yourself about self-injury. Cutting and other self-injurious behaviors are on the rise. Do your best to stay up to date. The resources at the end of this book are good places to begin your efforts.

Talk openly with students about self-injury. Acknowledge that cutting and other forms of self-injury are thought by some to be trendy or cool. Talk about the destructive nature of self-injury and encourage students to reject any peer pressure they might feel to engage in these behaviors.

Note: Self-injury represents a psychological problem that can lead to physical harm and medical consequences. In this way, the disorder is similar to an eating disorder. Many recommendations in chapter 15 are also relevant to students who self-injure.

 GET HELP! Distinguishing whether a student's scratches, burns, or scars are a result of self-injury or simply the signs of a recent accident can be difficult. It's always best to be proactive. If any marks on a student's body make you suspicious, get help from a school nurse or counselor and prepare to inform parents. If you have reason to believe marks are the result of parental abuse, report a student's injuries to the appropriate state agency. Visit www.childwelfare.gov for information on reporting child abuse in your state.

Suicide

The tragic act of taking one's life occurs too often among teenagers. About 18 percent of high school students have contemplated suicide, and 9 percent have attempted to end their lives.[7] In 2015, 2,061 teenagers between the ages of fifteen and nineteen killed themselves.[8] That's more than five teens per day. Among girls, suicides have doubled since 2007. These statistics compelled the authors of the *DSM-5* to propose a new diagnostic category, suicidal behavior disorder.[9] If the next edition of the *DSM* includes this as a permanent diagnosis, individuals who commit acts expected to lead to their deaths would be diagnosed with a suicidal behavior disorder. This diagnosis would not include acts of NSSI.

Most young people who attempt suicide are troubled. Ninety percent of them qualify for at least one *DSM-5* diagnosis.[10] The most common diagnoses are depression, disruptive behavior disorders, substance abuse, anxiety and depressive disorders, and bipolar disorder.[11] Other teens at an elevated risk of suicide are those who identify as gay, lesbian, bisexual, or transgender; those who have been sexual abused; and those who are or have been victims of bullying and cyberbullying.[12]

Behaviors and Symptoms to Look For

Four out of five students who attempt suicide give clear warning signs. These include:

Talking about or having recurrent thoughts about suicide. Students who talk about suicide ("I wish I were dead." "Things would be better if I weren't here.") are not just looking for attention. They're crying out for help and need immediate professional attention.

Feeling helpless or hopeless. Young people may feel overwhelmed and may talk about how there is no possible way for them to overcome problems. ("There's no point in anything without my girlfriend." "I'll never get over that abuse." "Life sucks.")

Prior suicide attempt(s). About 8 percent of teens who commit suicide have made one or more previous attempts.[13]

Feeling worthless or guilt-ridden. Students may express these feelings generally or in regard to a specific event. ("I can't do anything right." "My parents would still be together if it weren't for me.")

Engaging in risky behaviors. Students may seem to have little regard for their own safety. They may drive recklessly or otherwise act in ways that suggest they don't care about their own lives.

Suffering a recent loss or life-changing event. Students are at greater risk for depression and suicide attempts when experiencing a relationship breakup, serious health concerns, abuse, or another significant life event such as separation or divorce of parents.

Engaging in substance abuse. Ninety percent of teens who commit suicide have a substance abuse disorder.[14]

Possessing firearms. Nearly 45 percent of adolescent suicides in 2014 were committed with firearms.[15]

Saying goodbye or giving things away. Students may indirectly say goodbye or give prized possessions to friends. ("If I don't see you again, have a good life." "You can have my mp3 player—I won't need it anymore.")

WHAT'S YOUR SELF-INJURY AND SUICIDE IQ?

Choose *T* if the statement is true or *F* if the statement is false.

1. Suicide is the fourth most common cause of death among adolescents. T F

2. White people are more likely to commit suicide than people of color are. T F

3. Differences in brain stress chemicals have been found in suicidal individuals. T F

4. Adolescents who attempt suicide but don't succeed aren't likely to try again. T F

5. Asking people whether they've considered killing themselves may cause them to become suicidal. T F

6. Mental health professionals are good at predicting suicide attempts. T F

7. Boys are as likely as girls to engage in NSSI. T F

8. Teens who self-injure do not attempt to die, but these acts increase the likelihood of future suicide attempts. T F

9. Most young people who engage in self-injury will outgrow this behavior before adulthood. T F

10. When a teen commits suicide, it is a good idea to hold a school assembly to remember the student and learn about suicide. T F

Answers

1. **F.** Suicide is the second most common cause, behind traffic fatalities.

2. **T.** In 2014, more than 14,000 middle-aged white people killed themselves. That number is double the *combined* suicide totals for middle-aged African Americans, Hispanics, Asians, Pacific Islanders, American Indians, and Alaska Natives.[16]

3. **T.** Brain imaging studies found that a part of the brain associated with decision-making was less active in people who attempted suicide. In addition, cellular and molecular differences were observed in the brains of people who attempted suicide.[17]

4. **F.** Almost 25 percent will try again within one year.

5. **F.** There is no evidence that asking will give people the idea that suicide is an option.[18] In fact, asking may communicate that you take a person's problem very seriously.

6. **F.** Unfortunately, even trained professionals are not very good at predicting suicide. Recent research has found that computer algorithms based on people's social media language may predict suicidal behavior much better than humans can.[19]

7. **F.** Girls are two to three times more likely to commit NSSI than boys are.

8. **T.** Self-injury is a stronger predictor of future suicide attempts than previous suicide attempts are.[20]

9. **F.** Self-injury usually persists for ten to fifteen years without treatment. Fifty percent of adolescents will continue to self-injure as adults.

10. **F.** *After a Suicide: A Toolkit for Schools* created by the American Foundation for Suicide Prevention and the Suicide Prevention Resource Center recommends that school memorials or funerals take place outside of school after school hours. It is important to continue the normal school schedule, structure, and routine. In addition, holding a ceremony in a school room may connect that room to the student's death. School personnel should also monitor for a contagion or clustering effect—the possibility that other students might try to imitate a suicide attempt shortly after an incident has occurred.[21] Older teens are two to four times more likely to be influenced by these effects compared to other age groups.[22]

Responding to Signs of Suicide/Classroom Strategies and Interventions

Take all threats of suicide seriously. Don't dismiss suicidal talk or suspicious actions as attention-seeking behavior.

Listen to what students have to say. Be supportive and nonjudgmental in your responses to students. Avoid cliché responses that may sound insincere. Instead, genuinely empathize with students and listen to them. Affirm that sharing depressed or suicidal feelings is the first step toward getting help.

Don't agree to keep a student's secret. It is your responsibility to inform others at school about students' suicidal thoughts or wishes. Show appreciation for their trust in you and offer your full support. Also let students know that the responsibility you have to help them necessitates involving their parents and a counselor (or another specialist on staff).

Get immediate help. Don't take responsibility for a student's life. As soon as possible, get help from a counselor or school psychologist. If you feel a student is in imminent danger, do not leave the student alone.

Read guidelines for schools. *After a Suicide: A Toolkit for Schools* provides comprehensive strategies for teachers and schools to help students in the aftermath of a classmate's suicide. You can download the guide at the American Foundation for Suicide Prevention website (afsp.org).

PROFESSIONAL TREATMENTS

Students who self-injure or who contemplate or attempt suicide need treatment from a mental health professional. Dialectical behavior therapy (DBT) appears to be an effective treatment for these individuals. This therapy emphasizes mindfulness, emotion regulation, distress tolerance, and interpersonal communication skills.

CHAPTER 15

Eating Disorders

Including Anorexia Nervosa (AN), Bulimia Nervosa (BN), and Binge Eating Disorder (BED)

. . . .

> "If I'd gained like half a pound, I'd assume everyone was pointing and laughing at the fat girl. It was so hard to force myself to go to school and face the world those days."
>
> —*Adolescent with an eating disorder*

. . . .

In the United States and Europe, more than 50 percent of ten-year-old girls are worried about their weight. By adolescence, 46 to 80 percent report dissatisfaction with their weight. Many of these girls start dieting, which is the biggest predictor of an eating disorder in later years.[1]

Millions of young people have eating disorders, including anorexia nervosa (AN), bulimia nervosa (BN), and binge eating disorder (BED). AN and BN involve unrealistic perceptions that one is too heavy. Intense fear of gaining weight leads to restriction of food intake and inappropriate behaviors to prevent weight gain. Individuals with BED eat excessive amounts during short periods of time and feel a lack of control over their eating. Many other students not diagnosed with eating disorders obsessively exercise, severely restrict their diets, or have other unhealthy attitudes toward weight and food.

WHAT'S YOUR EATING DISORDER IQ?

Choose *T* if the statement is true or *F* if the statement is false.

1. It's possible to tell if people have an eating disorder by looking at them.　T　F
2. Eating disorders affect only middle-class girls.　T　F
3. Eating disorders are lifestyle choices individuals make.　T　F
4. Perfectionism causes eating disorders.　T　F
5. Many young people with eating disorders also engage in self-injury.　T　F
6. Eating disorders are a phase teenagers will grow out of.　T　F
7. Hospital or residential treatment is necessary for some individuals with eating disorders.　T　F
8. Parents cause eating disorders by focusing too much on food and weight in early childhood.　T　F
9. A person can never fully recover from an eating disorder.　T　F
10. Medication is frequently used in treating individuals with eating disorders.　T　F

Answers

1. **F.** People with AN will likely look too thin, but individuals with BN or BED may have normal weight or be overweight.

2. **F.** Eating disorders occur in people of all ethnicities, races, genders, and socioeconomic classes.

3. **F.** Eating disorders are serious, biologically influenced illnesses.

4. **F.** Perfectionism is common in individuals with eating disorders, but it does not cause eating disorders.

5. **T.** About 40 percent of individuals with eating disorders also self-injure. A number of similarities between eating disorders and self-injury are covered in the book *Self-Harm and Eating Disorders in Schools: A Guide to Whole-School Strategies and Practical Support* by Pooky Knightsmith.[2]

6. **F.** It is highly unlikely that someone with a diagnosed eating disorder will grow out of it without treatment.

7. **T.** Individuals who haven't been successful in outpatient therapy and those whose eating disorder puts them in medical danger will need hospital or residential treatment.

8. **F.** Some individuals with eating disorders claim that their parents were preoccupied with food and weight, but this alone does not cause the development of an eating disorder.

9. **F.** With treatment, many individuals partially or fully overcome eating disorders. AN is the most challenging eating disorder to overcome.

10. **T.** Antidepressants are commonly used to rebalance certain brain chemicals in people with eating disorders.

While it's common for people to be concerned about food and weight, those with eating disorders have extreme attitudes and behaviors that extend beyond a healthy diet and exercise. In general, this is not the only problem for these individuals. At least 50 percent and up to 90 percent of those affected have an additional diagnosable mental disorder. Depressive and anxiety disorders are most common.

About 90% of people with eating disorders are female.[5] Although only 0.3% of adolescent females have AN,[6] it is the third most prevalent chronic illness among adolescents.[7] Between 1% and 5% of adolescents experience BN, while just over 1% have BED.[8]

Multiple factors lead to eating disorders, including family history, biological brain differences, and childhood trauma and neglect.[3] Individuals with eating disorders may be perfectionistic, have difficulty expressing feelings, have low self-esteem, or come from a controlling family.[4]

A major influence for the development of eating disorders is society's thin ideal, emphasized by the media. Children as young as six years old become aware of society's preferences for personal appearance.[9] Elite athletes and dancers may also have a tendency to reduce their weight in unhealthy ways.

Students with eating disorders often don't realize their habits are self-destructive. They may even pride themselves on how they are much more disciplined than others are. In truth, eating disorders are potentially life-threatening. Individuals with eating disorders have a higher risk of death, either from suicide or medical complications.[10]

Behaviors and Symptoms to Look For

Adolescence is the age when eating disorders usually appear, though younger and younger children are now showing unhealthy attitudes toward food and diet. Students often are secretive about their eating habits. They may deny or try to cover up symptoms so they can continue their behavior. In addition to problems with food and weight, these students may engage in cutting or other self-harming behaviors (see chapter 14).

The three main types of eating disorders are:

Anorexia nervosa (AN). There are two types of AN. In the restricting type, students severely limit how much they eat, leading to a very low body weight. They have an intense fear of gaining weight, and they don't realize the severity of their low body weight. Body image is distorted in these children. They may perceive themselves to be "fat" regardless of how they look or how much weight they lose. In the binge eating/purging type, individuals binge-eat and purge through vomiting, laxatives, or diuretics.[11] These individuals develop AN as a result of their binging and purging. Individuals with BN or BED do not develop AN. Symptoms of AN may include:

- rapid weight loss
- frequent comments about being "fat," "gross," or "ugly"
- paleness, dark circles under eyes, and gaunt features
- dizziness and fainting spells
- complaints of being cold
- intense, dramatic mood swings
- hair loss
- abuse of laxatives, diuretics, and diet pills
- cessation of menstruation
- frequent excuses for not eating
- restricted eating
- preoccupation with food, calories, and cooking
- frequent self-weighing or measuring
- excessive and compulsive exercise
- wearing loose, baggy clothes

Bulimia nervosa (BN). People who have BN have episodes of binge eating. This means that within a two-hour period, they eat a much larger amount of (often unhealthy) food than most people would eat. They show a lack of control while bingeing. Shortly after a binge, they attempt to rid themselves of calories by purging through vomiting, laxatives, diuretics, fasting, or excessive exercise. Individuals with BN evaluate themselves according to their body shape and weight. Students with BN can be particularly difficult to observe, because they often maintain a normal weight. Like AN, BN can lead to medical illness and death. Symptoms of BN may include:

- bingeing and purging
- visits to the bathroom after meals
- secretive eating
- chewing lots of gum or drinking lots of water
- swollen glands in neck and puffiness in cheeks
- complaints of sore throat
- broken blood vessels in eyes
- tooth decay and erosion of enamel
- abuse of laxatives, ipecac, and diuretics
- excessive and compulsive exercise

Binge eating disorder (BED). Students with this disorder binge, but do not purge. They may eat much more quickly than normal and not stop until they're uncomfortably full. They may eat large amounts of food even when they don't feel hungry, or they may eat alone because they are embarrassed about how much they eat. Those who engage in these behaviors often feel disgusted, depressed, or guilty after overeating. Symptoms of binge eating disorder include:

- frequently eating abnormally large amounts of food until uncomfortably full
- inability to control eating
- secretive eating
- feelings of distress while bingeing
- frequently overweight

People do not always fall neatly into one category of eating disorders. Some people have more than one eating disorder or a combination of symptoms. For example, students with AN may periodically binge and purge in addition to limiting what they eat. Others may have some characteristics of eating disorders but not enough to qualify for a diagnosis.

Classroom Strategies and Interventions

Eating disorders affect cognitive functions, so students with eating disorders will likely have trouble with concentration, memory, and work production.

Eating disorders should be diagnosed only by a qualified health professional. If a student has not been diagnosed but you observe symptoms, it's important to report any concerning behaviors to the student's parents, counselors, the school nurse, and other school staff.

Following are some suggestions for helping students with eating disorders:

Build strong relationships with students. Students often are secretive about their unhealthy food attitudes and body image. Your best antidote to secrecy is to gain the confidence of your students. Showing empathy and genuine interest in a student can help you establish trust. A positive relationship is essential if you'll be talking with a student about your concerns.

Avoid insensitive comments. Eating disorders are serious and potentially deadly. Off-the-cuff remarks ("You look like a skeleton; you should eat something." "You could use some exercise.") can have a strong negative effect upon students.

Talk about unhealthy body image and model healthy eating habits. Regardless of whether you teach a health course, take opportunities to address the media's unrealistic portrayals of the "perfect" body. Shift students' thinking from looking a certain way to being healthy. Talk about healthy attitudes you have about body image, nutrition, and exercise.

Give students consistent reassurance. Compliment students on talents, accomplishments, creativity, and values. Teach students that they're much more than what they look like—that you value them based on what's on the inside, not on their appearances.

Address perfectionism in your classroom. Many students with eating disorders are perfectionistic. Their pursuit of a "perfect" body may coincide with being perfect in other areas—including schoolwork. Impress upon students that perfection is an impossible (and debilitating) goal.

Eliminate teasing. Students with eating disorders may get criticized about their weight. Establish a zero-tolerance policy on teasing, taunting, ridiculing, and other negative statements. Chapter 2 suggests ways you can address teasing and other bullying behaviors.

Allow for flexibility in a student's workload. Eating disorders and the physical problems they cause can make it difficult for students to focus on schoolwork. As appropriate, reduce classroom pressures.

What to Do If You're Concerned About a Student's Well-Being[12]

Be available when a student wants to talk. As an educator, you play an important role in students' lives. Closely monitor those students who seem troubled. Initiate conversations with them and be aware of times in which it seems they might want to talk with you. These students might appear anxious and come to class early, hang around after class, or start a conversation with you but seem to talk around a problem. If students do open up to you, make time to listen, avoid judgment, and share information as appropriate with parents and other school staff.

Schedule a time to speak to the student in private. Allow sufficient time for a lengthy conversation.

Communicate care and concern about the student. In a nonjudgmental way, describe observations that you're concerned about. For example, "Is everything okay?" or, "You don't seem to be like your old self these days." If a student has an eating disorder, it's not likely that he will disclose this. But your concern is important and may be an initial indication that a student can trust you with a further disclosure someday. If nothing changes, another inquiry in a week or two would impress the student with your concern.

Inform parents. You aren't legally required to report a student you suspect has an eating disorder. But if a student doesn't acknowledge a problem with eating and you remain concerned, call a meeting with your school counselor, nurse, and other educators who are familiar with the student. Let the group come to a consensus so the burden is not entirely on you. If the group's consensus is that a disorder is likely, ask the student what the next step might be. If the student is not sure, say that her parents should be informed. Ask the student whether she would prefer to tell them or have you talk with them. Be prepared to offer the student and family local resources, websites, and phone numbers.

Respond to a student's concerns about parents' reactions. Students might say, "They won't get it" or, "They'll get angry." Let students know you'll be their advocate and help parents understand why you're concerned. Your goal is to work as a team with students and their parents.

Follow up. If students choose to talk to their parents, give them a time frame and follow up with a phone call to parents asking if their child spoke with them and what the content of the conversation was. If students prefer that you communicate with their parents, attempt to set up a face-to-face meeting. If that is not possible, make a phone call.

Evaluate parents' reactions. Parents may say they've been aware of the problem. Ask what they're doing to help their child. If a professional evaluation has not been done, suggest one. If the parents become defensive or angry, reiterate your concern.

Keep a written record of all conversations and their outcomes. This is to ensure that you have documented your communications.

EATING DISORDERS AND TEACHER-STUDENT CONFIDENTIALITY

Teachers have a duty to prevent a student's death or serious medical complications from an eating disorder. How can you determine if a student is that ill? You can't. Only a mental health or medical professional can. If you suspect or observe signs of an eating disorder, inform your school nurse and counselor. School counselors have a duty to inform and protect students engaged in any self-destructive behavior. Legal and ethical considerations for school counselors are discussed in a paper included in the resource section titled "Duty to Warn and Protect Against Self-Destructive Behaviors and Interpersonal Violence."[13]

Supporting Students During and After Residential Treatment

Some young people with eating disorders, like other students with severe mental health disorders, will require months of residential treatment. Following are ways you can support these students during and after treatment:[14]

Arrange communication with the residential facility. With permission from the student's family, designate one person from your school who will receive updates and communicate them to classmates. If other children know that the student with an eating disorder is in residential treatment, ask them to write notes or letters to the student. If the facility allows mobile phones, classmates can text messages to the student.

Provide academic work if appropriate. The facility will let you know how capable the student is of performing academic work. If appropriate, arrange assignments and facilitate delivery of work materials.

Upon the student's discharge from residential treatment, meet with the student and parents. It has likely been several months since the student was in school. A smooth reintegration is essential for continued progress. A gradual return in phases may be appropriate.

Modify academic expectations. Allow for a range of accommodations ranging from very little work to a full course load, based on the opinions of the student, the family, and the treatment team. Students with eating disorders may be perfectionistic. If you know a student will get a lower-than-desired grade on a paper or test, offer reassurance. Note the remarkable performance, given what the student has been through. Be prepared to reduce the workload quickly and nonjudgmentally if it proves overwhelming.

Discuss potential triggers with the student. A student may identify triggers that provoke distress. These might include teasing, participating in physical education, speaking in front of the class, eating in the cafeteria, or pressures to perform academically. Reassure the student that you will arrange accommodations to eliminate these concerns.

Allow the student to leave class without permission. A student may still suffer anxiety and other negative emotions after treatment. Arrange for this student to leave class and go to the school counselor or another adult if the need arises.

Remain alert to ongoing signs of an eating disorder. Many individuals relapse after treatment. Without being obvious, continue to observe the student.

PROFESSIONAL TREATMENTS

Eating disorders are most effectively addressed by a multidisciplinary team that includes psychiatrists, psychologists, physicians, nutritionists, and other medical professionals. A student may continue to struggle with an eating disorder after beginning treatment. Full or partial recovery can be a long process.

CHAPTER 16

Trauma and Stressor-Related Disorders

Including Adverse Childhood Experiences (ACEs), Bullying and School Violence, and Post-Traumatic Stress Disorder (PTSD)

. . . .

"When I step back and consider the obstacles in my students' lives—poverty, trauma, chronic stress—it makes total sense that they are struggling to communicate, regulate their emotions, and make progress on learning."

—Alex Shevrin, teacher

. . . .

A large number of students are exposed to adverse childhood experiences (ACEs) such as abuse, parental separation, or divorce. Students may also witness domestic violence, substance abuse, mental illness, and adult incarceration. They may experience bullying or school violence. Some are exposed to actual or threatened death, serious injury, or sexual violence. These events are traumatic. They change the brain and interfere with academic and emotional functioning, and they may cause post-traumatic stress disorder (PTSD).

Adverse Childhood Experiences (ACEs)

People experience events differently. One student may experience a negative event with little adverse reaction, while the same event can adversely affect another child for life. Sometimes, students do not think an experience has harmed them, but it has actually affected their brain in ways that will influence their behavior. Therefore, trauma must be defined by the impact rather than the nature of an event.[1]

Some childhood experiences are almost always traumatic. The Adverse Childhood Experiences Study (ACE Study) in the 1990s showed that these experiences included multiple types of abuse, domestic violence, substance abuse, mental illness, separation or divorce, and adult incarceration.[2]

ACEs create a fight-or-flight response in the brain, causing the release of stress hormones, which cause changes in the brain. The more ACEs a student experiences, the more damaging the neurobiological changes in the brain are. These changes can create vulnerability to disease, psychological disorders, and cognitive disorders. Consider students who live in places where they often hear gunshots or who have lost family and friends to violence. These children live in a constant state of emergency, which has lasting physical and emotional effects.[3]

THE IMPACT OF ACES

The prevalence and consequences of ACEs are striking:[4]

- Almost two-thirds of adults report having at least one ACE by age sixteen; more than one in five report three or more ACEs.

- Students with lower socioeconomic statuses are much more vulnerable to ACEs.

- Students experiencing ACEs are at higher risk for ADHD, oppositional defiant disorder (ODD), depression, anxiety, and PTSD.

- ACEs are associated with lower grades, increased absences and dropouts, grade retention, lower test scores, increased suspensions and expulsions, and more special education referrals.

Bullying and School Violence

Schools are not necessarily safe places. While schools are addressing bullying, it still occurs too frequently. Bullying is abuse. It can be considered an ACE and may be traumatic for students. The effects of bullying can last a lifetime. Victims of bullying have higher rates of suicide, depression, low self-esteem, and anxiety.[5]

Additionally, school shootings reported in the media expose children to the potential danger of such events. Knowing that fellow students or someone outside of school can shoot students in school can cause some students to feel constant apprehension during the school day.

Recognizing that many students have experienced trauma from ACEs, including school bullying and violence, school districts have responded with policies and programs to help these children feel safe and supported. The terms used to describe these programs are *trauma-aware, trauma-sensitive,* and *trauma-informed schools*. These programs are designed to help all students—especially those who are most vulnerable—feel safe. Programs can be included in a school's Multi-Tiered System of Supports, or MTSS (see chapter 2), or they can be separate. You'll find more information about these programs in the resources on page 230.

High School Bullying and School Violence Statistics

- 20% of high school students have been bullied on school property; 16% have been victims of cyberbullying.

- 8% of students have participated in a fight at some point.

- 5% of students have refused to go to school on one or more days in the past thirty days because they feel unsafe.

- 4% of students carry a weapon on school property.

- 9% of teachers have been threatened with injury by a student; 5% have been physically attacked by a student.[6]

Post-Traumatic Stress Disorder (PTSD)

Students who experience PTSD have been exposed to traumatic events such as actual or threatened death, serious injury, or sexual violence. They have either directly experienced or witnessed the traumatic event, have learned that the event happened to a family member or close friend, or have been exposed to graphic details of the event. These students experience symptoms related to the event, which may include recurrent distressing memories, dreams, flashbacks, and intense psychological or physical distress when experiencing reminders. People who have PTSD also experience avoidance of memories, thoughts, feelings, or external reminders of the event.

NATURAL DISASTERS AND TRAUMA

Multiple natural disasters were traumatic experiences for many children in North America in 2017. Life-threatening hurricanes Harvey, Irma, and Maria; an earthquake in Mexico; and fires in California and Montana created homelessness and lack of schooling for thousands of students.

General changes in mood and thoughts are common in students with PTSD. Some students forget aspects of the traumatic event. Others develop cynical views about themselves (self-blame) or the world. Still others develop a persistent negative mood, a decreased interest in certain activities, or an inability to experience positive emotions. To be diagnosed with PTSD, a student must also experience at least two of the following changes: irritability and anger, reckless or self-destructive behavior, hypervigilance, startle responses, and problems with concentration or sleep.

RISK AND RESILIENCY FACTORS FOR POST-TRAUMATIC STRESS DISORDER

Risk Factors

- **Severity.** The more serious a trauma, the more likely it is to have long-lasting effects.

- **Physical injury.** A child who is physically injured in an event may feel trauma more intensely.

- **Involvement.** Those directly involved in a traumatic event (as opposed to witnessing it) are more likely to experience PTSD.

- **History.** Children who've experienced trauma in the past are more likely to be severely affected by another traumatic event.

- **Family.** Family instability or family dysfunction can make children more susceptible to PTSD. A family history of PTSD also increases the likelihood of PTSD because of a genetic predisposition to the disorder.[7]

Resiliency Factors

- **Social and family support.** Positive support from family members and others who care for a student can help reduce an event's effect.

- **Coping mechanisms.** These may include anxiety-reducing strategies a child has learned prior to the trauma.

- **Safety.** Children are not as hypervigilant if they perceive their school as a safe place and know their teachers will protect them.

Behaviors and Symptoms to Look For

You may not know whether a student has experienced an adverse or traumatic event. Even when you do know what's happened in a child's life, symptoms and triggers can vary widely among students.

ACEs and traumas might create specific triggers leading to emotional responses from students with PTSD.[8]

Students who have experienced trauma may have symptoms that include:

Fight, flight, or freeze behaviors. Fight behaviors include hyperactivity, verbal or physical aggression, limit testing, and oppositional behavior. Flight behaviors include withdrawal, avoidance, escaping, running away, and self-isolation. Freeze behaviors include watchfulness, looking dazed, daydreaming, forgetfulness, and shutting down emotionally.[9]

Constant fear and vigilance. Students may experience all-consuming terror and become hypervigilant of their surroundings. They believe constant alertness can help them avoid future trauma, and they are extremely sensitive to environmental cues they believe may signify danger.

Constant apprehension during the school day. Students who have been bullied worry constantly about being victimized again. All students (including those who have not been exposed to trauma) may worry about the possibility of a school shooter.

Separation anxiety. Young children who experience trauma may become overly attached to parents or caregivers. Children often fear that once they're outside the protection of parents or caregivers, the traumatic event will recur. See page 78 for more information on separation anxiety disorder.

Difficulty with confrontation, authority, or limit setting. These actions by an adult can remind students of abuse.

Tendency to experience overstimulation. The brains of traumatized students are constantly hyperaroused. Overstimulation can occur very easily.

Extreme moodiness. Trauma can create moodiness, depression, or anxiety. Most students with a PTSD diagnosis have significant anxiety and depression.

Loneliness. Students likely felt very alone when experiencing the trauma. No one prevented the event or protected them from it. Certain situations in school may evoke feelings of loneliness, which in turn can make these students feel vulnerable.

Sudden change or drop-off in interests. Students who were once outgoing and had many interests may suddenly become withdrawn and refrain from activities they previously enjoyed. Younger children may stop playing games they like. Older students may avoid or limit participation in extracurricular activities.

Stress associated with triggers. Students may have unexpected reactions to what seem like normal daily routines. Certain objects, places, or people at school may remind them of the trauma they've experienced. This association also can extend to conversations or ideas from the curriculum. Loud unknown noises may evoke the fear of gunshots. Students most often will attempt to avoid these triggers.

Overreaction to unpredictability or sudden change. Students likely were exposed to trauma(s) without warning. As a result, they may overreact to sudden changes in the classroom.

Anxiety over loss of control. Students had no control over the traumatic events they experienced. Situations in which they have no input or control can trigger anxiety.

Play that reenacts the trauma. Students, especially younger children, may begin to play in ways that include themes of the trauma. Young children who have been sexually abused may reenact this behavior with other children.

Abuse of alcohol or other drugs. Middle and high school students may use alcohol or other drugs to try to reduce the anxiety they feel.

Classroom Strategies and Interventions

PTSD can create problems with mood and anxiety. Family and teacher support are essential to help students overcome the effects of a traumatic experience. Even with this support, some students experience long-lasting effects from the trauma, which can influence how you teach and relate to them in the classroom.

In addition to the suggestions in this chapter, recommendations for other mood and anxiety disorders can be helpful (see chapters 8 and 10). Following are strategies to help you support students who have experienced trauma.

Monitor and support students you suspect may have experienced trauma. You may know students who have been bullied in school or cyberbullied. Monitor these students closely for further signs of bullying. In helping students with trauma, it would be ideal if you knew the trauma they experienced or witnessed. However, you may not have this information if families don't disclose it. Your best antidote to secrecy is to gain the confidence of your students. Showing empathy and genuine interest in a student can help you establish trust. If students share their situations with you, work with school staff to provide support. Supportive systems can be integrated in your MTSS procedures (see chapter 2).

Create a sense of safety and security in students. Children who have experienced a traumatic event can benefit a great deal from words of comfort and strong, trusting relationships. Make sure your school—and especially your classroom—is a place where students can feel safe. Point out safety features to students. Research your state's laws or policies regarding school bullying and harassment at www.stopbullying.gov. Encourage your administration to establish a school safety policy and clearly communicate it to students.[10]

Create a calm, predictable environment. Students with PTSD or those who have experienced bullying may become anxious when routines vary. Make your classroom a place of consistency where students know what to expect. Discuss with students schedule changes, field trips, or other special events well in advance. You can find more information on creating consistent routines in chapter 1.

Empower students. Students need to feel a sense of control over their environment. When possible, involve students in decisions and policies that affect them. Consider a student-centered approach to learning, giving students choices and some control over what and how they study.[11]

Consistently enforce limits. You will have to establish some policies and limits without students' input. Make sure these are enforced in a consistent, predictable way to minimize surprises.

Be especially sensitive to students' backgrounds. Students living in cities are more likely to experience trauma than their peers from suburban or rural environments are.[12] Students whose families have immigrated recently may have left countries where violence or war is common.

Provide a safe place for students who become overwhelmed. Traumatic memories and associations might be triggered by various stimuli within the classroom. Should this happen, allow the student to visit a previously designated place to escape the troubling stimuli. Calling on a school counselor or school psychologist who is familiar with the student's history might be helpful.

Modify academic requirements. Design curriculum accommodations according to the severity of a student's PTSD. If emotional difficulties are causing the student to struggle in the classroom, accommodations might include a reduction in workload, flexible deadlines, or alternative assignments.

Be flexible with students' classes and schedules. Allow a student to change a class or schedule to avoid bullying.

Speak with the school counselor, the student's parents, and outside professionals working with the child. Some students' families may not share information about a child's traumatic event. Try to open lines of communication with parents and any mental health professionals treating the student, so that all adults are well informed and working together.

EMILIA

Emilia entered sixth grade far away from home. Her family had been displaced in 2017 when Hurricane Maria destroyed their home and Emilia's school in Puerto Rico. The family was stranded for three days before being rescued. Emilia remembered standing on top of furniture to avoid the floodwaters.

She had been in her new school for a couple of months when teachers began to grow concerned. Emilia always looked very worried. Changes in routines upset her, as did ordinary classroom sounds. She frequently daydreamed, and teachers often had to remind her to pay attention. She also asked to be seated away from windows. She was especially anxious on very windy, cloudy, or rainy days.

The guidance counselor requested a meeting with Emilia's parents. They had noticed her anxiety whenever rain, thunder, or lightning occurred. She also became upset when she saw footage of hurricanes on television. Emilia often awoke to nightmares and would demand to sleep with her parents—something she hadn't done since she was four years old.

The guidance counselor spoke with the school psychologist, and the consensus was that Emilia was likely experiencing PTSD. The school team referred the family to a local social service agency for counseling and developed a plan for teachers to respond to Emilia's anxiety. These interventions included seating Emilia away from windows, preparing her for changes in schedules or activities, notifying her of predictable loud noises (such as scheduled fire drills), and repeating any instructions her inattention might cause her to miss.

PROFESSIONAL TREATMENTS

Students who experience PTSD may benefit from more than one type of therapy. Cognitive-behavioral therapy (CBT) is a technique that gradually exposes a child to a stimulus associated with the trauma while helping the child think in a different way about the event. Eye movement desensitization and reprocessing (EMDR) is another treatment shown to be effective, as is trauma incident reduction therapy (TIR). Therapists must be trained in these specialized techniques.

If an anxiety or a depressive disorder accompanies PTSD, medications for these disorders can be helpful. See chapters 8 and 10.

 GET HELP! Students with PTSD may experience terrifying trauma-related flashbacks at any time. These children may have other extreme emotional reactions that can frighten them and other students. Teachers should be prepared to get immediate assistance to safely accompany a student out of class to see a counselor or school psychologist.

CHAPTER 17

A Final Word

"I have come to a frightening conclusion. I am the decisive element in the classroom. It is my personal approach that creates the climate. It is my daily mood that makes the weather. As a teacher I possess tremendous power to make a child's life miserable or joyous. I can be a tool of torture or an instrument of inspiration. I can humiliate or humor, hurt or heal. In all situations, it is my response that decides whether a crisis will be escalated or de-escalated, and a child humanized or dehumanized."

—Haim Ginott, educator and author

In this revised and updated book, I hope to have provided you with the latest knowledge and best practices for teaching kids with mental health and learning disorders. I'd like to leave you with a final thought to remember: Students with mental health and learning disorders did not choose to experience their challenges. But you can choose to identify and respond to these students in ways that accommodate their needs and show that you understand. With your empathy and responsiveness, you can instill confidence in these students and motivate them to achieve their full potential. Thank you for being committed to the education of all children—especially those with mental health and learning disorders.

Glossary of Mental Health Disorders

adjustment disorder with depressed mood: This type of depressive disorder begins within three months of an identifiable stressful event. Changes in mood are out of proportion to the severity or intensity of the stressor. The depressed mood also creates impairment in an important area of functioning.

adverse childhood experiences (ACEs): Many types of harmful experiences in childhood predict a higher likelihood of adult mental health disorders. These events include physical, sexual, and substance abuse; domestic violence; mental illness; and parental separation or divorce.

agoraphobia: An intense fear triggered by exposure to at least two situations such as riding in cars, being in open or enclosed spaces, being in a crowd, or being away from home.

anorexia nervosa (AN): This potentially lethal disorder has three characteristics: ongoing restriction of food, extreme fear of weight gain or being fat or behavior that limits weight gain, and self-perceived distortion of body weight.

anxiety disorders: Anxiety disorders are the most common mental health disorders in the United States. Students affected by these disorders experience uncontrollable and persistent fears and worries that interfere significantly with their abilities to function academically or socially. Anxiety disorders include generalized anxiety disorder (GAD), panic disorder, school refusal, separation anxiety, social anxiety disorder (SAD), and specific phobia.

apraxia: This speech disorder, which makes it difficult for students to speak, is caused by the brain's inability to send messages to muscles in the mouth.

attention deficit hyperactivity disorder (ADHD): Students with this disorder have difficulty sustaining attention to nonstimulating activities. Some of these children are impulsive and hyperactive. Many have weaknesses in memory, organization, and planning. Very young children may show only impulsivity and hyperactivity since young students are not required to pay attention for long periods.

autism spectrum disorder (ASD): Persistent deficits in social communication and social interaction in multiple contexts characterize students with ASD. They also have restricted, repetitive patterns of behavior, interests, or activities. ASD can look very different in students depending on the severity of a child's disorder.

binge eating disorder (BED): Students who have this disorder eat a much greater amount of food in a two-hour period than most people would. They engage in this behavior at least once a week, have little control over it, and often feel distress over the behavior.

bipolar disorder: Students with bipolar disorder experience moods that alternate between irritability with increased energy for at least one week and a depressed mood or loss of interest or pleasure. These two moods occur during the same two-week period.

bullying and school violence: Bullying is unwanted verbal, physical, or relational aggression meant to harm another person. School violence includes bullying, fights, and shootings.

bulimia nervosa (BN): Students with BN have persistent episodes of binge eating, ongoing and inappropriate behaviors (purging) that limit weight gain, and a self-image excessively influenced by weight. They show little control over these behaviors.

childhood-onset fluency disorder (stuttering): Students with dysfluent speech omit sounds, repeat sounds or words, pause in the middle of words, substitute words, hesitate while speaking, or have broken speech.

communication disorders: These disorders involve difficulties with speech, language, and understanding and expressing thoughts and ideas.

conduct disorder (CD): Conduct disorder refers to students who engage in serious behavior violations such as showing aggression, destroying of property, lying, stealing, or breaking the law.

depressive disorders: These mood disorders cause sadness or irritability as well as other cognitive and physical changes depending on the specific depressive disorder.

disruptive and conduct disorders: These disorders refer to problems in the self-control of emotions and behaviors. Students with disruptive and conduct disorders create conflicts with others or society. These disorders include oppositional defiant disorder (ODD) and conduct disorder (CD).

disruptive mood dysregulation disorder (DMDD): This new diagnosis refers to students who have severe, recurrent verbal or physical outbursts that are out of proportion to the situation. In between outbursts, these children are irritable or angry on most days. The diagnosis is predicted to apply to many children who were previously diagnosed with bipolar disorder.

dyscalculia: A specific learning disorder with impairment in math.

dysgraphia: A specific learning disorder with impairment in written expression is sometimes referred to by this term (also called *developmental coordination disorder*).

dyslexia: Dyslexia is a specific type of reading disability characterized by poor word identification, phonetic decoding, and spelling.

eating disorders: Students with eating disorders have an ongoing pattern of eating and other behaviors that lead to a modified intake or absorption of food. This pattern typically impairs a student's physical health or social functioning. Eating disorders include anorexia nervosa (AN), bulimia nervosa (BN), and binge eating disorder (BED).

generalized anxiety disorder (GAD): Generalized anxiety disorder is a condition in which children worry excessively about many aspects of life. These students may feel anxiety even when there is no objective reason to be worried.

hairpulling (trichotillomania): Students frequently and compulsively pull hair from their scalps, eyebrows, and eyelashes. This disorder sometimes coexists with OCD.

language disorder: Students who have problems understanding language or experience difficulty expressing themselves verbally or in writing may have a language disorder.

major depressive disorder (MDD): This serious type of depression occurs when a depressed or irritable mood or loss of interest or pleasure is present for two weeks along with at least three of the following symptoms: weight loss, weight gain, sleeping problems, agitation, fatigue, concentration and decision-making problems, or feelings of worthlessness or guilt.

neurodevelopmental disorders: This new *DSM-5* category includes all conditions that begin in early childhood. These disorders are characterized by developmental deficits that impair a student's personal, social, or academic functioning. Neurodevelopmental disorders include attention deficit hyperactivity disorder (ADHD), autism spectrum disorder (ASD), specific learning disorder (SLD), tic disorders, and Tourette syndrome.

nonsuicidal self-injury disorder (NSSI): Individuals with this proposed diagnosis engage in intentional, self-inflicted damage to the surface of their bodies that causes bleeding, bruising, or pain. These are not suicidal acts. Self-injurious acts are performed to resolve an interpersonal difficulty, obtain relief from a negative feeling, or create a positive emotional state.

nonverbal learning disability (NVLD): This uncommon disability does not primarily affect academic skills. Students exhibit social skills weaknesses and some other characteristics similar to children with autism spectrum disorder.

obsessive-compulsive disorder (OCD): OCD is characterized by obsessions and compulsions. Obsessions are recurrent and persistent thoughts, urges, or images that are intrusive and unwanted and cause anxiety. Compulsions are repetitive behaviors or mental acts that reduce the anxiety caused by obsessions.

oppositional defiant disorder (ODD): Students with ODD are often angry, irritable, argumentative, and defiant. They may justify their behavior by blaming it on others.

panic disorder: Panic attacks are sudden, intense experiences of fear accompanied by physical symptoms such as rapid heartbeat, difficulty breathing, and trembling. When students begin to fear more panic attacks and change their behavior to avoid these attacks, they may have developed panic disorder.

persistent depressive disorder (PDD): Students with this disorder are depressed or irritable on most days over a two-year period. They may also have problems with sleep, appetite, energy, self-esteem, and concentration.

post-traumatic stress disorder (PTSD): Students who have witnessed or been threatened with death or serious injury may develop this disorder. Symptoms include distressing memories, nightmares, flashbacks, anxiety, and depression.

school refusal: School refusal is not a mental health disorder. Students can be afraid or unwilling to attend school for many reasons. In young children, separation anxiety disorder is a common reason for school refusal.

selective mutism: This severe social anxiety disorder results in an unwillingness to speak to individuals outside the child's family.

self-injury and suicide: This is a new proposed *DSM-5* category under "Conditions for Further Study." It includes nonsuicidal self-injury disorder (NSSI) and suicidal behavior disorder.

separation anxiety disorder: Students with separation anxiety disorder exhibit persistent, inappropriate, and excessive fear when separating from individuals to whom they are attached. Students experience excessive worry about the health of attachment figures, going to school, or being left with another caretaker. They may protest and refuse to engage in some activities if they have to separate from these individuals.

skin picking (excoriation): Students who pick at their own skin, nails, scabs, or pimples for at least one hour a day are diagnosed with this disorder. Excoriation sometimes coexists with OCD.

social anxiety disorder (SAD): Previously referred to as social phobia, social anxiety disorder occurs in both social and performance settings. Students become very anxious in these situations because they fear they will embarrass themselves or be judged critically by others.

social (pragmatic) communication disorder: Students with this disorder have poor social communication skills. They have difficulty with the unwritten rules of conversation and have trouble understanding subtleties of language such as sarcasm, idioms, and metaphors.

specific learning disorder (SLD): Students with SLD might have reading, math, or written language weaknesses with skills well below those of peers. Weaknesses cannot be explained by lack of instruction, intelligence, or other factors. SLD may include dycalculia, dysgraphia, dyslexia, or nonverbal learning disability (NVLD).

specific phobia: A phobia is an extreme fear of an object or a situation. Often students will avoid the object or situation.

speech sound disorder: Young children whose speech articulation is difficult to understand may have a speech sound disorder.

suicidal behavior disorder: An individual with this disorder has, within the previous two years, engaged in behavior that was expected to lead to his or her death.

tic disorders: A tic is a sudden, rapid, recurrent motor movement (motor tic) or vocalization (vocal tic). Motor and vocal tics can occur at the same or different times.

Tourette syndrome: Students are diagnosed with Tourette syndrome when multiple motor and one or more vocal tics occur (not necessarily at the same time).

trauma and stressor-related disorders: Certain events in childhood may be traumatic. These events can harm children psychologically and create a higher likelihood that students will have mental health disorders as adults. These disorders or experiences include adverse childhood experiences (ACEs), bullying and school violence, and post-traumatic stress disorder (PTSD).

NOTES

Introduction

1. Joshua J. Mark, "Heraclitus of Ephesus," *Ancient History Encyclopedia*, last modified July 14, 2010, www.ancient.eu/Heraclitus_of_Ephesos.

2. Center for Public Education, *The United States of Education: The Changing Demographics of the United States and Their Schools*, May 2012, www.centerforpubliceducation.org/You-May-Also-Be-Interested-In-landing-page -level/Organizing-a-School-YMABI/The-United-States-of-education-The-changing -demographics-of-the-United-States-and-their-schools.html.

3. Tim Walker, "Snapshot of the Teaching Profession: What's Changed Over a Decade?" *NEA Today*, May 19, 2016, neatoday.org/2016/05/19/snapshot-of-the -teaching-profession.

4. Jean M. Twenge, "Have Smartphones Destroyed a Generation?" *The Atlantic*, September 2017, www.theatlantic.com/magazine/archive/2017/09/has-the -smartphone-destroyed-a-generation/534198; Justin W. Patchin, "Summary of Our Cyberbullying Research (2004–2016)," Cyberbullying Research Center, November 26, 2016, cyberbullying.org/summary-of-our-cyberbullying-research.

5. "How Children's Social Competence Impacts Their Well-Being in Adulthood," Robert Wood Johnson Foundation, July 16, 2015, www.rwjf.org/en/library/research/2015/07 /how-children-s-social-competence-impacts-their-well-being-in-adu.html.

6. Room 241 Team, "Mainstreaming Special Education in the Classroom," *Room 241* (blog), Concordia University, January 6, 2016, education.cu-portland.edu/blog /special-ed/mainstreaming-special-education-in-the-classroom.

7. Jackie Mader, "Teacher Training Is Failing Students with Disabilities," *The Atlantic*, March 1, 2017, www.theatlantic.com/education/archive/2017/03/how-teacher -training-hinders-special-needs-students/518286.

8. Shannon Stagman and Janice L. Cooper, *Children's Mental Health: What Every Policymaker Should Know* (New York: National Center for Children in Poverty, 2010); Meg Anderson and Kavitha Cardoza, "Mental Health in Schools: A Hidden Crisis Affecting Millions of Students," NPR, August 31, 2016, www.npr.org/sections/ed /2016/08/31/464727159/mental-health-in-schools-a-hidden-crisis-affecting -millions-of-students; Emily Goldberg, "The New Focus on Children's Mental Health," *The Atlantic*, October 17, 2016, www.theatlantic.com/education/archive/2016/10 /the-new-focus-on-childrens-mental-health/504227/?utm_source=nl-atlantic -daily-101716; Kristin Souers with Pete Hall, *Fostering Resilient Learners: Strategies for Creating a Trauma-Sensitive Classroom* (Alexandria, VA: ASCD, 2016).

9. Stagman and Cooper, *Children's Mental Health*.

10. Candace Cortiella and Sheldon H. Horowitz, *The State of Learning Disabilities: Facts, Trends, and Emerging Issues* (New York: National Center for Learning Disabilities, 2014).

11. Stagman and Cooper, *Children's Mental Health*.

12. Stagman and Cooper, *Children's Mental Health*.

13. Anderson and Cardoza, "Mental Health in Schools"; TeenScreen, "Youth Mental Health and Academic Achievement," National Center for Mental Health Checkups at Columbia University, 2012, www.flgov.com/wp-content/uploads/childadvocacy /mental-health-and-academic-achievement-2-24-12.pdf.

14. Jessica Lahey, "The Failing First Line of Defense," *The Atlantic*, October 18, 2016, www.theatlantic.com/education/archive/2016/10/the-failing-first-line-of-defense/504485.

15. Thomas Boat and Joel Wu, *Mental Disorders and Disabilities Among Low-Income Children* (Washington, DC: National Academies Press, 2015).

16. Mark T. Greenberg, Joshua L. Brown, and Rachel M. Abenavoli, "Teacher Stress and Health," Robert Wood Johnson Foundation, September 1, 2016, www.rwjf.org/en/library/research/2016/07/teacher-stress-and-health.html.

17. John Meiklejohn et al., "Integrating Mindfulness Training into K–12 Education: Fostering the Resilience of Teachers and Students," *Mindfulness* 3 (March 2012): 291–307.

18. Building Collaboration for Mental Health Services in California Schools, "The Relationship of Mental Health and Academic Achievement: Current Research Findings," LAUSD School Mental Health, 2010, lausdsmh.net/wp-content/uploads/2010/11/Mental-Health-and-Academic-Achievement-Abstract.pdf.

19. Geneva Gay, *Culturally Responsive Teaching: Theory, Research, and Practice* (New York: Teachers College Press, 2010).

20. American Psychiatric Association, *Diagnostic and Statistical Manual of Mental Disorders: Fifth Edition (DSM-5)* (Arlington, VA: American Psychiatric Association Publishing, 2013).

CHAPTER 1

1. Ross W. Greene, *Lost at School: Why Our Kids with Behavioral Challenges Are Falling Through the Cracks and How We Can Help Them* (New York: Scribner, 2014).

2. Greene, *Lost at School.*

CHAPTER 2

1. Edward Fergus, "Common Causes of the Overidentification of Racial/Ethnic Minorities in Special Education: Understanding and Addressing Disproportionality," *The EDge* 31, no. 2 (Spring 2017).

2. "PBIS—What You Need to Know," Safe & Civil Schools, accessed October 5, 2017, www.safeandcivilschools.com/research/papers/pbs-pbis.php.

3. "Fast Facts: Students with Disabilities," National Center for Education Statistics, accessed December 27, 2017, nces.ed.gov/fastfacts/display.asp?id=64.

4. Room 241 Team, "Mainstreaming Special Education in the Classroom," *Room 241* (blog), Concordia University, January 6, 2016, education.cu-portland.edu/blog/special-ed/mainstreaming-special-education-in-the-classroom.

5. Joseph F. Kovaleski, Christina M. Marco-Fies, and Michael J. Boneshefski, "Treatment Integrity: Ensuring the '*I*' in RTI," RTI Action Network, accessed October 5, 2017, rtinetwork.org/getstarted/evaluate/treatment-integrity-ensuring-the-i-in-rti.

6. Kent McIntosh and Steve Goodman, *Integrated Multi-Tiered Systems of Support: Blending RTI and PBIS* (New York: The Guilford Press, 2016), 5.

7. US Office of Special Education Programs, *Supporting and Responding to Behavior: Evidence-Based Classroom Strategies for Teachers* (Washington, DC: US Office of Special Education Programs, 2015).

8. Edward S. Shapiro, "Tiered Instruction and Intervention in a Response-to-Intervention Model," RTI Action Network, accessed December 27, 2017, www.rtinetwork.org/essential/tieredinstruction/tiered-instruction-and-intervention-rti-model.

9. National Center on Response to Intervention, *Essential Components of RTI—A Closer Look at Response to Intervention* (Washington, DC: National Center on Response to Intervention, 2010).

10. "Building the Legacy: IDEA 2004," US Department of Education, accessed October 6, 2017, idea.ed.gov; US Department of Education, *Guiding Principles: A Resource Guide for Improving School Climate and Discipline* (Washington, DC: US Department of Education, 2014); Deanne A. Crone, Leanne S. Hawken, and Robert H. Horner, *Responding to Problem Behavior in Schools: The Behavior Education Program* (New York: The Guilford Press, 2010); National Association of School Psychologists, "Social Skills: Promoting Positive Behavior, Academic Success, and School Safety," NASP Center, 2002, www.naspcenter.org/factsheets/socialskills_fs.html; Linda Jucovy and Michael Garringer, *The ABCs of School-Based Mentoring: Effective Strategies for Providing Quality Youth Mentoring in Schools and Communities* (Portland, OR: National Mentoring Center, 2008); Cindy Sturtevant Borden, *Implementing Effective Youth Mentoring Relationships for High School Students*, Smaller Learning Communities Program, accessed October 6, 2017, www2.ed.gov/programs/slcp/finalimplem.pdf.

11. Jim Wright, *Developing Effective Tier 2 & Tier 3 RTI Reading Interventions: Guidelines for Schools*, Intervention Central, accessed December 27, 2017, www.jimwrightonline.com/mixed_files/CCIRA/wright_CCIRA__Feb_2013_Tier_2_Rdng_Guidelines_Internet_PPT.pdf.

12. Timothy Peil, "Problem Solving," accessed October 6, 2017, web.mnstate.edu/peil/M110/Worksheet/PolyaProblemSolve.pdf.

13. "Functional Behavior Assessment," Public Schools of North Carolina, accessed October 6, 2017, ec.ncpublicschools.gov/instructional-resources/behavior-support/resources/functional-behavior-assessment.docx/view.

14. "Functional Behavior Assessment."

15. National Center on Response to Intervention, *Essential Components of RTI*.

16. Ruth A. Ervin, "Considering Tier 3 Within a Response-to-Intervention Model," RTI Action Network, accessed October 6, 2017, www.rtinetwork.org/essential/tieredinstruction/tier3/consideringtier3.

17. Douglas Fuchs and Donald D. Deshler, "What We Need to Know About Responsiveness to Intervention (and Shouldn't Be Afraid to Ask)," *Learning Disabilities Research and Practice* 22, no. 2 (May 2007): 129–136.

18. "Evidence-Based Intervention Network," University of Missouri, 2011, ebi.missouri.edu; National Center for Education Evaluation and Regional Assistance, "Appendix A: Where to Find Evidence-Based Interventions" in *Identifying and Implementing Educational Practices Supported by Rigorous Evidence: A User Friendly Guide* (Washington, DC: US Department of Education, 2003); "Ideas That Work: Preparing Children and Youth with Disabilities for Success," US Department of Education, accessed October 6, 2017, ccrs.osepideasthatwork.org.

19. Legal Information Institute, "34 CFR 104.33—Free Appropriate Public Education," Cornell Law School, accessed October 6, 2017, www.law.cornell.edu/cfr/text/34/104.33.

20. "Fact Sheet on the EEOC's Final Regulations Implementing the ADAAA," US Equal Employment Opportunity Commission, accessed October 6, 2017, www.eeoc.gov/laws/regulations/adaaa_fact_sheet.cfm.

CHAPTER 4

1. D'Vera Cohn, "It's Official: Minority Babies Are the Majority Among the Nation's Infants, but Only Just," Pew Research Center, June 23, 2016, www.pewresearch.org/fact-tank/2016/06/23/its-official-minority-babies-are-the-majority-among-the-nations-infants-but-only-just.

2. National Center for Education Statistics, "Table 203.50: Enrollment and Percentage Distribution of Enrollment in Public Elementary and Secondary Schools, by Race/Ethnicity and Region: Selected Years, Fall 1995 Through Fall 2023," in *Digest of Education Statistics 2013* (Washington, DC: US Department of Education, 2015).

3. Greg Toppo and Mark Nichols, "Decades After Civil Rights Gains, Black Teachers a Rarity in Public Schools," *USA Today*, February 1, 2017, www.usatoday.com/story /news/nation-now/2017/02/01/decades-after-civil-rights-gains-black-teachers -rarity-public-schools/96721684.

4. Samantha Allen, "Just How Many LGBT Americans Are There?" *The Daily Beast*, January 14, 2017, www.thedailybeast.com/just-how-many-lgbt-americans-are-there.

5. Geneva Gay, *Culturally Responsive Teaching: Theory, Research, and Practice* (New York: Teachers College Press, 2010), 31.

6. Milaney Leverson et al., *PBIS Cultural Responsiveness Field Guide: Resources for Trainers and Coaches* (Washington, DC: OSEP Technical Assistance Center on PBIS, 2016).

7. Tachelle Banks and Festus E. Obiakor, "Culturally Responsive Positive Behavior Supports: Considerations for Practice," *Journal of Education and Training Studies* 3, no. 2 (March 2015): 83–90.

8. Todd Bertani et al., *Culturally Responsive Classrooms: A Toolkit for Educators*, July 2010, www.sbbh.pitt.edu/files/pdf/Culturally%20Responsive%20Classrooms010412.pdf.

9. Matthew Lynch. "6 Ways Teachers Can Foster Cultural Awareness in the Classroom" *Education Week* (blog), November 6, 2014, blogs.edweek.org/edweek/education _futures/2014/11/6_ways_teachers_can_foster_cultural_awareness_in_the _classroom.html.

10. Leverson et al., *PBIS Field Guide.*

11. Bertani et al., *Culturally Responsive Classrooms.*

12. Bertani et al., *Culturally Responsive Classrooms.*

13. Tary J. Tobin and Claudia G. Vincent, "Culturally Competent School-Wide Positive Behavioral Support: From Theory to Evaluation Data" (presentation, 7th International Conference on Positive Behavior Support, Saint Louis, MO, March 26, 2010), www.ocde.us/PEI/Documents/Culturally-Competent-School-wide-Positive -Behavior-Support-From-Theory+to-Evaluation-Data.pdf.

14. Bertani et al., *Culturally Responsive Classrooms.*

15. Linda Flanagan, "How to Develop a School Culture That Helps Curb Bullying," *MindShift*, April 7, 2016, ww2.kqed.org/mindshift/2016/04/07 /how-to-develop-a-school-culture-that-helps-curb-bullying.

16. Rick Nauert, "School Culture Can Factor into Bullying," Psych Central, October 6, 2015, psychcentral.com/news/2013/11/29/school-culture-can-factor-into-bullying /62573.html; Australia's Safe and Supportive School Communities Working Group, *Research Snapshot from a Literature Review* (City East, Queensland: Bullying. No Way!, 2014).

17. Jesse Singal, "The Key to Stop Bullying: Popular Kids," CNN, January 19, 2016, www.cnn.com/2016/01/19/health/popular-kids-can-stop-bullying/index.html.

18. Amos Clifford, *Teaching Restorative Practices with Classroom Circles*, Center for Restorative Process, accessed February 13, 2018, www.healthiersf.org /RestorativePractices/Resources/documents/RP%20Curriculum%20and%20 Scripts%20and%20PowePoints/Classroom%20Curriculum/Teaching%20 Restorative%20Practices%20in%20the%20Classroom%207%20lesson%20 Curriculum.pdf.

CHAPTER 5

1. John Payton et al., *The Positive Impact of Social and Emotional Learning for Kindergarten to Eighth-Grade Students: Findings from Three Scientific Reviews* (Chicago, IL: CASEL, 2008).

2. Johns Hopkins School of Nursing, "Social-Behavioral Readiness in Kindergarteners Impacts Long-Term Success," ScienceDaily, March 17, 2016, www.sciencedaily.com /releases/2016/03/160317190319.htm.

3. "How Children's Social Competence Impacts Their Well-Being in Adulthood," Robert Wood Johnson Foundation, July 16, 2015, www.rwjf.org/en/library/research /2015/07/how-children-s-social-competence-impacts-their-well-being-in-adu.html.

4. Payton et al., *Positive Impact of Social and Emotional Learning*.

5. Payton et al., *Positive Impact of Social and Emotional Learning*.

6. "How SEL Improves School Climate and Achievement," Channing-Bete Company, accessed October 13, 2017, www.channing-bete.com/prevention-programs/paths /SEL.html.

7. Walter Mischel, *The Marshmallow Test: Mastering Self-Control* (New York: Little, Brown and Company, 2014).

8. Frank Porter Graham Child Development Institute, "Federal Report Recommends Teaching Self-Regulation in Schools: Teachers and Parents Can Help Children Build the Skills They Need for the Rest of Their Lives," ScienceDaily, December 6, 2016, www.sciencedaily.com/releases/2016/12/161206110156.htm.

9. Andrew Reiner, "The Education Issue: Believing Self-Control Predicts Success, Schools Teach Coping," *Washington Post*, April 11, 2013, www.washingtonpost.com /sf/feature/wp/2013/04/11/the-education-issue-believing-self-control-predicts -success-schools-teach-coping.

10. Gwen Dewar, "Teaching Self-Control: Evidence-Based Tips," Parenting Science, last modified November 2015, www.parentingscience.com/teaching-self-control.html.

11. Kelly McGonigal, *The Willpower Instinct: How Self-Control Works, Why It Matters, and What You Can Do to Get More of It* (New York: Avery Press, 2012).

12. Dewar, "Teaching Self-Control."

13. Allison Dimick, Amity Noltemeyer, and Suzanne Klatt, *School-Based Mindfulness Interventions*, Project AWARE Ohio, June 2016, education.ohio.gov/getattachment /Topics/Other-Resources/School-Safety/Building-Better-Learning-Environments /PBIS-Resources/Project-AWARE-Ohio/Project-AWARE-Ohio-Statewide-Resources /Mindfulness-in-Schools.pdf.aspx; Jon Kabat-Zinn, "Mindfulness-Based Interventions in Context: Past, Present, and Future" *Clinical Psychology: Science and Practice* 10, no. 2 (Summer 2003): 145.

14. Daniel J. Siegel, "The Science of Mindfulness," Mindful, September 7, 2010, www.mindful.org/the-science-of-mindfulness; Jeffrey M. Greeson, "Mindfulness Research Update: 2008," *Journal of Evidence-Based Complementary and Alternative Medicine* 14, no. 1 (January 2009): 10–18.

15. John Meiklejohn et al. "Integrating Mindfulness Training into K–12 Education: Fostering the Resilience of Teachers and Students," *Mindfulness* 3 (March 2012): 291–307.

16. Dan Jones, "Mindfulness in Schools," *The Psychologist* 24, no. 10 (October 2011): 736–739; John Meiklejohn et al., "Integrating Mindfulness Training," 291–307; Dimick, Noltemeyer, and Klatt, *School-Based Mindfulness Interventions*; "Research on Mindfulness," Mindful Schools, accessed October 16, 2017, www.mindfulschools.org /about-mindfulness/research.

17. John Meiklejohn et al., "Integrating Mindfulness Training," 291–307.

18. "Large-Scale Trial Will Assess Effectiveness of Teaching Mindfulness in UK Schools," Wellcome Trust, July 16, 2015, wellcome.ac.uk/press-release /large-scale-trial-will-assess-effectiveness-teaching-mindfulness-uk-schools.

19. Mark Greenberg, Joshua Brown, and Rachel Abenavoli, "Teacher Stress and Health," Robert Wood Johnson Foundation, September 1, 2016, www.rwjf.org/en/library /research/2016/07/teacher-stress-and-health.html.

20. Audrey Breen, "Curry Study: Reducing Teachers' Stress Leads to Higher-Quality Classrooms," *UVAToday*, May 2, 2016, news.virginia.edu/content/curry-study -reducing-teachers-stress-leads-higher-quality-classrooms; John Meiklejohn et al., "Integrating Mindfulness Training," 291–307.

21. Carol S. Dweck, *Mindset: The New Psychology of Success* (New York: Random House, 2016).

22. Bill Murphy Jr., "Want to Raise Successful Kids? Science Says Praise Them Like This (But Most Parents Do the Opposite)," Inc., November 28, 2016, www.inc.com /bill-murphy-jr/want-to-raise-successful-kids-science-says-praise-them-like-this -most-parents-do.html.

23. Lin Bian, Sarah-Jane Leslie, and Andrei Cimpian, "Gender Stereotypes About Intellectual Ability Emerge Early and Influence Children's Interests," *Science* 355, no. 6323 (January 2017): 389–391.

24. Jim Wright, "How to Encourage Students to Try: Growth Mindset Statements," Intervention Central, 2016, www.interventioncentral.org /student_motivation_growth_mindset.

25. Nicole Shechtman et al., *Promoting Grit, Tenacity, and Perseverance: Critical Factors for Success in the 21st Century* (Washington, DC: US Department of Education, 2013).

26. "How SEL Improves School Climate and Achievement"; Shechtman et al., *Promoting Grit.*

27. National Association of School Psychologists, "Social Skills: Promoting Positive Behavior, Academic Success, and School Safety," NASP Center, 2002, www.naspcenter.org/factsheets/socialskills_fs.html.

28. Diane E. McClellan and Lilian G. Katz, *ERIC Digests: Assessing Young Children's Social Competence* (Champaign: IL: ERIC Clearinghouse on Elementary and Early Childhood Education, 2001).

29. "Yoga 4 Classrooms Supporting Research," Yoga 4 Classrooms, accessed October 17, 2017, www.yoga4classrooms.com/supporting-research.

30. Bethany Butzer et al., "School-Based Yoga Programs in the United States: A Survey," *Advances in Mind/Body Medicine* 29, no. 4 (April 2016): 18–26.

31. Beate Chung, "The Benefits of Yoga for Kids," DOYOUYOGA, accessed December 27, 2017, www.doyouyoga.com/why-yoga-is-perfect-for-kids.

32. Jane Rosen, "Yoga in Schools Isn't Just for Kids: How Teachers Benefit," Kripalu Center for Yoga & Health, accessed December 27, 2017, kripalu.org/resources /yoga-schools-isn-t-just-kids-how-teachers-benefit.

33. April Bowling et al., "Cybercycling Effects on Classroom Behavior in Children with Behavioral Health Disorders: An RCT," *Pediatrics* 139, no. 2 (January 2017); Kirsten Weir, "The Exercise Effect," *Monitor on Psychology* 42, no. 11 (December 2011): 48.

34. Viatcheslav Wlassoff, "Can Physical Exercise Improve Cognitive Abilities?" *BrainBlogger* (blog), February 4, 2015, brainblogger.com/2015/02/04 /can-physical-exercise-improve-cognitive-abilities.

35. Rebecca Wylie, "The Average Amount of Kids That Get Exercise in the U.S." Livestrong, September 11, 2017, www.livestrong.com/article/387136-the -average-amount-of-kids-that-get-exercise-in-the-u-s.

36. Robert Murray and Catherine Ramstetter, "The Crucial Role of Recess in School," *Pediatrics* 131, no. 1 (January 2013): 183–188.

37. Institute of Medicine, *Educating the Student Body: Taking Physical Activity and Physical Education to School* (Washington, DC: Institute of Medicine, 2013).

38. Centers for Disease Control and Prevention and SHAPE America, *Strategies for Recess in Schools* (Atlanta, GA: Centers for Disease Control and Prevention, 2017).

39. New South Wales Education, "Motivating Lazy Children," School A to Z, accessed December 27, 2017, www.schoolatoz.nsw.edu.au/wellbeing/fitness /motivating-lazy-children; Sarah Henry, "Kid Fitness: When Your Child Won't Exercise," WebMD, accessed December 27, 2017, www.webmd.com/parenting /features/kid-fitness-when-your-child-wont-exercise#1.

40. Evie Blad, "Principals Like Social-Emotional Learning. Here's Why Schools Struggle with It," *Education Week* (blog), November 7, 2017, blogs.edweek.org /edweek/rulesforengagement/2017/11/principals_like_social-emotional _learning_heres_why_schools_struggle_with_it.html.

41. Blad, "Principals Like Social-Emotional Learning."

42. "Program," Compassionate Schools Project, accessed December 17, 2017, www.compassionschools.org/program.

CHAPTER 6

1. Olivia Goldhill, "The Concept of Different 'Learning Styles' Is One of the Greatest Neuroscience Myths," Quartz, January 3, 2016, qz.com/585143/the-concept-of -different-learning-styles-is-one-of-the-greatest-neuroscience-myths; Harold Pashler et al., "Learning Styles: Concepts and Evidence" *Psychological Science in the Public Interest* 9, no. 3 (December 2009): 105–119.

2. Tracy Alloway, "10% Students May Have Working Memory Problems: Why Does It Matter?" *SharpBrains* (blog), May 10, 2009, sharpbrains.com/blog/2009/05/10/10 -students-may-have-working-memory-problems-why-does-it-matter.

3. "Is Working Memory More Important Than IQ?" *UCanConnect* (blog), November 7, 2013, blog.ucanconnect.org/is-working-memory-more-important-than-iq.

4. Psych Central Staff, "Memory and Mnemonic Devices," Psych Central, last modified July 17, 2016, psychcentral.com/lib/memory-and-mnemonic-devices.

5. Kathleen Lynne Lane et al., *Managing Challenging Behaviors in Schools: Research-Based Strategies That Work* (New York: The Guilford Press, 2011).

CHAPTER 7

1. "About Behavioral Risk Factor Surveillance System ACE Data," Centers for Disease Control and Prevention, last modified April 1, 2016, www.cdc.gov /violenceprevention/acestudy/ace_brfss.html.

2. National Center for Learning Disabilities, "RTI Action Network Position Statement on Determination of Specific Learning Disabilities," RTI Action Network, accessed December 15, 2017, www.rtinetwork.org/about-us /position-statement-on-determination-of-specific-learning-disabilities.

3. Genevieve Mackenzie, "Person-First Language Promotes Healthier Self-Understanding in Those with ADHD," *The ADHD Report* 25, no 6 (September 2017): 6–11.

CHAPTER 8

1. "Any Anxiety Disorder," National Institute of Mental Health, accessed October 24, 2017, www.nimh.nih.gov/health/statistics/prevalence/any-anxiety-disorder -among-children.shtml; Charmaine K. Higa-McMillan, Sarah E. Francis, and Bruce F. Chorpita, "Anxiety Disorders," in *Child Psychopathology*, edited by Eric J. Mash and Russell A. Barkley (New York: The Guilford Press, 2014), 345–428; Kathleen Ries Merikangas et al., "Lifetime Prevalence of Mental Disorders in US Adolescents: Results from the National Comorbidity Study-Adolescent Supplement (NCS-A)," *Journal of the American Academy of Child and Adolescent Psychiatry* 49, no. 10 (October 2010): 980–989; "Prevalence," Youth.gov, accessed October 24, 2017, youth.gov/youth-topics/youth-mental-health/prevalance-mental-health-disorders -among-youth; Ruth Perou et al., "Mental Health Surveillance Among Children— United States, 2005–2011: Supplements," *Morbidity and Mortality Weekly Report (MMWR)* 62, no. 02 (May 2013): 1–35; Cathy Creswell and Polly Waite, "Recent Developments in the Treatment of Anxiety Disorders in Children and Adolescents," *Evidence-Based Mental Health* 19, no. 3 (July 2016): 65–68.

2. Katja Beesdo, Susanne Knappe, and Daniel S. Pine. "Anxiety and Anxiety Disorders in Children and Adolescents: Developmental Issues and Implications for DSM-V," *Psychiatric Clinics of North America* 32, no. 3 (September 2009): 483–524; Higa-McMillan, Francis, and Chorpita, "Anxiety Disorders," 345–428; American Psychiatric Association, *Diagnostic and Statistical Manual of Mental Disorders: Fifth Edition (DSM-5)* (Arlington, VA: American Psychiatric Association Publishing, 2013).

3. American Psychiatric Association, *DSM-5*; Higa-McMillan, Francis, and Chorpita, "Anxiety Disorders," 345–428.

4. Todd B. Kashdan and James D. Herbert, "Social Anxiety Disorder in Childhood and Adolescence: Current Status and Future Directions," *Clinical Child and Family Psychology Review* 4, no. 1 (March 2001): 37–61.

5. Deborah C. Beidel and Samuel M. Turner, *Shy Children, Phobic Adults: Nature and Treatment of Social Anxiety Disorder* (Washington, DC: American Psychological Association, 2007).

6. Philip G. Zimbardo and Shirley Radl, *The Shy Child: Overcoming and Preventing Shyness from Infancy to Adulthood* (Los Altos, CA: Malor, 2015).

7. American Psychiatric Association, *DSM-5*; Higa-McMillan, Francis, and Chorpita, "Anxiety Disorders," 345–428.

8. American Psychiatric Association, *DSM-5*; Higa-McMillan, Francis, and Chorpita, "Anxiety Disorders," 345–428.

9. Higa-McMillan, Francis, and Chorpita, "Anxiety Disorders," 345–428.

10. "Any Anxiety Disorder," National Institute of Mental Health.

11. Pooky Knightsmith, *Self-Harm and Eating Disorders in Schools: A Guide to Whole-School Strategies and Practical Support* (London: Jessica Kingsley Publishers, 2015).

12. Knightsmith, *Self-Harm and Eating Disorders*.

13. American Psychiatric Association, *DSM-5*; Higa-McMillan, Francis, and Chorpita, "Anxiety Disorders," 345–428.

14. Higa-McMillan, Francis, and Chorpita, "Anxiety Disorders," 345–428.

15. Beidel and Turner, *Shy Children*.

16. Bettina E. Bernstein, "Separation Anxiety and School Refusal," Medscape, October 6, 2016, emedicine.medscape.com/article/916737-overview#a5.

17. Eleanor Barkhorn, "'160,000 Kids Stay Home from School Each Day to Avoid Being Bullied'" *The Atlantic*, October 3, 2013, www.theatlantic.com/education/archive/2013/10/160-000-kids-stay-home-from-school-each-day-to-avoid-being-bullied/280201.

CHAPTER 9

1. American Psychiatric Association, *Diagnostic and Statistical Manual of Mental Disorders: Fifth Edition (DSM-5)* (Arlington, VA: American Psychiatric Association Publishing, 2013).

2. John Piacentini et al., "Obsessive-Compulsive Spectrum Disorders," in *Child Psychopathology*, edited by Eric J. Mash and Russell A. Barkley (New York: The Guilford Press, 2014), 429–475.

3. American Psychiatric Association, *DSM-5*.

4. Piacentini et al., "Obsessive-Compulsive Spectrum Disorders," 429–475.

5. Piacentini et al., "Obsessive-Compulsive Spectrum Disorders," 429–475.

6. Piacentini et al., "Obsessive-Compulsive Spectrum Disorders," 429–475.

7. American Psychiatric Association, *DSM-5*.

8. American Psychiatric Association, *DSM-5*.

Chapter 10

1. "Dysthymic Disorder Among Children," National Institute of Mental Health, accessed December 15, 2017, www.nimh.nih.gov/health/statistics/prevalence/dysthymic -disorder-among-children.shtml; Constance L. Hammen, Karen D. Rudolph, and Jamie L. Abaied, "Child and Adolescent Depression," in *Child Psychopathology*, edited by Eric J. Mash and Russell A. Barkley (New York: The Guilford Press, 2014), 225–263; Sara G. Miller, "More US Teens May Be Facing Depression: Here's Why," LiveScience, August 10, 2016, www.livescience.com/55706-depression-rates -adolescents-teens.html.

2. Hammen, Rudolph, and Abaied, "Child and Adolescent Depression," 225–263.

3. Jean M. Twenge et al., "Increases in Depressive Symptoms, Suicide-Related Outcomes, and Suicide Rates Among U.S. Adolescents After 2010 and Links to Increased New Media Screen Time," *Clinical Psychological Science* 6, no. 1 (November 2017).

4. "Facts & Stats," The Jason Foundation, accessed November 3, 2017, jasonfoundation.com/youth-suicide/facts-stats.

5. Nahama Broner et al., *Mandatory Reporting and Keeping Youth Safe* (Washington, DC: Administration on Children, Youth, and Families, 2013).

6. Jeffrey S. Forrest, "Pediatric Persistent Depressive Disorder (Dysthymia)," Medscape, last modified October 14, 2016, emedicine.medscape.com/article /913941-overview#a6.

7. "Major Depression," National Institute of Mental Health, last modified November 2017, www.nimh.nih.gov/health/statistics/prevalence/major-depression-among -adolescents.shtml; Thomas Huberty, "Depression: Supporting Students at School," in *Helping Children at Home and School III: Handouts for Families and Educators* (Bethesda, MD, National Association of School Psychologists, 2010).

8. American Psychiatric Association, *Diagnostic and Statistical Manual of Mental Disorders: Fifth Edition (DSM-5)* (Arlington, VA: American Psychiatric Association Publishing, 2013).

9. Forrest, "Pediatric Persistent Depressive Disorder."

10. Hammen, Rudolph, and Abaied, "Child and Adolescent Depression," 225–263.

11. American Psychiatric Association, *DSM-5*.

12. Forrest, "Pediatric Persistent Depressive Disorder."

13. Karen Dineen Wagner, "Exercise and Depression in Youth," *Psychiatric Times*, February 24, 2017, www.psychiatrictimes.com/child-adolescent-psychiatry /exercise-and-depression-youth/page/0/2.

14. Karen Weintraub, "Most Antidepressants Don't Work on Kids, Teens, Study Finds," *STAT*, June 8, 2016, www.statnews.com/2016/06/08/antidepressants-teens-kids; Emily Karanges and Iain McGregor, "Antidepressants and Adolescent Brain Development," *Future Neurology* 6, no. 6 (October 2011): 783–808.

Chapter 11

1. American Psychiatric Association, *Diagnostic and Statistical Manual of Mental Disorders: Fifth Edition (DSM-5)* (Arlington, VA: American Psychiatric Association Publishing, 2013).

2. Bettina E. Bernstein, "Pediatric Bipolar Affective Disorder," Medscape, last modified February 10, 2017, emedicine.medscape.com/article/913464-overview#a5.

3. American Psychiatric Association, *DSM-5*; Eric A. Youngstrom and Guillermo Pérez Algorta, "Pediatric Bipolar Disorder," in *Child Psychopathology*, edited by Eric J. Mash and Russell A. Barkley (New York: The Guilford Press, 2014), 264–316.

4. Youngstrom and Algorta, "Pediatric Bipolar Disorder," 264–316.

5. Youngstrom and Algorta, "Pediatric Bipolar Disorder," 264–316.

6. Guillermo Pérez Algorta et al., "Suicidality in Pediatric Bipolar Disorder: Predictor or Outcome of Family Processes and Mixed Mood Presentation?" *Bipolar Disorders* 13, no. 1 (February 2011): 76–86.

CHAPTER 12

1. Kevin Mitchell, *Wiring the Brain* (blog), accessed November 8, 2017, www.wiringthebrain.com.

2. Ruth Perou et al., "Mental Health Surveillance Among Children—United States, 2005–2011: Supplements," *Morbidity and Mortality Weekly Report (MMWR)* 62, no. 02 (May 2013): 1–35; Joel T. Nigg and Russell A. Barkley, "Attention Deficit/Hyperactivity Disorder," in *Child Psychopathology*, edited by Eric J. Mash and Russell A. Barkley (New York: The Guilford Press, 2014), 75–144.

3. Nigg and Barkley, "Attention Deficit/Hyperactivity Disorder," 75–144.

4. Boudien C.T. Flapper, Suzanne Houwen, and Marina M. Schoemaker, "Fine Motor Skills and Effects of Methylphenidate in Children with Attention-Deficit-Hyperactivity Disorder and Developmental Coordination Disorder," *Developmental Medicine & Child Neurology* 48, no. 3 (March 2006): 165–169.

5. Radboud University Nijmegen Medical Centre, "Brain Differences in ADHD," ScienceDaily, February 16, 2017, www.sciencedaily.com/releases/2017/02/170216105919.htm.

6. Frye, Devon, "The Doctor Is Not In: ADHD's Pediatrician Problem," *ADDitude: Strategies and Support for ADHD & LD* (Fall 2017); Rabiner, David, "Pediatric Care for Children with ADHD—Discouraging New Findings," The A.D.D. Resource Center, May 22, 2016, www.addrc.org/pediatric-care-for-children-with-adhd.

7. W. Barlow Soper and Mark J. Miller, "Junk-Time Junkies: An Emerging Addiction Among Students," *The School Counselor* 31, no. 1 (September 1983): 40–43.

8. Jennifer Golbeck, "Video Gaming Disorder Is Now a Mental Health Condition," *Psychology Today* (blog), December 26, 2017, www.psychologytoday.com/blog/your-online-secrets/201712/video-gaming-disorder-is-now-mental-health-condition.

9. University of Bergen, "Videogame Addiction Linked to ADHD," ScienceDaily, April 25, 2016, www.sciencedaily.com/releases/2016/04/160425095529.htm.

10. Stuart Passmore, *The ADHD Handbook* (Wollombi, Australia: Exisle Publishing, 2014), 56.

11. Russell A. Barkley, *Attention-Deficit Hyperactivity Disorder: A Handbook for Diagnosis and Treatment* (New York: The Guilford Press, 2006).

12. James Greenblatt and Bill Gottlieb, *Finally Focused: The Breakthrough Natural Treatment Plan for ADHD That Restores Attention, Minimizes Hyperactivity, and Helps Eliminate Drug Side Effects* (New York: Harmony Books, 2017); Joel T. Nigg, *Getting Ahead of ADHD: What Next-Generation Science Says About Treatments That Work—and How You Can Make Them Work for Your Child* (New York: The Guilford Press, 2017).

13. Ayman Mukerji Househam and Mary V. Solanto, "Mindfulness as an Intervention for ADHD," *The ADHD Report* 24, no. 2 (March 2016): 1–13.

14. John Piacentini et al., "Obsessive-Compulsive Spectrum Disorders," in *Child Psychopathology*, edited by Eric J. Mash and Russell A. Barkley (New York: The Guilford Press, 2014), 429–475.

15. Piacentini et al., "Obsessive-Compulsive Spectrum Disorders," 429–475.

16. Michael L. Sulkowski, Joseph F. McGuire, and Andrew Tesoro, "Treating Tics and Tourette's Disorder in School Settings," *Canadian Journal of School Psychology* 31, no. 1 (March 2016): 47–62.

17. Sulkowski, McGuire, and Tesoro, "Treating Tics and Tourette's Disorder," 47–62.

18. Sulkowski, McGuire, and Tesoro, "Treating Tics and Tourette's Disorder," 47–62.

19. Sulkowski, McGuire, and Tesoro, "Treating Tics and Tourette's Disorder," 47–62.

20. Candace Cortiella and Sheldon H. Horowitz, *The State of Learning Disabilities: Facts, Trends, and Emerging Issues* (New York: National Center for Learning Disabilities, 2014).

21. Cortiella and Horowitz, *The State of Learning Disabilities.*

22. Understood Team, "Understanding Dyslexia," Understood.org, accessed November 20, 2017, www.understood.org/en/learning-attention-issues/child-learning-disabilities/dyslexia/understanding-dyslexia.

23. Understood Team, "Dyslexia Fact Sheet," Understood.org, accessed November 20, 2017, www.understood.org/en/learning-attention-issues/child-learning-disabilities/dyslexia/dyslexia-fact-sheet.

24. "Dyslexia Basics," International Dyslexia Association, accessed November 20, 2017, dyslexiaida.org/dyslexia-basics.

25. Barbara Foorman, Jack Fletcher, and David Francis, "A Scientific Approach to Reading Instruction," LD OnLine, 1997, www.ldonline.org/article/6251.

26. National Association of School Psychologists, *NASP Position Statement on Identification of Students with Specific Learning Disabilities* (Bethesda, MD: National Association of School Psychologists, 2007).

27. Dyslexic Advantage Team, "The LD That Won't Be Named," Dyslexic Advantage, August 21, 2017, www.dyslexicadvantage.org/the-ld-that-wont-be-named; Emily Hanford, "Hard to Read: How American Schools Fail Kids with Dyslexia," *APM Reports*, September 11, 2017, www.apmreports.org/story/2017/09/11/hard-to-read.

28. Geoff Nixon, "Why Schools Are Avoiding the Dyslexia Label," *Inside Learning* (blog), Gemm Learning, January 6, 2015, www.gemmlearning.com/blog/education_trends/schools-avoiding-dyslexia-label.

29. Michael K. Yudin, "Dear Colleague: Dyslexia Guidance," US Department of Education, October 23, 2015, www2.ed.gov/policy/speced/guid/idea/memosdcltrs/guidance-on-dyslexia-10-2015.pdf.

30. Bridget Dalton and Dana L. Grisham, "eVoc Strategies: 10 Ways to Use Technology to Build Vocabulary," *The Reading Teacher* 64, no. 5 (February 2011): 306–317.

31. National Center for Learning Disabilities, "Dyscalculia," LD OnLine, 2007, www.ldonline.org/article/13709.

32. Lawrence J. Lewandowski and Benjamin J. Lovett, "Learning Disabilities," in *Child Psychopathology*, edited by Eric J. Mash and Russell A. Barkley (New York: The Guilford Press, 2014), 625–672.

33. Danielle Paquette, "Even the Most Empowered Girls Are More Anxious About Math Than Boys," *Wonkblog* (blog), *The Washington Post*, May 5, 2016, www.washingtonpost.com/news/wonk/wp/2016/05/05/the-victims-of-math-anxiety.

34. American Psychiatric Association, *Diagnostic and Statistical Manual of Mental Disorders: Fifth Edition (DSM-5)* (Arlington, VA: American Psychiatric Association Publishing, 2013).

35. Kouichi Yoshimasu et al., "Written-Language Disorder Among Children with and Without ADHD in a Population-Based Birth Cohort," *Pediatrics* 128, no. 3 (September 2011): e605–e612.

36. "Disorders of Reading and Writing," American Speech-Language-Hearing Association, accessed December 21, 2017, www.asha.org/Practice-Portal/Clinical-Topics/Written-Language-Disorders/Disorders-of-Reading-and-Writing.

37. Elizabeth Babbin, "Is Dysgraphia the Same Thing as Disorder of Written Expression?" Understood.org, accessed December 21, 2017, www.understood.org/en/learning-attention-issues/child-learning-disabilities/dysgraphia/is-dysgraphia-the-same-thing-as-disorder-of-written-expression.

38. American Psychiatric Association, *DSM-5.*

39. "Dysgraphia," Learning Disabilities Association of America, ldaamerica.org
/types-of-learning-disabilities/dysgraphia; National Center for Learning Disabilities,
"What Is Dysgraphia?" LD OnLine, 2007, www.ldonline.org/article/12770.

40. Understood Team, "Software Programs for Kids with Writing Issues," Understood.org,
September 12, 2016, www.understood.org/en/school-learning/assistive-technology
/finding-an-assistive-technology/software-programs-for-kids-with-writing-issues.

41. Erica Patino, "Understanding Nonverbal Learning Disabilities,"
Understood.org, accessed November 22, 2017, www.understood.org/en
/learning-attention-issues/child-learning-disabilities/nonverbal-learning
-disabilities/understanding-nonverbal-learning-disabilities.

42. American Psychiatric Association, *DSM-5.*

43. American Speech-Language-Hearing Association, "Almost 8 Percent of US Children
Have a Communication or Swallowing Disorder," *The ASHA Leader,* August 1,
2015, leader.pubs.asha.org/article.aspx?articleid=2423605.

44. National Institutes of Health, "Phonological Disorder," MedlinePlus, last modified
October 3, 2017, medlineplus.gov/ency/article/001541.htm; American Psychiatric
Association, *DSM-5.*

45. Becca Jarzynski, "Child Speech Sound Development: Part 1," *Child Talk* (blog), April
12, 2011, www.talkingkids.org/2011/04/speech-sounds-and-kids-part-1.html.

46. Julie A. Daymut, *Types of Articulation Errors—A Simple Guide,* Super
Duper Publications, 2009, www.superduperinc.com/handouts/pdf/201
_TypesofArticulationErrors.pdf.

47. "Quick Statistics About Voice, Speech, Language," National Institutes of Health,
last modified May 19, 2016, www.nidcd.nih.gov/health/statistics/quick-statistics
-voice-speech-language.

48. American Psychiatric Association, *DSM-5.*

CHAPTER 13

1. American Psychiatric Association, *Diagnostic and Statistical Manual of Mental
Disorders: Fifth Edition (DSM-5)* (Arlington, VA: American Psychiatric Association
Publishing, 2013).

2. American Psychiatric Association, *DSM-5.*

3. Eva R. Kimonis, Paul J. Frick, and Robert J. McMahon, "Conduct and Oppositional
Defiant Disorders," in *Child Psychopathology,* edited by Eric J. Mash and Russell A.
Barkley (New York: The Guilford Press, 2014), 145–179.

4. Kimonis, Frick, and McMahon, "Conduct and Oppositional Defiant
Disorders," 145–179.

5. American Psychiatric Association, *DSM-5.*

6. Maria P. Cantu, "Chapter 8: Qualities of Culturally Sensitive Teachers," in
Culturally Responsive Classroom Management & Motivation Handbook,
accessed November 27, 2017, sites.google.com/site/crmmprojectsite/Home
/chapter-4--qualities-of-culturally-sensitive-teachers.

7. Ross W. Greene, *Lost at School: Why Our Kids with Behavioral Challenges Are Falling
Through the Cracks and How We Can Help Them* (New York: Scribner, 2014).

8. US Office of Special Education Programs, *Supporting and Responding to Behavior:
Evidence-Based Classroom Strategies for Teachers* (Washington, DC: US Office of
Special Education Programs, 2015).

9. US Office of Special Education Programs, *Supporting and Responding to Behavior.*

10. US Office of Special Education Programs, *Supporting and Responding to Behavior.*

11. Ray Levy, Bill O'Hanlon, and Tyler Norris Goode, *Try and Make Me! Simple Strategies That Turn Off the Tantrums and Create Cooperation* (New York: Berkley Publishing, 2002).

12. Levy, O'Hanlon, and Goode, *Try and Make Me!*

13. Greene, *Lost at School.*

14. Ross W. Greene, "ALSUP," Lives in the Balance, February 1, 2016, www.livesinthebalance.org/sites/default/files/ALSUP216.pdf.

15. Ross W. Greene, *Lost and Found: Helping Behaviorally Challenging Students (and, While You're at It, All the Others)* (San Francisco: Jossey-Bass, 2016).

16. Susannah Everett et al., *School-Wide Tier II Interventions: Check-In Check-Out Getting Started Workbook* (Washington, DC: OSEP Center on PBIS, 2011).

CHAPTER 14

1. Hal Arkowitz and Scott O. Lilienfeld, "Self-Cutters May Be Seeking Pain Relief," *Scientific American*, November 1, 2013, www.scientificamerican.com/article /self-cutters-may-be-seeking-pain-relief.

2. Christine B. Cha and Matthew K. Nock, "Suicidal and Nonsuicidal Self-Injurious Thoughts and Behaviors," in *Child Psychopathology*, edited by Eric J. Mash and Russell A. Barkley (New York: The Guilford Press, 2014), 317–344.

3. Cha and Nock, "Suicidal and Nonsuicidal Self-Injurious Thoughts and Behaviors," 317–344.

4. Romuald Brunner et al., "Life-Time Prevalence and Psychosocial Correlates of Adolescent Direct Self-Injurious Behavior: A Comparative Study of Findings in 11 European Countries," *Journal of Child Psychology and Psychiatry* 55, no. 4 (April 2014): 337–348; Maria Zetterqvist, Lars-Gunnar Lundh, and Carl Goran Svedin, "A Comparison of Adolescents Engaging in Self-Injurious Behaviors with and Without Suicidal Intent: Self-Reported Experiences of Adverse Life Events and Trauma Symptoms," *Journal of Youth and Adolescence* 42, no. 8 (August 2013): 1257–1272; Michael J. Sornberger et al., "Nonsuicidal Self-Injury and Gender: Patterns of Prevalence, Methods, and Locations Among Adolescents," *Suicide and Life-Threatening Behavior* 42, no. 3 (June 2012): 266–278; Cha and Nock, "Suicidal and Nonsuicidal Self-Injurious Thoughts and Behaviors," 317–344.

5. Cha and Nock, "Suicidal and Nonsuicidal Self-Injurious Thoughts and Behaviors," 317–344.

6. Cha and Nock, "Suicidal and Nonsuicidal Self-Injurious Thoughts and Behaviors," 317–344.

7. "Suicidal Teens," Child Trends Databank, December 2016, www.childtrends.org /indicators/suicidal-teens.

8. "QuickStats: Suicide Rates for Teens Ages 15–19 Years, by Sex—United States, 1975–2015," *Morbidity and Mortality Weekly Report (MMWR)* 66, no. 30 (August 2017): 816.

9. Cha and Nock, "Suicidal and Nonsuicidal Self-Injurious Thoughts and Behaviors," 317–344; American Psychiatric Association, *Diagnostic and Statistical Manual of Mental Disorders: Fifth Edition (DSM-5)* (Arlington, VA: American Psychiatric Association Publishing, 2013).

10. Cha and Nock, "Suicidal and Nonsuicidal Self-Injurious Thoughts and Behaviors," 317–344.

11. Cha and Nock, "Suicidal and Nonsuicidal Self-Injurious Thoughts and Behaviors," 317–344; American Psychiatric Association, *DSM-5.*

12. Cha and Nock, "Suicidal and Nonsuicidal Self-Injurious Thoughts and Behaviors," 317–344; Kristen Clements-Nolle et al., "Sexual Identity, Adverse Childhood Experiences, and Suicidal Behaviors," *Journal of Adolescent Health* 62, no. 2 (February 2018): 198–204.

13. Benjamin Shain, "Suicide and Suicide Attempts in Adolescents," *Pediatrics* 138, no. 1 (July 2016): e1–e11.

14. "The Link Between Drug Use and Teen Suicide," The Recovery Village, accessed February 21, 2018, www.therecoveryvillage.com/drug-addiction /drugs-and-suicide/#gref.

15. Kenneth D. Kochanek et al., "Deaths: Final Data for 2014," *National Vital Statistics Reports* 65, no. 4 (April 2017).

16. "US Suicide Rate Surges, Particularly Among White People," BBC News, April 22, 2016, www.bbc.com/news/world-us-canada-36116166.

17. Nadia Whitehead, "The Suicidal Brain," *Undark*, June 28, 2016, undark.org/article /suicidal-brain-biology-depression.

18. Kavitha Cardoza, "6 Myths About Suicide That Every Educator and Parent Should Know," NPR, September 2, 2016, www.npr.org/sections/ed/2016/09/02/478835539 /6-myths-about-suicide-that-every-educator-and-parent-should-know.

19. Peter Holley, "Teenage Suicide Is Extremely Difficult to Predict. That's Why Some Experts Are Turning to Machines for Help," *The Washington Post*, September 26, 2017, www.washingtonpost.com/news/innovations/wp/2017/09/25/teenage -suicide-is-extremely-difficult-to-predict-thats-why-some-experts-are-turning-to -machines-for-help.

20. Cha and Nock, "Suicidal and Nonsuicidal Self-Injurious Thoughts and Behaviors," 317–344.

21. American Foundation for Suicide Prevention and Suicide Prevention Resource Center, *After a Suicide: A Toolkit for Schools* (Waltham, MA: Suicide Prevention Resource Center, 2011).

22. Max Kutner, "Teen Suicide Is Contagious, and the Problem May Be Worse Than We Thought," *Newsweek*, October 29, 2016, www.newsweek.com/2016/10/28 /teen-suicide-contagious-colorado-springs-511365.html.

Chapter 15

1. Kristin M. Von Ranson and Laurel M. Wallace, "Eating Disorders," in *Child Psychopathology*, edited by Eric J. Mash and Russell A. Barkley (New York: The Guilford Press, 2014), 801–847.

2. Pooky Knightsmith, *Self-Harm and Eating Disorders in Schools: A Guide to Whole-School Strategies and Practical Support* (London: Jessica Kingsley Publishers, 2015).

3. Annalisa M. Pignatelli et al., "Childhood Neglect in Eating Disorders: A Systematic Review and Meta-Analysis," *Journal of Trauma and Dissociation* 18, no. 1 (2017): 110–115.

4. Von Ranson and Wallace, "Eating Disorders," 801–847.

5. Von Ranson and Wallace, "Eating Disorders," 801–847.

6. "Prevalence and Correlates of Eating Disorders in Adolescents," National Eating Disorders Association, 2011, www.nationaleatingdisorders.org/prevalence-and -correlates-eating-disorders-adolescents.

7. National Eating Disorders Association, *Educator Toolkit* (New York: National Eating Disorders Association).

8. National Eating Disorders Association, *Educator Toolkit.*

9. Von Ranson and Wallace, "Eating Disorders," 801–847.

10. National Eating Disorders Association, *Educator Toolkit*; Von Ranson and Wallace, "Eating Disorders," 801–847.

11. American Psychiatric Association, *Diagnostic and Statistical Manual of Mental Disorders: Fifth Edition (DSM-5)* (Arlington, VA: American Psychiatric Association Publishing, 2013); "Prevalence and Correlates of Eating Disorders in Adolescents," National Eating Disorders Association.

12. Lauren Muhlheim, "Addressing Eating Disorders in Middle and High Schools," F.E.A.S.T., February 2, 2012, www.feast-ed.org/news/253577/Addressing-Eating-Disorders-in-Middle-and-High-Schools.htm; Students FIRST Project, "School and Classroom Strategies: Eating Disorders," Students FIRST Project, accessed December 6, 2017, studentsfirstproject.org/wp-content/uploads/ED-Quick-Fact-Sheet-Strategies.pdf; National Eating Disorders Association, *Educator Toolkit*.

13. Danica G. Hays et al., "Duty to Warn and Protect Against Self-Destructive Behaviors and Interpersonal Violence," *Journal of School Counseling* 7, no. 11 *(2009)*.

14. Knightsmith, *Self-Harm and Eating Disorders*.

CHAPTER 16

1. "The Problem: Impact," Helping Traumatized Children Learn, Trauma and Learning Policy Initiative, accessed December 7, 2017, traumasensitiveschools.org/trauma-and-learning/the-problem-impact.

2. "The Problem: Prevalence of Trauma," Helping Traumatized Children Learn, Trauma and Learning Policy Initiative, accessed December 7, 2017, traumasensitiveschools.org/trauma-and-learning/the-problem-prevalence.

3. Maura McInerney and Amy McKlindon, *Unlocking the Door to Learning: Trauma-Informed Classrooms and Transformational Schools* (Philadelphia, PA: Education Law Center, 2014).

4. "About Behavioral Risk Factor Surveillance System ACE Data," Centers for Disease Control and Prevention, last modified April 1, 2016, www.cdc.gov/violenceprevention/acestudy/ace_brfss.html; National Child Traumatic Stress Network Schools Committee, *Child Trauma Toolkit for Educators* (Los Angeles: National Center for Child Traumatic Stress, 2008).

5. Stephanie Pappas, "The Pain of Bullying Lasts into Adulthood," *Live Science*, February 20, 2013, www.livescience.com/27279-bullying-effects-last-adulthood.html.

6. National Center for Injury Prevention and Control, "Understanding School Violence Fact Sheet" (Atlanta, GA: Centers for Disease Control and Prevention, 2016).

7. Marilyn C. Cornelis et al., "Genetics of Post-Traumatic Stress Disorder: Review and Recommendations for Genome-Wide Association Studies," *Current Psychiatry Reports* 12, no. 4 (August 2010): 313–326.

8. National Child Traumatic Stress Network Schools Committee, *Child Trauma Toolkit*.

9. National Child Traumatic Stress Network Schools Committee, *Child Trauma Toolkit*.

10. "Safe Schools Week" National School Safety Center, 2017, www.schoolsafety.us/safe-schools-week.

11. Alfie Kohn, "Choices for Children: Why and How to Let Students Decide," alfiekohn.org, September 1993, www.alfiekohn.org/article/choices-children.

12. Kathryn Collins et al., *Understanding the Impact of Trauma and Urban Poverty on Family Systems: Risks, Resilience, and Interventions* (Baltimore, MD: Family Informed Trauma Treatment Center, 2010).

Resources

Schoolwide Behavior and Academic Supports

Brown-Chidsey, Rachel, and Rebekah Bickford. *Practical Handbook of Multi-Tiered Systems of Support: Building Academic and Behavioral Success in Schools.* New York: The Guilford Press, 2016. Shows how to build a Multi-Tiered System of Supports (MTSS), describing every component of MTSS including effective instruction, the role of school teams, assessment, implementation, problem-solving, and data-based decision-making.

Burns, Matthew K., T. Chris Riley-Tillman, and Natalie Rathvon. *Effective School Interventions: Evidence-Based Strategies for Improving Student Outcomes.* New York: The Guilford Press, 2017. Fully revised and updated, this classic text offers eighty-three interventions that can be implemented by teachers and other staff in K through 12 classrooms as part of an MTSS program. Provides reproducible forms and online resources.

Evidence Based Intervention Network. ebi.missouri.edu. This website is devoted to the selection and implementation of evidence-based interventions for classrooms.

Hawken, Leanne S., and Kimberli Breen. *Check-In, Check-Out: A Tier 2 Intervention for Students at Risk* DVD Program. New York: The Guilford Press, 2017. Also known as the *Behavior Education Program*, this process is the most widely implemented Tier 2 intervention. The DVD offers step-by-step instructions for implementing this process.

Jucovy, Linda, and Michael Garringer. *The ABCs of School-Based Mentoring: Effective Strategies for Providing Quality Youth Mentoring in Schools and Communities.* Washington, DC: Hamilton Fish Institute on School and Community Violence, 2008. This is an excellent resource for a widely used Tier 3 MTSS strategy for high-risk students.

McIntosh, Kent, and Steve Goodman. *Integrated Multi-Tiered Systems of Support: Blending RTI and PBIS.* New York: The Guilford Press, 2016. A comprehensive text for schools, this book shows how RTI and PBIS can be combined to form a seamless Multi-Tiered System of Supports.

Simonsen, Brandi, and Diane Myers. *Classwide Positive Behavior Interventions and Supports: A Guide to Proactive Classroom Management.* New York: The Guilford Press, 2015. Provides practical, step-by-step instructions for implementing PBIS in K through 12 classrooms, regardless of whether a schoolwide PBIS program exists.

Culturally Responsive Education

Bal, Aydin, Kathleen King Thorius, and Elizabeth Kozleski. *Culturally Responsive Positive Behavioral Support Matters.* Tempe, AZ: The Equity Alliance at ASU, 2012. This policy article addresses the increasing diversity in public schools and emphasizes that schoolwide systems of support must be culturally responsive.

"Equity and PBIS." OSEP Technical Assistance Center for PBIS. www.pbis.org /school/equity-pbis. Offers many practice guides and other resources to help educators ensure that MTSS minimizes discipline disproportionality and is culturally responsive.

Hollie, Sharroky. *Culturally and Linguistically Responsive Teaching and Learning: Classroom Practices for Student Success.* Huntington Beach, CA: Shell Education, 2012. This book provides teachers with strategies and suggestions to support their culturally and linguistically diverse students at all grade levels.

Scholastic. www.scholastic.com/teachers. Search "Multiculturalism in the Classroom Collection" for a wealth of resources on cultural sensitivity, multicultural literacy, and teaching about different cultures.

Social-Emotional Learning

CASEL. *Effective Social and Emotional Learning Programs: Middle and High School Edition.* Chicago, IL: CASEL, 2015. Covers evidence-based social and emotional programs for middle school through high school.

CASEL. *Effective Social and Emotional Learning Programs: Preschool and Elementary School Edition.* Chicago, IL: CASEL, 2013. Covers evidence-based social and emotional programs for preschool through elementary school.

Duckworth, Angela. *Grit: The Power of Passion and Perseverance.* New York: Simon and Schuster, 2016. Psychologist Angela Duckworth explains that the secret to outstanding achievement is not talent, but a blend of passion and persistence she calls *grit.*

Durlak, Joseph A., et al., eds. *Handbook of Social and Emotional Learning: Research and Practice.* New York: The Guilford Press, 2016. Covers state-of-the-art interventions and prevention programs designed to build students' skills for managing emotions, showing empathy, making responsible decisions, and forming positive relationships.

Ferlazzo, Larry. "The Best Resources for Learning About 'Grit.'" *Larry Ferlazzo's Websites of the Day . . .* (blog). May 17, 2011. larryferlazzo.edublogs.org/2011/05/17 /the-best-resources-for-learning-about-the-importance-of-grit. Offers links to articles and interviews with Angela Duckworth, Ph.D., the originator of the concept of grit.

Gresham, Frank M. *Effective Interventions for Social-Emotional Learning.* New York: The Guilford Press, 2017. This book describes evidence-based, multi-tiered practices for promoting social-emotional learning with typically developing students and those with special needs. Provides advice on assessment of social skills in students in grades K through 12 as well as on planning and implementing interventions.

Jones, Stephanie, et al. *Navigating SEL from the Inside Out: Looking Inside & Across 25 Leading SEL Programs—A Practical Resource for Schools and OST Providers (Elementary School Focus).* New York: The Wallace Foundation, 2017. This report offers detailed information on twenty-five leading SEL programs for elementary schools.

Schargel, Franklin. "Bullying: What Schools, Parents, and Students Can Do." *HuffPost: The Blog* (blog). *Huffington Post*, October 10, 2013. www.huffingtonpost. com/franklin-schargel/bullying-what-schools-par_b_4103901.html. A former teacher, counselor, and school administrator lists a host of strategies for teachers, administrators, staff, and parents to address bullying and cyberbullying.

Walker, Hill M., and Frank M. Gresham, eds. *Handbook of Evidence-Based Practices for Emotional and Behavioral Disorders: Applications in Schools.* New York: The Guilford Press, 2016. A compilation from multiple experts on screening, assessments, and interventions for students with emotional and behavioral disorders.

Identifying and Supporting Students with Executive Function Difficulties

Adults

Branstetter, Rebecca. *The Conscious Parent's Guide to Executive Functioning Disorder: A Mindful Approach for Helping Your Child Focus and Learn.* New York: Adams Media, 2016. A school psychologist helps parents teach children essential skills necessary for academic success. Parents accomplish this goal through building a relationship with children rather than controlling children's behavior.

Cooper-Kahn, Joyce, and Laurie Dietzel. *Late, Lost, and Unprepared: A Parents' Guide to Helping Children with Executive Functioning.* Bethesda, MD: Woodbine Press, 2008. Written by psychologists, this book emphasizes helping children with impulse control, short-term memory, planning, and organizing so they can more effectively manage responsibilities. It's full of practical strategies for parents to use with K through 12 students.

Dawson, Peg, and Richard Guare. *Smart but Scattered: The Revolutionary "Executive Skills" Approach to Helping Kids Reach Their Potential.* New York: The Guilford Press, 2009. This original, best-selling book defines executive functions and instructs parents on how to teach them to children ages four to thirteen.

Guare, Richard, Peg Dawson, and Colin Guare. *Smart but Scattered Teens: The "Executive Skills" Program for Helping Teens Reach Their Potential.* New York: The Guilford Press, 2012. This best-selling book for parents of teens with executive function difficulties provides alternatives to micromanaging and constantly reminding teens of their responsibilities. Parents, tutors, or educational coaches can use these step-by-step strategies to help teens strengthen executive functions.

Kaufman, Christopher. *Executive Function in the Classroom: Practical Strategies for Improving Performance and Enhancing Skills for All Students.* Baltimore, MD: Brookes Publishing, 2010. A psychologist defines all executive functions and describes how each function affects students' learning and behavior. Provides research-based strategies so teachers can teach and develop accommodations for students in grades K through 12 with weaknesses in these functions.

Meltzer, Lynn. *Promoting Executive Function in the Classroom.* New York: The Guilford Press, 2010. Advises how to teach planning, prioritizing, self-monitoring, and organizing to K to 12 students. Includes strategies for differentiating learning for certain students, along with many reproducible forms.

Students

Cook, Julia. *I Can't Find My Whatchamacallit!!* Chattanooga, TN: National Center for Youth Issues, 2015. This storybook describes cousins Cletus and Bocephus, who are very different in their neatness and organization. When Bocephus helps Cletus clean his room so the boys can play together, the benefits of being organized become obvious.

Cook, Julia. *Planning Isn't My Priority . . . and Making Priorities Isn't in My Plans!* Chattanooga, TN: National Center for Youth Issues, 2016. This storybook for eight- to twelve-year-olds tells about Cletus and Bocephus, who are working together on their science fair project. The boys are opposites—one hates to plan while the other loves to plan. The boys have trouble working with each other, but each learns a valuable lesson about planning and prioritizing.

Nadeau, Kathleen G. *Learning to Plan and Be Organized: Executive Function Skills for Kids with AD/HD.* Washington, DC: Magination Press, 2016. Teaches seven- to eleven-year-olds how to plan and organize using checklists and activities.

Smith, Bryan. *What Were You Thinking? A Story About Learning to Control Your Impulses.* Boys Town, NE: Boys Town Press, 2016. Third grader Braden gets lots of attention from his classmates. The problem is that his behavior gets him into trouble because he acts before he thinks. Eight- to twelve-year-olds will relate to this funny story that tells how Braden's teachers and his mother attempt to teach him to control his impulses.

Anxiety Disorders

Generalized Anxiety Disorder (GAD)
Adults

Anxiety and Depression Association of America. adaa.org. This national nonprofit organization is dedicated to improving the research, education, and treatment of anxiety, depression, and related disorders. The website provides links to numerous articles, a therapist locator, and outside resources.

Anxiety Disorders Association of Canada. www.anxietycanada.ca. This nonprofit organization works with government and research institutions in Canada to improve the quality of services for people suffering from anxiety disorders.

Chansky, Tamar E. *Freeing Your Child from Anxiety: Practical Strategies to Overcome Fears, Worries, and Phobias and Be Prepared for Life—from Toddlers to Teens.* New York: Harmony Publishing, 2014. This revision of a classic book helps parents teach children how to overcome worries and deal with the pressures of our competitive, test-driven educational system.

Childhood Anxiety Network. www.childanxiety.net. This website is dedicated to providing professionals and other adults current, practical information about anxiety in children.

Dacey, John S., Martha D. Mack, and Lisa B. Fiore. *Your Anxious Child: How Parents and Teachers Can Relieve Anxiety in Children.* New York: John Wiley & Sons, 2016. Provides a step-by-step program for teachers and parents to help children manage a variety of anxiety problems.

Josephs, Sheila Achar. *Helping Your Anxious Teen: Positive Parenting Strategies to Help Your Teen Beat Anxiety, Stress, and Worry.* Oakland, CA: New Harbinger, 2017. Helps parents understand adolescent worries and effectively respond to teens in ways that help them manage anxieties.

Manassis, Katharina. *Keys to Parenting Your Anxious Child.* Hauppauge, NY: Barron's Educational Series, 2015. Discusses how to recognize anxiety problems in children and help them deal with anxiety in specific situations at home and at school.

Rapee, Ronald M., et al. *Helping Your Anxious Child: A Step-by-Step Guide for Parents.* Oakland, CA: New Harbinger, 2008. Explains the causes of childhood anxiety and offers practical strategies for parents to help children cope.

Spencer, Elizabeth DuPont, Robert L. DuPont, and Caroline M. DuPont. *The Anxiety Cure for Kids: A Guide for Parents and Children.* New York: John Wiley & Sons, 2014. Helps parents learn how to recognize anxiety in children, how to talk about anxiety with children, and how to be a supportive parent. This book also offers advice for teachers, therapists, and other school staff.

Students

Alter, Robin, and Crystal Clarke. *The Anxiety Workbook for Kids: Take Charge of Fears & Worries Using the Gift of Imagination.* Oakland: CA: Instant Help Books, 2016. Teaches five- to eleven-year-olds to use their imaginations and creativity to rid themselves of fears and worries.

Hoopmann, Kathy. *All Birds Have Anxiety.* Philadelphia, PA: Jessica Kingsley Publishers, 2017. This delightful book depicts how birds worry about airplanes, getting enough worms, and crashing into windows. Helps five- to eight-year-olds understand that others worry, too.

Schab, Lisa M. *The Anxiety Workbook for Teens: Activities to Help You Deal with Anxiety & Worry.* Oakland, CA: Instant Help Books, 2008. This workbook for teens helps them develop skills to control their anxiety.

Shannon, Jennifer. *The Anxiety Survival Guide for Teens: CBT Skills to Overcome Fear, Worry & Panic.* Oakland, CA: Instant Help Books, 2015. Helps teens identify their "monkey mind," the part of the brain that creates anxiety. Using cognitive-behavioral techniques, this illustrated manual helps teens work through anxiety-provoking situations.

Sisemore, Timothy A. *I Bet I Won't Fret: A Workbook to Help Children with Generalized Anxiety Disorder*. Oakland, CA: Instant Help Books, 2008. This workbook is filled with activities to help kids manage worrying.

Tompkins, Michael A., and Katherine Martinez. *My Anxious Mind: A Teen's Guide to Managing Anxiety and Panic*. Washington, DC: Magination Press, 2009. Offers middle and high school students tools and strategies to overcome worries.

Willard, Christopher. *Mindfulness for Teen Anxiety: A Workbook for Overcoming Anxiety at Home, at School & Everywhere Else*. Oakland, CA: Instant Help Books, 2014. Teaches teens mindfulness-based exercises to help them cope with anxiety.

Zelinger, Laurie, and Jordan Zelinger. *Please Explain Anxiety to Me! Simple Biology and Solutions for Children and Parents*. Ann Arbor, MI: Loving Healing Press, 2014. A dinosaur explains the connection between our brains and bodies and helps children use techniques to overcome anxiety. Great book for adults to read to elementary and middle school students.

Social Anxiety Disorder (SAD)
Adults
Selective Mutism Association. www.selectivemutism.org. Selective mutism is an extreme form of social anxiety. This website provides information on the disorder and advice for helping those who have it.

Social Anxiety Association. socialphobia.org. This nonprofit organization was founded in 1997 to meet the needs of people with social anxiety. Its website contains articles, essays, and links to resources about social anxiety.

Students
Brozovich, Richard, and Linda Chase. *Say Goodbye to Being Shy: A Workbook to Help Kids Overcome Shyness*. Oakland, CA: Instant Help Books, 2008. Describes forty fun activities for children and parents to do together that will increase children's confidence and assertiveness.

Freeland, Claire A.B., and Jacqueline B. Toner. *What to Do When You Feel Too Shy: A Kid's Guide to Overcoming Social Anxiety*. Washington, DC: Magination Press, 2016. Teaches eight- to twelve-year-olds how to use cognitive-behavioral techniques to overcome social anxiety. Includes an introduction for parents.

Shy Kids. www.shykids.com. This website for shy children and adolescents helps them deal with their social worries and fears. Contains a section for parents and teachers on social anxiety and provides links to outside resources.

Specific Phobia
Students
Umbach, Andrea. *Conquer Your Fears and Phobias for Teens: How to Build Courage & Stop Fear from Holding You Back*. Oakland, CA: Instant Help Books, 2015. A psychologist describes evidence-based strategies that teens will find useful in dealing with many different phobias.

PANIC DISORDER

Students

Kissen, Debra, Bari Goldman Cohen, and Kathi Fine Abitbol. *The Panic Workbook for Teens: Breaking the Cycle of Fear, Worry & Panic Attacks.* Oakland, CA: Instant Help Books, 2015. Helps teens understand that panic sensations are uncomfortable—not dangerous. Instead of fighting these feelings, teens learn how to observe and accept them, which minimizes their impact.

SEPARATION ANXIETY DISORDER AND SCHOOL REFUSAL

Adults

Eisen, Andrew R., and Linda B. Engler. *Helping Your Child Overcome Separation Anxiety or School Refusal: A Step-by-Step Guide for Parents.* Oakland, CA: New Harbinger, 2006. The only book with evidence-based advice and a plan for helping parents get their children back to school.

Kearney, Christopher A. *Getting Your Child to Say "Yes" to School: A Guide for Parents of Youth with School Refusal Behavior.* New York: Oxford University Press, 2007. A foremost authority on school refusal gives step-by-step instructions and worksheets for families with children who refuse school.

Students

Chang, Hae-Kyung. *Oh No, School!* Washington, DC: Magination Press, 2014. This book for kindergartners and first graders offers reassurance about going to school. A young girl's mother offers comfort and coaching to encourage the girl to think differently about the things that bother her at school.

Cosmo, A.J. *I Don't Want to Go to School.* Los Angeles: Thought Bubble Publishing, 2015. On the first day of school, Joey has lots of reasons for not going. His mother tries to convince him to go. Great illustrated book for first graders.

Penn, Audrey. *The Kissing Hand.* Indianapolis, IN: Tanglewood Press, 2006. A best-selling, classic story about Chester Raccoon, who's afraid to go to school. His mother gives him a special kiss on his hand. When he feels afraid at school, he presses his hand to his cheek to comfort himself. For children ages four to seven.

Obsessive-Compulsive and Related Disorders

Adults

International OCD Foundation. iocdf.org. An international nonprofit organization for people with OCD and their families and friends. The website contains fact sheets about OCD, weekly newsletters, and resources for educators.

Students

Burns, Ellen Flanagan. *Ten Turtles on Tuesday: A Story for Children About Obsessive-Compulsive Disorder.* Washington, DC: Magination Press, 2014. This book tells the story of Sarah, an eleven-year-old girl who believes she has to count things to prevent something bad from happening. With the help of her family and a psychotherapist, Sarah learns how to break free from her OCD. For eight- to twelve-year-olds. Includes useful notes for parents.

Dotson, Alison. *Being Me with OCD: How I Learned to Obsess Less and Live My Life.* Minneapolis, MN: Free Spirit Publishing Inc., 2014. A memoir and self-help book for teenagers with OCD.

Huebner, Dawn. *What to Do When Bad Habits Take Hold: A Kid's Guide to Overcoming Nail Biting and More.* Washington, DC: Magination Press, 2008. For children ages six to twelve, this book describes five keys to help children free themselves from nail-biting, thumb-sucking, hair twirling, scab picking, shirt chewing, and more.

Huebner, Dawn. *What to Do When Your Brain Gets Stuck: A Kid's Guide to Overcoming OCD.* Washington, DC: Magination Press, 2007. This best-selling, award-winning workbook provides step-by-step instructions for children to fight back and win the battle against OCD. Best for children ages eight to twelve—to be read and completed with parents or a therapist.

March, John S., with Christine M. Benton. *Talking Back to OCD: The Program That Helps Kids and Teens Say "No Way"—and Parents Say "Way to Go."* New York: The Guilford Press, 2006. Describes the well-researched, most effective therapy for OCD. The first half of the book teaches children and adolescents how to manage their OCD. The second half shows parents and other adults how to be supportive and encouraging of children's efforts to manage the disorder.

Sisemore, Timothy A. *Free from OCD: A Workbook for Teens with Obsessive-Compulsive Disorder.* Oakland, CA: Instant Help Books, 2010. A psychologist describes ways for teens to become aware of obsessive thoughts and stop their compulsive behaviors.

Wagner, Aureen Pinto. *Up and Down the Worry Hill: A Children's Book About Obsessive-Compulsive Disorder and Its Treatment.* Rochester, NY: Lighthouse Press, 2013. Explains OCD and treatment methods to children ages seven to ten.

Depressive Disorders

Adults

Depression and Bipolar Support Alliance. www.dbsalliance.org. A nonprofit organization that provides up-to-date, scientific information about depressive and bipolar disorders. The website includes information about treatment plans and directs readers to support centers all over the United States.

International Foundation for Research and Education on Depression. www.ifred.org. This organization offers support to people dealing with depression and combats the stigma associated with the disease. The website contains articles and fact sheets about depression and links to many outside resources.

Mondimore, Francis Mark, and Patrick Kelly. *Adolescent Depression: A Guide for Parents.* Baltimore, MD: Johns Hopkins University Press, 2015. Discusses depressive disorders, bipolar disorder, and their differences. Includes sections on eating disorders, attention disorders, alcohol and drug abuse, and cutting.

Reilly, Nadja. *Anxiety and Depression in the Classroom: A Teacher's Guide to Fostering Self-Regulation in Young Students.* New York: W.W. Norton & Company, 2015. A psychologist discusses how depression can limit one's ability to control emotions and behaviors. Offers practical strategies to help teachers improve self-regulation in students.

Serani, Deborah. *Depression and Your Child: A Guide for Parents and Caregivers.* Lanham, MD: Rowman & Littlefield, 2013. Having had depression as a child, the author emphasizes depression as an illness and covers research and treatment along with real-life cases of depressed children.

Travis, Richard L. *Overcoming Depression in Teens and Pre-Teens: A Parent's Guide.* Fort Lauderdale, FL: RLT Publishing, 2012. This basic introductory book covers the various types of depression that adolescents may experience.

Students

Abblett, Mitch R., and Christopher Willard. *Mindfulness for Teen Depression: A Workbook for Improving Your Mood.* Oakland, CA: Instant Help Books, 2016. This workbook helps teens learn and use mindfulness skills to improve their moods. Skills, activities, and exercises include mindful meditations, walking, yoga, healthy eating, and sleeping tips.

Crist, James J. *What to Do When You're Cranky and Blue.* Minneapolis, MN: Free Spirit Publishing Inc., 2014. Gives children ages nine to thirteen strategies and tips to beat the blues and get a handle on their feelings. Covers feelings of sadness and more serious problems like depression and bipolar disorder.

Foley, James M. *Danny and the Blue Cloud.* Washington, DC: Magination Press, 2016. Danny the bear was born under a blue cloud that makes him sad. Barnaby the rabbit teaches him some "Feel Good Rules" that change the way Danny thinks and improve his mood. Best for children four to eight years old.

Toner, Jacqueline B., and Claire A.B. Freeland. *Depression: A Teen's Guide to Survive and Thrive.* Washington, DC: Magination Press, 2016. This self-help book for teens discusses depression and provides guidelines for a cognitive-behavioral approach that teens can use to deal with their depressed thinking and mood. The book is intended to be used in addition to therapy.

Towery, Jacob. *The Anti-Depressant Book: A Practical Guide for Teens and Young Adults to Overcome Depression and Stay Healthy.* Palo Alto, CA: Jacob Towery, 2016. A psychiatrist offers the latest information about evidence-based, non-drug treatments for depression. His conversational writing style makes this a reader-friendly book.

Bipolar Disorder

Adults

The Bipolar Child. bipolarchild.com. Authors of the book *The Bipolar Child,* Janice and Demitri Papolos, provide links to multiple resources on bipolar disorder.

Bipolar Child Support. bipolarchildsupport.com. Offers practical tips for parents and teachers and covers laws governing the rights of children with bipolar disorder in schools.

BPChildren. www.bpchildren.com. Provides articles and lists resources about bipolar disorder for parents, teachers, and children.

Juvenile Bipolar Research Foundation. www.jbrf.org. The first charitable organization dedicated to supporting the study of bipolar disorder in children. Its website has many downloadable articles reflecting the most current research on the topic.

McDonnell, Mary Ann, and Janet Wozniak with Judy Fort Brenneman. *Positive Parenting for Bipolar Kids: How to Identify, Treat, Manage, and Rise to the Challenge.* New York: Bantam Books, 2009. Focuses on scientific facts about bipolar children and adolescents to help parents cope and manage children's treatment with professionals.

Papolos, Demitri, and Janice Papolos. *The Bipolar Child: The Definitive and Reassuring Guide to Childhood's Most Misunderstood Disorder.* New York: Broadway Books, 2006. Research pioneers discuss the diagnosis, treatment methods, and long-term care of children with bipolar disorder. Includes a discussion about the emotional challenges that parents face when raising a child with bipolar disorder.

Pavuluri, Mani. *What Works for Bipolar Kids: Help and Hope for Parents.* New York: The Guilford Press, 2008. In this book, a clinician and researcher discusses how to manage sleep deprivation, aggression, and depression and describes why the best treatment combination for bipolar disorder is medication and psychotherapy.

Students

Anglada, Tracy. *Brandon and the Bipolar Bear: A Story for Children with Bipolar Disorder.* Murdock, FL: BPChildren, 2009. Helps children ages four to twelve understand bipolar disorder and its treatment.

Van Dijk, Sheri, and Karma Guindon. *The Bipolar Workbook for Teens: DBT Skills to Help You Control Mood Swings.* Oakland, CA: Instant Help Books, 2010. Two therapists describe how teens can use dialectical behavior therapy techniques to deal with their emotions and moods.

Neurodevelopmental Disorders

ATTENTION DEFICIT HYPERACTIVITY DISORDER (ADHD)

Note: See "Identifying and Supporting Students with Executive Function Difficulties" on page 211 for additional resources to help students with ADHD.

Adults

A.D.D. WareHouse. addwarehouse.com. This website is a clearinghouse for hundreds of publications, videos, and training programs on ADHD and related developmental disorders. Resources are available for parents, teachers, and students. Find short comic-like books explaining ADHD and other disorders to children.

"Attention Deficit Hyperactivity Disorder." National Institute of Mental Health. www.nimh.nih.gov. This website provides information and resources on ADHD, plus information on how to enroll in clinical trials on ADHD.

Barkley, Russell A. *Taking Charge of ADHD: The Complete, Authoritative Guide for Parents.* New York: The Guilford Press, 2013. A comprehensive resource on ADHD by a leading authority on ADHD, this book includes a step-by-step plan for behavior management, information on the multitude of available treatments (including medications), and other practical advice for parents of children with ADHD.

Children and Adults with Attention Deficit/Hyperactivity Disorder (CHADD). www.chadd.org. CHADD is of the largest organizations in the United States serving individuals with ADHD. Chapters around the country allow parents, educators, professionals, and others interested in the disorder to connect and share insights. The website has lots of information on ADHD as well as membership and conference opportunities. Also available through the organization is the *CHADD Educator's Manual.* Published in 2006, this resource is full of strategies for helping students with ADHD in the classroom.

Rief, Sandra F. *The ADHD Book of Lists: A Practical Guide for Helping Children and Teens with Attention Deficit Disorders.* San Francisco: Jossey-Bass, 2015. Full of strategies and interventions for helping children who have difficulties with attention, impulsivity, and hyperactivity, this book is a comprehensive resource for K to 12 educators as well as parents. Reproducible forms, checklists, and tools make the book very easy to use.

Segal, Jeanne, and Melinda Smith. "Teaching Students with ADHD." HelpGuide. Last updated March 2018. helpguide.org/articles/add-adhd/teaching-students -with-adhd-attention-deficit-disorder.htm. This page for educators provides strategies and resources for teaching students with ADHD.

Understood. www.understood.org. This is a website developed by parents for parents of children ages three to twenty. It provides resources and advice for learning and attention problems. Digital simulations of various learning problems give parents an idea of how a child experiences these problems.

US Department of Education, Office of Special Education Programs. *Teaching Children with Attention Deficit Hyperactivity Disorder: Instructional Strategies and Practices.* Washington, DC: US Department of Education, 2008. This guide from the federal government offers many ideas for accommodating the needs of students with ADHD in the classroom.

Tic Disorders
Adults
Chowdhury, Uttom, and Tara Murphy. *Tic Disorders: A Guide for Parents and Professionals.* Philadelphia, PA: Jessica Kingsley Publishers, 2017. The authors of this book have treated many individuals with tic disorders and provide a wealth of information on the cause and treatment of these disorders. The book provides valuable advice to parents and educators who deal with these children.

Conners, Susan. *The Tourette Syndrome & OCD Checklist: A Practical Reference for Parents and Teachers.* San Francisco: Jossey-Bass, 2011. Written by the founder of the Tourette Syndrome Association of Greater New York State, this book provides many suggestions for parents and teachers to advocate for these children, manage their classroom behavior, and help them with homework.

Marsh, Tracy Lynne, ed. *Children with Tourette Syndrome: A Parents' Guide.* Bethesda, MD: Woodbine Press, 2007. This update of a classic book provides information on the biochemistry of tics and medications to treat severe tics. A summary of habit reversal training (HRT), a behavioral technique that is useful for some tics, is also covered.

Okun, Michael S, ed. *Tourette Syndrome: 10 Secrets to a Happier Life.* Seattle, WA: Books4Patients, 2017. This book brings together ten experts and researchers who provide up-to-date information and advice for families and educators dealing with children who have Tourette syndrome.

Tourette Association of America. www.tourette.org. This national organization devoted to informing people about Tourette syndrome and advocating for people with the disorder offers information on current research and treatment options at its website. It is a useful resource for educators, parents, and others involved in the care of students with the Tourette syndrome.

Students

Chowdhury, Uttom, and Mary Robertson. *Why Do You Do That? A Book About Tourette Syndrome for Children and Young People.* Philadelphia, PA: Jessica Kingsley Publishers, 2014. This short book for eight- to fourteen-year-olds explains Tourette syndrome for children and gives advice on dealing with teasing and bullying.

Peters, Dylan. *Tic Talk: Living with Tourette Syndrome.* Seymour, MO: Heartland Publishing, 2009. A child describes living with Tourette syndrome for five years. His experience helps sufferers as well as other children understand and accept the condition.

AUTISM SPECTRUM DISORDER (ASD)

Adults

Asperger's Disorder Homepage. www.aspergers.com. This online resource, maintained by Dr. R. Kaan Ozbayrak for more than twenty years, answers frequently asked questions about Asperger's syndrome (now called *high-functioning autism,* or *HFA*).

Attwood, Tony. *The Complete Guide to Asperger's Syndrome.* London: Jessica Kingsley Publishers, 2007. A comprehensive resource full of cutting-edge information on Asperger's syndrome (now called *high-functioning autism,* or *HFA*) and its treatment. The author, a foremost authority on HFA, maintains a website (www.tonyattwood.com.au) that provides guidance for parents, professionals, and individuals with HFA.

Autism Asperger Publishing Company. www.aapcpublishing.net. This independent publishing company provides hands-on, practical information about autism spectrum disorders to parents and educators.

Autism Spectrum Connection. www.aspergersyndrome.org. This website contains information, articles, and a message board for parents who have children with HFA.

Bashe, Patricia Romanowski. *Asperger Syndrome: The OASIS Guide.* New York: Harmony Books, 2014. With survey input from thousands of parents, the author of this book offers practical information, true stories, and support to anyone raising a child with Asperger's syndrome (now called *high-functioning autism,* or *HFA*).

Carol Gray Social Stories. carolgraysocialstories.com. This website provides information about Social Stories, a tool for helping students with social and communication problems strengthen their understanding of social cues and expectations.

Cumine, Val, Julia Dunlop, and Gill Stevenson. *Asperger Syndrome: A Practical Guide for Teachers.* New York: Routledge, 2010. Provides effective strategies for teaching children with Asperger's syndrome (now called *high-functioning autism,* or *HFA*) in regular classes.

Faherty, Catherine. *Autism . . . What Does It Mean to Me?* Arlington, TX: Future Horizons, 2014. One of the best books for parents and teachers to help them understand and provide interventions for children of all ages. Activities help kids ages nine through twelve with HFA understand their differences.

Future Horizons, Inc. fhautism.com. This leading publisher of books about HFA has titles for individuals, families, and professionals.

Ozonoff, Sally, Geraldine Dawson, and James C. McPartland. *A Parent's Guide to High-Functioning Autism Spectrum Disorder: How to Meet the Challenges and Help Your Child Thrive.* New York: The Guilford Press, 2015. Provides advice for parents from leading psychologists about how to foster the strengths of children with HFA and cope with the challenges. Contains strategies for helping affected children interact with peers and understand the expectations of appropriate behavior.

Social Thinking. www.socialthinking.com. This organization is dedicated to helping adults understand social-cognitive problems in children.

Students

Crist, James J. *The Survival Guide for Making and Being Friends.* Minneapolis, MN: Free Spirit Publishing Inc., 2014. This book offers lots of tips for kids to learn and improve social skills.

Grossberg, Blythe. *Asperger's Rules! How to Make Sense of School and Friends.* Washington, DC: Magination Press, 2012. For middle school students, this book covers how to behave in common school situations that create difficulty for children with HFA.

O'Toole, Jennifer Cook. *The Asperkid's Secret Book of Social Rules: The Handbook of Not-So-Obvious Social Guidelines for Tweens and Teens with Asperger Syndrome.* Philadelphia, PA: Jessica Kingsley Publishers, 2013. This award-winning book for ten- to seventeen-year-olds makes hidden social rules explicit.

Rice, Ethan. *Ethan's Story: My Life with Autism.* New York: Anchor Books, 2012. Written by an eight-year-old boy with autism, this book can provide other kids with a realistic understanding of autism. Great to read to an entire class.

Verdick, Elizabeth, and Elizabeth Reeve. *The Survival Guide for Kids with Autism Spectrum Disorders (and Their Parents).* Minneapolis, MN: Free Spirit Publishing Inc., 2012. Explains the various ways students display symptoms of autism and encourages them to understand and accept these differences. Offers lots of advice on daily activities as well as how to handle intense emotions.

Specific Learning Disorders (SLD)

Adults

Harwell, Joan M., and Rebecca Williams Jackson. *The Complete Learning Disabilities Handbook: Ready-to-Use Strategies & Activities for Teaching Students with Learning Disabilities.* San Francisco: Jossey-Bass, 2008. Provides helpful tips and strategies for teachers to use with struggling students. Includes diagnostic tools, intervention techniques, and an overview of the various learning disabilities teachers may encounter in their classrooms.

LD OnLine. www.ldonline.org. A great website that features hundreds of articles, monthly columns, first-person stories, and a substantial list of LD resources. Includes sections especially for educators, parents, and students.

Learning Disabilities Association of America. ldaamerica.org. The largest nonprofit volunteer organization advocating for people with learning disorders. Its website contains a wealth of information for parents, teachers, and other professionals.

Reid, Robert, Torri Ortiz Lienemann, and Jessica L. Hagaman. *Strategy Instruction for Students with Learning Disabilities.* New York: The Guilford Press, 2013. A practical, step-by-step guide for using instructional techniques to improve the cognitive development of students with learning disabilities.

Understood.org. www.understood.org. A parent-friendly website with a wealth of suggestions for parents on how to help children at home and how to navigate the educational system.

What Works Clearinghouse (WWC). ies.ed.gov/ncee/wwc. A clearinghouse of math and reading interventions for teachers.

Winebrenner, Susan, with Lisa M. Kiss. *Teaching Kids with Learning Difficulties in Today's Classroom: How Every Teacher Can Help Struggling Students Succeed.* Minneapolis, MN: Free Spirit Publishing Inc., 2014. A goldmine of practical, easy-to-use teaching methods, strategies, and tips to help teachers differentiate curriculum in all subject areas to meet the needs of all learners.

Students

Stern, Judith, and Uzi Ben-Ami. *Many Ways to Learn: A Kid's Guide to LD.* Washington, DC: Magination Press, 2011. Uses the analogy of mountain climbing to explain learning disabilities to children ages nine to twelve.

Specific Learning Disorder with Impairment in Reading (Including Dyslexia)

Harvey, Stephanie, and Anne Goudvis. *Strategies That Work: Teaching Comprehension for Understanding and Engagement.* Portland, ME: Stenhouse Publishers, 2007. An excellent presentation of specific strategies classroom teachers can use to improve reading comprehension in students.

International Dyslexia Association. dyslexiaida.org. An international organization dedicated to the study and treatment of dyslexia. In addition to information on dyslexia, the website contains useful information about students with general reading problems.

Reading Rockets. www.readingrockets.org. A national multimedia project offering information on how children learn to read, why some students struggle with reading, and how adults can help.

Reid, Gavin. *Dyslexia: A Complete Guide for Parents and Those Who Help Them.* New York: John Wiley & Sons, 2011. Helps parents identify dyslexia in their children, navigate the school system, and find the support they need.

Scanlon, Donna M., Kimberly L. Anderson, and Joan M. Sweeney. *Early Intervention for Reading Difficulties: The Interactive Strategies Approach.* New York: The Guilford Press, 2017. Describes the interactive strategies approach to help struggling readers in grades K through 2 through whole-class, small-group, or individual settings.

Shaywitz, Sally. *Overcoming Dyslexia: A New and Complete Science-Based Program for Reading Problems at Any Level.* New York: Vintage Books, 2003. A leading authority and researcher on dyslexia discusses the biology of this disability, gives tips on how to help struggling readers, and offers practical ways to help young people overcome the disability.

Stahl, Katherine A. Dougherty, and Michael C. McKenna. *Reading Assessment in an RTI Framework.* New York: The Guilford Press, 2013. Offers a practical model for K to 8 screening and progress monitoring through all tiers of RTI.

Walpole, Sharon, and Michael C. McKenna. *How to Plan Differentiated Reading Instruction: Resources for Grades K–3.* New York: The Guilford Press, 2017. This book provides a model for differentiated small-group instruction for students in grades K through 3. Reproducible materials from the book can be downloaded from the companion website.

Yale Center for Dyslexia & Creativity. dyslexia.yale.edu. A wealth of information for parents and educators from one of the world's largest dyslexia research and educational institutions.

Specific Learning Disorder with Impairment in Math (Dyscalculia)

Boaler, Jo. *What's Math Got to Do with It? How Teachers and Parents Can Transform Mathematics Learning and Inspire Success.* New York: Penguin Books, 2015. A math professor offers inspiring ideas and practical suggestions for students who hate or fear math. Suggestions include teaching a growth mindset to convince students that they can achieve in math. Especially useful for girls who don't believe they can be good at math.

Burns, Marilyn. *About Teaching Mathematics: A K–8 Resource.* Sausalito, CA: Math Solutions, 2015. Offers creative ways to teach math to reluctant students.

Codding, Robin S., Robert J. Volpe, and Brian C. Poncy. *Effective Math Interventions: A Guide to Improving Whole-Number Knowledge.* New York: The Guilford Press, 2017. Offers step-by-step guidelines for designing and implementing classwide, small-group, and math interventions for K to 5 students.

Forbringer, Linda L., and Wendy W. Fuchs. *RtI in Math: Evidence-Based Interventions for Struggling Students.* New York: Routledge, 2014. This book for teachers of grades K through 8 describes practical strategies that will improve students' math skills.

Willis, Judy. *Learning to Love Math: Teaching Strategies That Change Student Attitudes and Get Results.* Alexandria, VA: ASCD, 2010. A former teacher turned neurologist, professor, and researcher uses her knowledge of how the brain works to prescribe methods for teaching and increasing interest in math.

SPECIFIC LEARNING DISORDER WITH IMPAIRMENT IN WRITTEN EXPRESSION

Harris, Karen R., et al. *Powerful Writing Strategies for All Students.* Baltimore, MD: Brookes Publishing, 2008. Includes twenty- to fifty-minute lesson plans to supplement curriculum for students in grades K to 8.

Jones, Susan. "Dysgraphia Accommodations and Modifications." LD OnLine. www.ldonline.org/article/6202. An excellent article for teachers that outlines the symptoms of dysgraphia and offers suggestions on how to accommodate students who have dysgraphia in the classroom.

Mather, Nancy, Barbara J. Wendling, and Rhia Roberts. *Writing Assessment and Instruction for Students with Learning Disabilities.* San Francisco: Jossey-Bass, 2009. Offers practical advice for teaching mechanical and expressive aspects of writing to students struggling with writing.

Richards, Regina G. "Strategies for Dealing with Dysgraphia." LD OnLine. www.ldonline.org/article/5890. This excellent article for teachers offers practical classroom strategies for helping students with dysgraphia.

NONVERBAL LEARNING DISABILITY (NVLD)

Cornoldi, Cesare, Irene C. Mammarella, and Jodene Goldenring Fine. *Nonverbal Learning Disabilties.* New York: The Guilford Press, 2016. In one of the few texts available on nonverbal learning disabilities, the authors address the challenges of the disorder inside and outside of the classroom. They also discuss how NVLD is different from autism and why the diagnosis is not included in the *DSM-5.*

Stewart, Kathryn. *Helping a Child with Nonverbal Learning Disorder or Asperger's Disorder.* Oakland, CA: New Harbinger, 2007. Helps parents develop the skills they need to support their child with NVLD.

Thompson, Sue. "Developing an Educational Plan for the Student with NLD." LD OnLine. www.ldonline.org/article/6119. Gives practical strategies for teachers to help students with NVLD function in the classroom.

COMMUNICATION DISORDERS

SPEECH SOUND DISORDER

Bernthal, John E., Nicholas W. Bankson, and Peter Flipsen Jr. *Articulation and Phonological Disorders: Speech Sound Disorders in Children.* Upper Saddle River, NJ: Pearson, 2017. This updated version of the classic textbook on speech sound disorders provides the latest information on the causes, assessment, and treatment of these communication problems.

Playing with Words 365. "Resources and Products I Recommend if You Treat Phonological Delays." www.playingwithwords365.com/resources-products-i -recommend-if-you-treat-phonological-delays. This post on a speech-language pathologist's blog lists helpful resources for parents and teachers of young children with speech sound disorders.

Williams, A. Lynn, Sharynne McLeod, and Rebecca J. McCauley, eds. *Interventions for Speech Sound Disorders in Children.* Baltimore, MD: Brookes Publishing, 2010. Offers detailed discussion and videos of many interventions for speech sound disorders.

CHILDHOOD-ONSET FLUENCY DISORDER (STUTTERING)

Guitar, Barry. *Stuttering: An Integrated Approach to Its Nature and Treatment.* Baltimore, MD: Lippincott Williams & Wilkins, 2014. This is the definitive text for undergraduate and graduate courses on stuttering. The latest revision covers new methodologies for working with students who stutter.

Stuttering Foundation of America. www.stutteringhelp.org. This nonprofit organization is dedicated to providing the most up-to-date information about the prevention and treatment of stuttering. The website contains fact sheets, speech-language pathologist referrals, and sections especially for children, adolescents, parents, and teachers.

LANGUAGE DISORDER

Hamaguchi, Patricia McAleer. *Childhood Speech, Language & Listening Problems: What Every Parent Should Know.* New York: John Wiley & Sons, 2010. An overview of language problems found in children and advice on where to go for help.

Kester, Ellen Stubbe. *Difference or Disorder? Understanding Speech and Language Patterns in Culturally and Linguistically Diverse Students.* Austin, TX: Bilinguistics, 2014. This unique book offers advice on how to differentiate between communication errors related to second-language influence and those related to a communication disorder.

SOCIAL (PRAGMATIC) COMMUNICATION DISORDER

Note: See "Autism Spectrum Disorder (ASD)" on page 220 for additional resources for helping students with this communication disorder.

Social Thinking. www.socialthinking.com. This organization is dedicated to helping adults understand social-cognitive problems in students.

Disruptive and Conduct Disorders

Adults

Barkley, Russell A., and Arthur L. Robin. *Your Defiant Teen: 10 Steps to Resolve Conflict and Rebuild Your Relationship.* New York: The Guilford Press, 2014. Psychologists show how to establish authority, enforce nonnegotiable rules, solve problems, and address relationship issues with defiant, acting-out teens. Covers new research describing why some students have more problems with self-control than others do.

Barkley, Russell A., and Christine M. Benton. *Your Defiant Child: 8 Steps to Better Behavior.* New York: The Guilford Press, 2013. This book for parents of defiant children offers a full program of positive, concrete strategies parents can use to promote positive behavior. Educators may also benefit from reading this book.

Bernstein, Jeffrey. *10 Days to a Less Defiant Child: The Breakthrough Program for Overcoming Your Child's Difficult Behavior.* Boston: Da Capo Press, 2015. This psychologist recommends letting defiant children know you understand their frustration and then responding in a calm, firm manner. Addresses defiance related to technology.

Duffy, Patrick M. *Parenting Your Delinquent, Defiant, or Out-of-Control Teen: How to Help Your Teen Stay in School and Out of Trouble Using an Innovative Multisystemic Approach.* Oakland, CA: New Harbinger, 2014. This book offers helpful guidance for parents of children with conduct disorders.

Elvén, Bo Hejlskov. *Disruptive, Stubborn, Out of Control? Why Kids Get Confrontational in the Classroom, and What to Do About It.* Philadelphia, PA: Jessica Kingsley Publishers, 2017. Offers insight into why students misbehave and ways to react using a low arousal approach. Describes this approach in the context of many useful scenarios.

Faber, Adele, and Elaine Mazlish. *How to Talk So Kids Will Listen & Listen So Kids Will Talk.* New York: Scribner, 2012. This classic, best-selling book emphasizes how to communicate with children to engage cooperation, set limits, and promote self-discipline instead of punishment.

Fabiano, Gregory A. *Interventions for Disruptive Behaviors: Reducing Problems and Building Skills.* New York: The Guilford Press, 2016. Gives educators interventions and parent training programs to address students whose disruptive behaviors interfere with their own learning and others' ability to learn. Many reproducible forms are available.

Greene, Ross W. *The Explosive Child: A New Approach for Understanding and Parenting Easily Frustrated, Chronically Inflexible Children.* New York: HarperCollins, 2014. The author believes that children misbehave because they lack skills to behave appropriately. He proposes a method called Collaborative and Proactive Solutions in which parents solve behavior problems *with* their children instead of imposing consequences *on* children.

Gresham, Frank M. *Disruptive Behavior Disorders: Evidence-Based Practice for Assessment and Intervention.* New York: The Guilford Press, 2016. Describes evidence-based procedures for assessing, implementing, and evaluating interventions within a multi-tiered framework. Home and primary prevention strategies are also covered.

Kazdin, Alan E. *The Kazdin Method for Parenting the Defiant Child.* New York: Mariner Books, 2009. This renowned Yale psychologist offers his well-researched program for managing defiant children that focuses on what parents want children *to* do instead of telling them what *not* to do.

Pantley, Elizabeth. *Kid Cooperation: How to Stop Yelling, Nagging & Pleading and Get Kids to Cooperate.* Oakland, CA: New Harbinger, 2002. The primary focus of this book is helping parents foster cooperation in the family. Many of the concepts, however, can also be useful in the classroom.

Phelan, Thomas W. *1-2-3 Magic: Effective Discipline for Children 2–12*. Naperville, IL: Sourcebooks, 2016. This award-winning book gives parents a simple yet effective strategy for getting children to stop or start doing something.

Phelan, Thomas W., and Sarah Jane Schonour. *1-2-3 Magic in the Classroom: Effective Discipline for Pre-K Through Grade 8*. Naperville, IL: Sourcebooks, 2016. This simple yet effective approach to behavior helps teachers stay in charge of the classroom and promote positive student involvement.

Siegel, Daniel J., and Tina Payne Bryson. *No-Drama Discipline: The Whole-Brain Way to Calm the Chaos and Nurture Your Child's Developing Mind*. New York: Bantam Books, 2016. This best-selling book uses cartoon illustrations to describe what is happening in children's brains when they're upset. Instead of punishment, the book proposes empathetic responses and problem-solving methods as the most effective ways to respond to children's misbehavior in order to maintain a loving parent-child relationship. Authors also list twenty discipline mistakes most parents make.

Walker, Hill M., and Frank M. Gresham, eds. *Handbook of Evidence-Based Practices for Emotional and Behavioral Disorders: Applications in Schools*. New York: The Guilford Press, 2015. Provides best practices for K through 12 students who have emotional and behavioral disorders (sometimes labeled *EBD*). This book covers laws and multicultural issues related to supporting these students along with interventions for specific disorders and schoolwide programs.

Students

Agassi, Martine. *Hands Are Not for Hitting*. Minneapolis, MN: Free Spirit Publishing Inc., 2009. This book teaches children ages four to eight that there are many positive, constructive ways to use their hands and that hurting others is never okay.

Verdick, Elizabeth, and Marjorie Lisovskis. *How to Take the Grrrr Out of Anger*. Minneapolis, MN: Free Spirit Publishing Inc., 2015. For ages eight to thirteen, this book gives students tools they can use to handle strong emotions in a constructive way that doesn't harm others.

Self-Injury and Suicide

Adults

Bowman, Susan, and Kaye Randall. *See My Pain! Creative Strategies and Activities for Helping Young People Who Self-Injure*. Chapin, SC: YouthLight, 2012. With a focus on therapy through the creative arts, this book can be used in classroom or guidance settings. The emphasis is on helping young people express the feelings that can cause them to cut or otherwise injure themselves.

Hays, Danica G., et al. "Duty to Warn and Protect Against Self-Destructive Behaviors and Interpersonal Violence." *Journal of School Counseling* 7, no. 11 (2009). School counselors have a duty to inform and protect students engaged in any self-destructive behavior. Legal and ethical considerations for school counselors are discussed.

Hollander, Michael. *Helping Teens Who Cut: Using DBT Skills to End Self-Injury.* New York: The Guilford Press, 2017. An expert on dialectical behavior therapy (DBT) describes how and why this therapy is effective for self-injury. Includes guidelines for parents on how to talk to children who self-injure and how to find a good therapist.

SAMHSA. *Preventing Suicide: A Toolkit for High Schools.* HHS Publication No. SMA-12-4669. Rockville, MD: Center for Mental Health Services, SAMHSA, 2012. A comprehensive guide with sample policies and forms for screening students and helping those at risk. Covers prevention programs, dealing with students after a suicide, and staff education programs.

Walsh, Barent W. *Treating Self-Injury: A Practical Guide.* New York: The Guilford Press, 2012. This comprehensive book has been updated to include new research and how to match interventions to individual students' needs.

Students

Ferentz, Lisa. *Letting Go of Self-Destructive Behaviors: A Workbook of Hope and Healing.* New York: Routledge, 2015. A book of exercises for individuals who self-injure that can be used alone or with a therapist.

Nelson, Richard E., and Judith C. Galas. *The Power to Prevent Suicide: A Guide for Teens Helping Teens.* Minneapolis, MN: Free Spirit Publishing Inc., 2006. Provides guidance for teens on recognizing signs of suicidality and steps to take if they know someone is contemplating suicide.

Self-Injury Outreach and Support. sioutreach.org. This website is full of information for those who self-injure and their families. It offers tips on what to do when urges to self-injure occur, as well as a TED talk by an adult male who began cutting at age fifteen.

Smith, Melinda, et al. "Cutting and Self-Harm: How to Feel Better Without Hurting Yourself." HelpGuide. Last updated March 2018. www.helpguide.org/articles /anxiety/cutting-and-self-harm.htm. A page discussing myths versus facts, signs and symptoms, alternative ways to calm down, and helping friends and family members who self-injure. Lists other valuable resources on self-harm.

Eating Disorders

Adults

Alliance for Eating Disorders Awareness. www.allianceforeatingdisorders.com. This website is a great source for information on eating disorders and their treatment. It also provides resources and contacts for getting help for students and families.

Anorexia Nervosa & Related Eating Disorders. www.anred.com. With dozens of articles and documents, this website provides a primer on eating disorders and their prevalence as well as tips for helping people who are affected by them. Resources point the way to additional information.

Grace on the Moon. www.graceonthemoon.com. This website is for people interested in learning more about eating disorders. It offers bulletin boards moderated by individuals who have recovered from eating disorders, information on treatment options, and articles and inspirations for sufferers.

Gürze Books. gurzebooks.com. A cataloger and online retailer, this company specializes in books on eating disorders for both adults and young people.

Lagasse, Shannon. *Why Can't You Just Eat? A Look Inside the Mind of Anorexia, Bulimia, and Binge Eating Disorder.* Create Space, 2015. The author of this book was an overachieving high school student who developed a severe eating disorder. She describes the thoughts and emotions she experienced to help readers understand the minds of those who suffer from eating disorders.

Lock, James, and Daniel Le Grange. *Help Your Teenager Beat an Eating Disorder.* New York: The Guilford Press, 2015. Featuring current research, this resource for parents will also be helpful for educators looking to help students with eating disorders.

Morton, Cindy. "It's Not About Food: Eating Disorder Awareness." *For High School Counselors* (blog). February 21, 2016. forhighschoolcounselors.blogspot.com /2016/02/its-not-about-food-eating-disorders.html. This blog post for high school counselors was written during National Eating Disorders Awareness Week 2016. It offers descriptions, videos, and other resources about different eating disorders and teens.

National Association of Anorexia Nervosa and Associated Disorders (ANAD). www.anad.org. The website of this national organization is a great source for information on eating disorders and treatment options. It provides links to many other support groups and resources.

National Eating Disorders Association (NEDA). www.nationaleatingdisorders.org. The largest nonprofit organization in the United States with a focus on eating disorders, the NEDA website is a clearinghouse for information on anorexia, bulimia, binge eating disorder, and other topics related to body image. Find referral options and links in your area for adolescents with these disorders.

Steil, Rachael Rose. *Running in Silence: My Drive for Perfection and the Eating Disorder That Fed It.* Virginia Beach, VA: Köehler Books, 2016. In this book, an all-American collegiate runner discloses her journey and struggle with an eating disorder. She learns how to define herself outside of being a successful runner.

Students

Taylor, Julia V. *The Body Image Workbook for Teens: Activities to Help Girls Develop a Healthy Body Image in an Image-Obsessed World.* Oakland, CA: Instant Help Books, 2014. This book is full of exercises for adolescents on appreciating who they are and not comparing themselves to others.

Wachter, Andrea. *Getting Over Overeating for Teens.* Oakland, CA: Instant Help Books, 2016. An eating disorder specialist who herself struggled with an eating disorder as a teen teaches adolescents cognitive-behavioral thinking and mindfulness techniques to help them overcome an eating disorder.

Trauma and Stressor-Related Disorders

Adults

Blaustein, Margaret E., and Kristine M. Kinniburgh. *Treating Traumatic Stress in Children and Adolescents: How to Foster Resilience Through Attachment, Self-Regulation, and Competency.* New York: The Guilford Press, 2010. This comprehensive guide to treating children and adolescents also provides handouts, worksheets, and forms for photocopying.

Brooks, Barbara, and Paula M. Siegel. *The Scared Child: Helping Kids Overcome Traumatic Events.* New York: John Wiley & Sons, 2007. Describes and explains the various traumatic events that can cause kids and teens to become afraid. Covers trauma related to abuse, divorce, natural disasters, world events, and more.

National Center on Safe Supportive Learning Environments. *Trauma-Sensitive Schools Training Package.* Washington, DC: National Center on Safe Supportive Learning Environments, forthcoming. This training package will provide interactive documents and online modules for understanding trauma and for leading and creating trauma-sensitive schools.

Redford, James, dir. *Paper Tigers.* Austin, TX: Tugg Edu, 2016. DVD. This powerful documentary follows six students in an alternative high school, illustrating the effects of poverty, violence, and disease on students. By abandoning most punitive discipline, this school had fewer fights among students and more college applications.

Schiraldi, Glenn R. *The Post-Traumatic Stress Disorder Sourcebook: A Guide to Healing, Recovery, and Growth.* New York: McGraw-Hill, 2009. Even though this book addresses adult PTSD, it provides a great deal of insight about causes, symptoms, and treatment methods for the illness.

Sidran Institute for Traumatic Stress Education and Advocacy. www.sidran.org. This national nonprofit organization is a leader in traumatic stress education and advocacy. The website contains fact sheets, articles, and resource links about traumatic stress in children.

Trauma and Learning Policy Initiative: Helping Traumatized Children Learn. traumasensitiveschools.org. This website offers information on advocating for and creating trauma-sensitive schools. Includes policies, publications, and videos.

Treatment and Services Adaptation Center. traumaawareschools.org. This comprehensive website provides an evidence-based intervention (Support for Students Exposed to Trauma, or SSET) to help schools manage students' distress from trauma.

Students

Lohmann, Raychelle Cassada, and Sheela Raja. *The Sexual Trauma Workbook for Teen Girls: A Guide to Recovery from Sexual Assault & Abuse.* Oakland, CA: Instant Help Books, 2016. With reassurance that healing is possible, the authors offer strategies and activities to show victims that they can be strong and resilient.

Mather, Cynthia L., and Kristina Debye. *How Long Does It Hurt? A Guide to Recovering from Incest and Sexual Abuse for Teenagers, Their Friends, and Their Families.* San Francisco: Jossey-Bass, 2014. Written by an incest survivor, this step-by-step guide for teens helps them work through their feelings in healthy ways. Includes powerful first-person testimonials from other teens recovering from sexual abuse.

Palmer, Libbi. *The PTSD Workbook for Teens: Simple, Effective Skills for Healing Trauma.* Oakland, CA: Instant Help Books, 2012. Describes symptoms of PTSD to validate what teens are feeling and includes worksheets and activities teaching cognitive-behavioral techniques to help teens deal with trauma.

Straus, Susan Farber. *Healing Days: A Guide for Kids Who Have Experienced Trauma.* Washington, DC: Magination Press, 2013. A short book for nine- to twelve-year-olds showing them that they're not alone and that they can find ways to move beyond a traumatic experience.

INDEX

Page numbers in **bold** refer to reproducible pages.

psychotherapies for, 68, 74, 77
separation anxiety, 78–79
of stuttering, 145, 147
of vomiting, 63, 73
See also Anxiety disorders
Feelings, managing. *See* Social-emotional learning (SEL)
Fidgeting, 105
Fighting. *See* Aggressive behavior; Bullying; Disruptive and
conduct disorders
Fight-or-flight responses, 75, 181
Filler words, 145, 150
Fine motor skills, 116, 137
Firearms, suicide and, 169
504 plans, 25, 27
Fixed mindset, 44
Flashbacks, 183, 187
Flexible deadlines classroom strategy
dyscalculia, 130, 132
generalized anxiety disorder, 66
nonverbal learning disorder (NVLD), 141
obsessive-compulsive disorder, 86
post-traumatic stress disorder, 186
reading disability, 127
school refusal, 82
tic disorders, 111
written expression, impairment in, 136
Flexible workloads strategy
bipolar disorder, 99
depressive disorders, 95
dyscalculia, 132
eating disorders, 177, 179
obsessive-compulsive disorder, 86
panic disorder, 76
post-traumatic stress disorder, 186
Fluency, reading, 123
Fluency disorder
anecdotal example, 148
behaviors and symptoms, 145–146
classroom strategies, 146–147
overview and statistics, 145, 191
professional treatments, 147
resources, 225
Food, preoccupation with, 175
See also Eating disorders
Foreign-language learning, 127
Formal language, use of, 115
Friendships. *See* Social interaction difficulties
Functional behavior assessment (FBA), 24
Funerals, location for, 170

G

Gaming disorder, 104
Gauntness, 175
Gay, lesbian, bisexual, or transgender students
sensitivity to, 1
suicide and, 168
Gender differences
attention deficit hyperactivity disorder, 102
depression and, 92
disciplinary disproportionality, 35
disruptive and conduct disorders, 157
eating disorders, 173, 174
fixed versus growth mindset, 44
internet gaming disorder, 104
self-injury and, 170
smartphone use, 91
General education classrooms
special needs students in, 2
See also Classroom management
Generalization of information, difficulties with, 139
Generalized anxiety disorder (GAD)
behaviors and symptoms, 64–65
classroom strategies, 65–67
overview and statistics, 64, 191
professional treatments, 68
resources, 212–214

Genetic factors
as causes of mental health/learning disorders, 59
disruptive and conduct disorders, 157
post-traumatic stress disorder, 184
Germs, avoiding, 84, 90
Gestures
as feedback, 13
in obsessive-compulsive disorders, 87
use of in place of words, 150
Giddiness, 98
Glands, swollen, 176
Goode, Tyler Norris, 161, 162
Grading assignments, 87, 127, 134, 135, 136, 141
Graduated exposure plans, 79–80
Graduation rates, 1
Grandiose thinking, 97, 98, 99
Graphic organizers, 125, 137
Graph paper, 132, 136, 140–141
Greene, Ross W., 10, 13, 162–163
Grimacing, 146
Grit, fostering, 45
Grit: The Power of Passion and Perseverance (Duckworth), 45
Group counseling, autism spectrum disorder, 119
Groups, joining, 47
Growth mindset, 44
Grunting vocal tics, 110
Guidance counselors. *See* Counselors; School psychologists
Guilt, feelings of
after overeating, 176
depressive disorders and, 91, 92, 94
lack of, 158
suicidal thoughts and, 168
Gurgling vocal tics, 158

H

Habit reversal training (HRT), 111, 112
Hair loss, 175
Hairpulling, 88–89, 191
Hallway behavior, 117
Hand fatigue, 134
Handwashing, excessive, 84, 85, 87
Handwriting difficulties, 134–137, 191
Harassment. *See* Bullying
Headaches
generalized anxiety disorder, 64
medication-related, 31, 68, 72, 77, 90, 95, 100, 108, 119
separation anxiety disorder, 78
Head turning motor tic, 110, 111
Healthy eating, modeling, 177
Heart palpitations, 75
Helplessness, feelings of, 166, 168
HFA. *See* High-functioning autism (HFA)
Higher education, social-emotional skills and, 39
High-functioning autism (HFA)
anecdotal example, 119
behaviors and symptoms, 115–116
classroom strategies, 116–118
executive function challenges, 51, 55
overview, 114–119, 190
professional treatments, 119
resources, 220–221
vs. attention deficit hyperactivity disorder, 116
vs. nonverbal learning disability, 138, 140
vs. social (pragmatic) disorder, 154
Hissing vocal tics, 110
Home, difficulties at, 81, 158
Hopelessness, feelings of, 91, 92, 168
Horowitz, Sheldon, 120
HRT. *See* Habit reversal training (HRT)
Hyperactive behavior
strategies and accommodations, 12–13, 40–42
See also Attention deficit hyperactivity disorder (ADHD)
Hypersensitivity, 114, 116, 118
Hypersexual thoughts, 98
Hypervigilance, 183, 184

I

IDEA. *See* Individuals with Disabilities Education Act (IDEA)
Idioms, difficulty understanding, 115, 139
IEPs. *See* Individualized education plans (IEPs)
Illegible writing, 134
Images
    in language instruction, 151
    in reading instruction, 124
Impatience, 85
Impulse control
    attention deficit hyperactivity disorder, 105, 109
    disruptive and conduct disorders, 157, 158
    dyscalculia and, 131
    See also Self-control and self-regulation
Inattention. *See* Attention, problems with
Incarceration, as adverse childhood experience, 181
Inclusion
    benefits of, 21–22
    distinguished from mainstreaming, 2
    of students with learning disabilities, 120
Incomplete words or phrases, 150
Indecision, 84, 92, 94
Independence, encouraging, 151
Individualized education plans (IEPs), 25, 27, 114
Individuals with Disabilities Education Act (IDEA), 21, 120, 124
Inference drawing, modeling, 152
Inferiority, feelings of, 94
    See also Self-esteem
Initiating tasks
    academic problems and, 51
    strategies for, 54
Injuries. *See* Post-traumatic stress disorder (PTSD); Self-injury
Insomnia. *See* Sleep disturbances
Institute of Medicine, report on physical exercise, 48
Instructions. *See* Directions, following
Intensive PBIS, 23–24
Interest, loss of, 93, 185
Interests, of students
    asking about, 34, 94, 167
    fostering grit and passion, 45
    preoccupation with, 115
    sudden changes in, 185
Internalizing disorders, 25
Internet gaming disorder, 104
Interpersonal relationships. *See* Social interaction difficulties; Social skills
Interrupting, 114
Intervention
    consulting with specialists about, 28, 29
    importance of early intervention, 27–28
    team approach, 30
Intruding on others, 105
Ipecac, 176
Irritability
    bipolar disorder, 97, 98
    depressive disorders, 91, 92, 93, 94
    disruptive and conduct disorders, 157–158
    disruptive mood dysregulation disorder, 92, 93, 97
    generalized anxiety disorder, 64
    medication-related, 108
    obsessive-compulsive disorder, 85
    post-traumatic stress disorder, 183
    social anxiety disorder, 70
Isolation, communication disorders and, 142, 146
"I told you so," avoiding, 162

J/K

Jaw snapping motor tics, 110
Jennings, Patricia A., 3
Jerking motor tics, 110
Journaling assignments, 137
Kabat-Zinn, Jon, 42
Kindergarten readiness, 39
Kinesthetic learners, 53, 124, 132
Knightsmith, Pooky, 174

L

Labels/labeling, 60
Language differences, cultural awareness, 34
Language disorder
    anecdotal example, 153
    behaviors and symptoms, 149–150
    classroom strategies, 150–152
    overview, 149, 192
    professional treatment, 153
    resources, 225
    vs. attention deficit hyperactivity disorder, 149
Language use
    autism spectrum disorder, 115
    nonverbal learning disability, 139
    See also Written expression, impairment in
Laughing/giggling, 98
Laxatives, 175, 176
Learning Ally (www.learningally.org), 127
Learning disorders
    causes of, 59
    classification of, 59
    executive function challenges, 51
    gathering information about students, 27–28
    identifying student needs, 27–28
    overview and statistics, 2, 120
    See also specific learning disorders (SLD)
Learning modalities, importance of varying, 53
Lecture notes/outlines, providing, 136, 140
Lecturing, avoiding, 162
Legislation, 21, 25
Lethargy, 92, 93
Letter formation, 135
Levy, Ray, 161, 162
Lip licking motor tics, 110
Literacy. *See* Reading disability (RD)
Loneliness
    post-traumatic stress disorder and, 185
    smartphone use and, 1, 91
Long sleeves/pants, wearing, 166
Lost at School (Greene), 10, 13, 162–163
Low-functioning autism, 114
Lunchtime
    consistency of rules during, 10
    facilitating social relationships during, 66, 71
    monitoring behavior during, 41, 118, 141, 161
    sensory hypersensitivity, 118
Lying, 157

M

Mader, Jackie, 2
Mainstreaming, 2
Major depressive disorder (MDD), 92, 192
Manic behavior. *See* Bipolar disorder
Mapping example, 152
Marshmallow test, 40
Math, impairment in
    behaviors and symptoms, 130–131
    classroom strategies, 131–133
    executive function and, 52
    overview and statistics, 130
    resources, 223–224
Medications
    antidepressants, 95, 100, 174
    antipsychotics, 100
    attention deficit hyperactivity disorder, 104, 108
    autism spectrum disorder, 119
    bipolar disorder, 100
    generalized anxiety disorder, 68
    mood stabilizers, 100
    obsessive-compulsive disorders, 90
    panic disorder, 77
    post-traumatic stress disorder, 187
    reporting side effects to parents, 31–32
    selective serotonin reuptake inhibitors (SSRIs), 68, 72, 77, 90, 95
    serotonin and norepinephrine reuptake inhibitors (SNRIs), 95
    social anxiety disorder, 72

P

Pain
- depressive disorders, 91, 94
- dysgraphia, 136
- generalized anxiety disorder, 64
- panic disorder, 75
- self-injury and, 166
- separation anxiety disorder, 78
- *See also* Headaches; Stomachaches

Paleness, 175

Panic disorder
- anecdotal example, 77
- behaviors and symptoms, 75–76
- classroom strategies, 76–77
- overview and statistics, 75, 192
- professional treatments, 77
- resources, 215
- school refusal, 81

Parents
- checking homework, 54, 55
- communicating with, 11–12, 29–31
- defensive/confrontational, 30, 178
- desired traits for children with ADHD, 107–108
- meetings with, 29
- reporting eating disorders to, 178
- reporting medication side effects to, 31–32
- strategies for behavior management, 164
- suggestions for increasing physical activity, 48–49

PBIS. *See* Positive Behavioral Interventions and Supports (PBIS)

PDD. *See* Persistent depressive disorder (PDD)

PEACE meditation process, 43

Peer interactions. *See* Social interaction difficulties; Social skills

Peer pressure
- self-injury and, 167
- *See also* Bullying

Peer relationship qualities, 46

Pencil grips, 135, 136

Perfectionism
- eating disorders, 174, 177
- generalized anxiety disorder, 64
- obsessive-compulsive disorder, 84, 86

Performance anxiety, 69–70, 81

Persistent depressive disorder (PDD), 92, 192

Person-first language, 60–61

Phobias, 73–74

Physical activity
- benefits of, 48, 95
- for depressive disorders, 95
- excessive, 174, 175, 176
- as self-control strategy, 41
- strategies for increasing, 48–49

Physical symptoms
- depressive disorders, 91
- eating disorders, 175, 176
- fluency disorder, 146
- generalized anxiety disorder, 64–65
- medication side effects, 31, 68, 72, 77, 90, 95, 100, 108, 119
- panic disorder, 75
- separation anxiety disorder, 78
- social anxiety disorder, 70

Pictures. *See* Images

Piercing, 166

Planning
- academic problems and, 51
- strategies for, 54
- *See also* Organizational skills

Play
- adults joining in, 48
- games teaching self-control, 40
- recess, importance of, 48
- reenacting trauma, 185
- therapy, 68, 95

Plurals, incorrect use of, 150

Policies, classroom. *See* Classroom management

Positive behavior, supportive strategies for, 10–13

Positive Behavioral Interventions and Supports (PBIS)
- compared to RTI, 22
- functional behavior assessment, 24
- historical perspective, 21–22
- increased use of, 3
- resources, 209
- rewards for students, 14
- tiers, 23–24

Positive reinforcement. *See* Praise

Possessions, giving away, 169

Possessives, incorrect use of, 150

Post-traumatic stress disorder (PTSD)
- adverse childhood experiences and, 182
- anecdotal example, 187
- behaviors and symptoms, 184–185
- classroom strategies and interventions, 185–186
- overview, 183, 192
- professional treatments, 187
- resources, 230–231
- risk and resiliency factors, 183–184

Power struggles, avoiding, 162

Practicing rule compliance, 11

Pragmatic language disorder, 154–155, 193, 225

Praise
- for academic success, 82
- in Academy approach, 161
- attention deficit hyperactivity disorder, 106
- depressive disorders, 94
- fixed versus growth mindset examples, 44
- generalized anxiety disorder, 65
- importance of, 11
- for physical activity, 49
- for reading progress, 126
- relative to negative feedback, 14, 159–160
- self-control, teaching about, 42
- social anxiety disorder, 71
- *See also* Positive Behavioral Interventions and Supports (PBIS)

Prewriting strategies, 137, 152

Privacy. *See* Confidentiality

Private/invisible experiences
- panic disorder, 75
- worry/anxiety, 64

Problem-solving difficulties, dyscalculia and, 130

Procedures, classroom. *See* Classroom management

Procrastination
- executive function and, 52
- obsessive-compulsive disorder and, 86

Professional treatments
- behavior therapy, 112
- cognitive-behavioral therapy (CBT), 68, 72, 77, 89, 95, 187
- counselors, consulting with, 28, 29
- crisis management, 29, 99, 158, 164, 187
- dialectical behavior therapy (DBT), 68, 95, 171
- exposure and response prevention (ERP) therapy, 74, 89
- eye movement desensitization and reprocessing (EMDR), 187
- group counseling, 119
- habit reversal training (HRT), 111, 112
- occupational therapy, 118, 119, 137, 141
- play therapy, 68, 95
- psychotherapy, 100, 109
- reading specialists, 128
- relaxation techniques, 68, 72, 74, 77, 89, 100
- speech-language therapy, 141, 144, 147, 153, 155
- team approach, 30, 99
- trauma incident reduction therapy (TIR), 187
- *See also* Medications

Pronouns, incorrect use of, 150

Pronunciation. *See* Speech sound disorder

Property destruction, 157, 158

Psychologists
- terminology used by, 59–60
- *See also* School psychologists

Psychotherapy
- attention deficit hyperactivity disorder, 109
- bipolar disorder, 100
- *See also* Professional treatments

To download the reproducible forms for this book, visit **freespirit.com/MHLD-forms**.
Use the password **2help**.

About the Author

Myles L. Cooley, Ph.D., ABPP, is a board-certified clinical psychologist licensed in Florida, where he has had a private practice for more than thirty-five years. For the second half of his career, Myles has specialized in learning, behavioral, and developmental disorders in children and adolescents. He has provided training on these topics to pediatricians, educators, school psychologists, and school counselors. He has served as a consultant to private and public schools and has published articles on ADHD, giftedness, and learning disabilities.

Myles and his wife live in Palm Beach Gardens, Florida, but escape hurricanes in the summer by visiting their grandchildren in San Diego. Myles enjoys tennis, pickleball, piano, and lecturing on cruises. For more information on speaking engagements, consultation, or training, you can contact Myles through his website www.drmylescooley.com.

Other Great Resources from Free Spirit

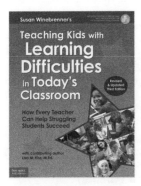

Teaching Kids with Learning Difficulties in Today's Classroom
How Every Teacher Can Help Struggling Students Succeed (Revised & Updated 3rd Edition)
by Susan Winebrenner, M.S., with Lisa M. Kiss, M.Ed.

For K–12 teachers, administrators, higher education faculty.
288 pp.; PB; 8½" x 11"; includes digital content

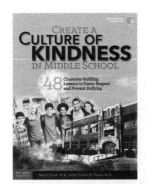

Create a Culture of Kindness
48 Character-Building Lessons to Foster Respect and Prevent Bullying
by Naomi Drew, M.A., with Christa M. Tinari, M.A.

For middle school educators.
272 pp.; PB; 8½" x 11"; includes digital content

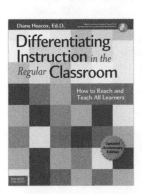

Differentiating Instruction in the Regular Classroom
How to Reach and Teach All Learners (Updated Anniversary Edition)
by Diane Heacox, Ed.D.

For grades K–12.
176 pp.; PB; 8½" x 11"; includes digital content

Boost Emotional Intelligence in Students
30 Flexible Researched-Based Activities to Build EQ Skills (Grades 5–9)
by Maurice J. Elias, Ph.D., and Steven E. Tobias, Psy.D.

For teachers and counselors of grades 5–9.
192 pp.; PB; 8½" x 11"; includes digital content

Self-Regulation in the Classroom
Helping Students Learn How to Learn
by Richard M. Cash, Ed.D.

For K–12 teachers, administrators, counselors.
184 pp.; PB; 8½" x 11"; includes digital content

Free PLC/Book Study Guide
freespirit.com/PLC

Uncover the Roots of Challenging Behavior
Create Responsive Environments Where Young Children Thrive
by Michelle Salcedo, M.Ed.

For early childhood educators.
208 pp.; PB; 8½" x 11"; includes digital content

Free PLC/Book Study Guide
freespirit.com/PLC

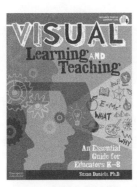

Visual Learning and Teaching
An Essential Guide for Educators K–8
by Susan Daniels, Ph.D.

For educators, K–8.
272 pp.; PB; 8½" x 11"; includes digital content

Free PLC/Book Study Guide
freespirit.com/PLC

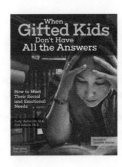

When Gifted Kids Don't Have All the Answers
How to Meet Their Social and Emotional Needs (Revised & Updated Edition)
by Judy Galbraith, M.A., and Jim Delisle, Ph.D.

For teachers, gifted coordinators, guidance counselors, and parents of gifted children K–9.
288 pp.; PB; 7¼" x 9¼"; B&W photos; includes digital content

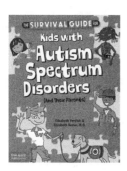

The Survival Guide for Kids with Autism Spectrum Disorders (And Their Parents)
by Elizabeth Verdick and Elizabeth Reeve, M.D.

For ages 9–13.
240 pp.; PB; 7" x 9";
color illust.

The Survival Guide for Kids with Behavior Challenges
How to Make Good Choices and Stay Out of Trouble (Revised & Updated Edition)
by Thomas McIntyre, Ph.D. (Dr. Mac)

For ages 9–14.
192 pp.; PB; 7" x 9";
two-color; illust.

The Survival Guide for Kids with ADHD
(Updated Edition)
by John F. Taylor, Ph.D.

For ages 8–12.
128 pp.; PB; 6" x 9";
two-color; illust.

The Survival Guide for Kids in Special Education (And Their Parents)
Understanding What Special Ed Is & How It Can Help You
by Wendy L. Moss, Ph.D., and Denise M. Campbell, M.S.

For ages 8–14.
184 pp.; PB; 6" x 9";
two-color; illust.

Being Me with OCD
How I Learned to Obsess Less and Live My Life
by Alison Dotson

For ages 15 & up.
152 pp.; PB; 6" x 9"

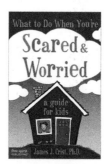

What to Do When You're Scared & Worried
A Guide for Kids
by James J. Crist, Ph.D.

For ages 9–13.
128 pp.; PB; 5⅜" x 8⅜"; two-color;
illust.

Stress Can Really Get on Your Nerves!
(Revised & Updated Edition)
by Trevor Romain and Elizabeth Verdick

For ages 8–13.
104 pp.; PB; 5⅛" x 7"; color illust.

What Do You Really Want?
How to Set a Goal and Go for It!
A Guide for Teens (Revised & Updated Edition)
by Beverly K. Bachel

For ages 11 & up.
160 pp.; PB; 6" x 9"; two-color

For pricing information, to place an order, or to request a free catalog, contact:

Free Spirit Publishing Inc. • 6325 Sandburg Road, Suite 100 • Minneapolis, MN 55427-3674
toll-free 800.735.7323 • local 612.338.2068 • fax 612.337.5050
help4kids@freespirit.com • www.freespirit.com